Lynn Pan, who also writes as Pan Ling, was born and brought up in Shanghai. She was first taught English by her mother, who was educated at an American missionary college in Shanghai, and then studied at the universities of London and Cambridge. She teaches Chinese and travels frequently to China, and has published two other books on China: *Old Shanghai: Gangsters in Paradise* and *China's Sorrow: Journeys around the Yellow River*.

p 35

# The New Chinese Revolution

by
LYNN PAN

*Revised and Updated*

SPHERE BOOKS LIMITED

SPHERE BOOKS LTD

Published by the Penguin Group
27 Wrights Lane, London W8 5TZ, England
Viking Penguin Inc., 40 West 23rd Street, New York, New York 10010, USA
Penguin Books Australia Ltd, Ringwood, Victoria, Australia
Penguin Books Canada Ltd, 2801 John Street, Markham, Ontario, Canada L3R 1B4
Penguin Books (NZ) Ltd, 182–190 Wairau Road, Auckland 10, New Zealand

Penguin Books Ltd, Registered Offices: Harmondsworth, Middlesex, England

First published in Great Britain by Hamish Hamilton Ltd, 1987
Revised and updated edition published by Sphere Books Ltd, 1988

Copyright © Lynn Pan, 1987, 1988

Printed and bound in Great Britain by
Richard Clay Ltd, Bungay, Suffolk

# Contents

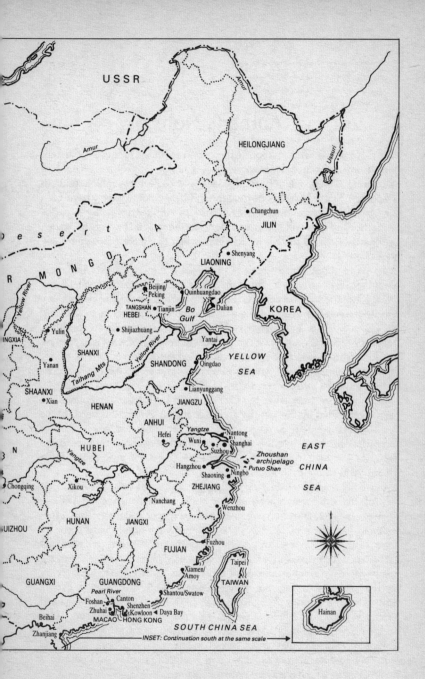

# Author's Note

An Anglo-Saxon writing about China will obviously produce a different book from mine, if only because, as a Chinese, I can't be accused of harbouring 'superior' European attitudes, and so feel less inhibited about criticising Chinese manners of thought and behaviour. I hope I have been fair, although I know that, however hard an author tries to be impartial suggestions of bias will sometimes occur in the imagination of the reader. And partiality is all the harder to avoid when the subject is so intensely political.

To write about China today is to pursue a moving target. The rapid changes keep her always ahead of the writer. Interested readers will, I hope, call my attention to inaccuracies, of which there are no doubt many. I am only too conscious that, in trying to describe the changes in so vast and old a society, there are grave risks of not doing justice to its complexities. But I believe that the reader will gain a truer impression of what is happening in China from a selective rather than an exhaustive account; and where possible or illuminating, I have chosen here and there to narrow my focus to the individual instance or profile.

The matter of translating the Chinese yuan into dollars or pounds has been complicated by the fact that in the course of writing this book, China decided to devalue her currency by 15·8 per cent against a basket of major currencies; so that while the rate of exchange was about 3 yuan to the dollar (or 4·7 yuan to the £) in autumn 1985, it was 3·7 yuan to the dollar (or 5·4 yuan to the £) in July 1986 .

I owe my thanks to many friends, acquaintances and strangers for giving help of one kind or another with this book. My first debt is to Thomas Kampen, whose unending supplies of newspaper clippings and other materials have been invaluable. I was also lucky enough to have come by some restricted Chinese papers, the ones they call *neibu*, or 'internally circulated' documents; and for this I must thank Michael Schoenhals. Among many who have given generously of their time, knowledge and hospitality are the following: in Europe, Henry Sacker, Ip Kung Sau, Frances Wood, Britta Kinnemark and Wilburg Kleff; in Hong Kong, Nick Elliot, Fatana and Jeremy Waller, John Minford, Geremie Barmé, Steven N. S. Cheung, Liao Xi, Leong Mo Ling, Billy Ma and above all Leong Ka Chai; and in China, Trevor Mound, Douglas and Claire Tomlinson, Aileng Soo, Bernd and Dorothee Kadura, Harold Goldin, Peng Hong, Liu Baohui, and numerous other Chinese who have asked not to be named.

# PART ONE

*

# A WORLD SO CHANGED

The mountain goddess,
Were she still about,
Would marvel to find
A world so changed.

from *Swimming*, a poem by Mao Zedong, 1956

When Confucius went to Wei, Ruan You drove for
him. Confucius said, 'How numerous are the people!'
  Ruan You said, 'When they are thus numerous,
what further benefit can one add?'
  'Make them rich,' was the Master's reply.

*The Analects*

# 1

# TWO CYCLES OF CATHAY

The ancient Chinese numbered the years by assigning two characters to each twelvemonth, one taken from a set of twelve signs, one from a set of ten. As the lowest common multiple of 10 and 12 is 60, a repetition of the first pair of characters becomes necessary after sixty years. The series of sixty years thus formed is known as the Chinese Cycle of Sixty, or the Cycle of Cathay.

In June 1981 the Chinese Communist Party, founded at a secret meeting in Shanghai in 1921, completed its first cycle of sixty and began on its next. The opening of the sixth plenum of the eleventh Central Committee, at which Deng Xiaoping, Hu Yaobang and Zhao Ziyang were confirmed as the undisputed leaders of China, was timed to coincide with this anniversary, to underline its importance as a watershed between one period and the next. A new chapter, marked by change so profound that Deng Xiaoping has called it a 'second revolution', opened in the People's Republic of China.

In calling his the second revolution, Deng Xiaoping took the communist triumph over Chiang Kai-shek's Kuomintang government in 1949 as the first. In fact the Chinese have been through more than two revolutions, and if there is one word to sum up their entire experience in the twentieth century, it is 'revolution'. The very first was in 1911, when the last of the Chinese dynasties, the Qing or Manchu, was overthrown and an empire reaching as far back as 221 BC was ended. The second, thirty-eight years later, saw the creation of the People's Republic. To these two upheavals one might add a third. The Great Proletarian Cultural Revolution spanned the years between 1966 and 1976, and will be remembered with a shudder by millions of Chinese as the nadir of their experience; beginning with the emergence of the Red Guards and ending with the fall of the so-called Gang of Four, it saw clashes and confusion of such magnitude as to suggest national chaos and the complete breakdown of political authority.

In the last hundred years, then, China has experienced internal violence on a scale unsurpassed by any other nation. And among all the communist regimes in the postwar period, none has been as politically volatile as the Chinese. The struggle continues still, and China remains a nation in search of a political form she can call her own.

All visitors to China can see at least a few of the outward signs of this new struggle. Many of them appear astonishing to anyone who knew the country in the previous two decades. In the spring of 1985, George Michael

and Andrew Ridgeley of the British pop duo Wham! played to bemused
Chinese audiences in Peking and Canton—this in a country where, not all
that long ago, rock and roll and jazz were thought to be examples of
Western vice and degeneracy. In Peking just a month later, a football match
which China lost to Hong Kong ended in such mayhem that Chinese fans
were compared to Liverpool soccer hooligans in the international press—
a world away from the days of ping-pong diplomacy, when Chinese table-
tennis stars would deliberately throw away a winning position to show
their sportsmanship, uncompetitiveness and superiority. Meanwhile, away
in the old southern town of Suzhou, nimble fingers finished off a double-
sided embroidery. The subject was exotic for a folk-art which has habitually
gone in for pandas and portraits of Mao Zedong: the embroidery, which it
had taken 300 days of careful and dedicated work to complete, pictured
Prince Charles on one side and Princess Diana on the other.

It is possible to go on and on. Almost everywhere one looks there are
symptoms of a country in transition. China is embarked on an enterprise,
we learn, the aim of which is to quadruple the value of her production by
the year 2000. If she succeeds, she will pass from rags to what millions of
Chinese see as riches in just one short generation. Not only is she trying
to modernise with forty times the number of people Europe had when *it*
industrialised, but she is trying to do so in less than a fifth of the time. It
is, said *The Economist* in the spring of 1986, 'the most exhilarating thing
that has happened to the world in the past ten years'. This was roughly the
sensation it left with an American who worked as a foreign expert in Peking:
'There were many times,' he said, 'when I told myself I was in the midst of
an important historical moment—China's first steps toward power and
prosperity.' Something unique was emerging, he continued, and the world
was watching, 'awaiting the test results on China's experiment.'

Yet it is easy enough to find in a country whatever you want to see in
it; and in China, as everywhere else, good and bad come mixed, so that
depending on your preconceptions or what catches your fancy, condemnation can seem as appropriate as panegyric. If the changes leave some
visitors heartened, they leave others unsettled. Chief among the latter are
those who, looking in the Third World for the realisation of the socialist
promise, thought they had found it in China in the 1960s and 1970s. They
found China politically appealing without her Coca Cola signs and rampant
advertising; they were ready to see Maoism as a true socialist alternative
to what they considered to be the disappointing failure of the Soviet
exemplar. Though many of them underwent a change of heart when the
Cultural Revolution was revealed in its true horror, some people cannot
help but be appalled by what seems to be happening today in China. Once
so aloof to materialistic ways, China seems to be moving headlong towards
commercial vulgarity with the rest of the Third World. What purist could

remain unruffled by the spectacle of Chinese waiters and waitresses dressed up as cowboys and cowgirls in Levi's and Resistol ten-gallon hats, to lend a Wild West American air to a tourist restaurant in Peking on the 4th of July?

If the world watches China, one of the reasons is certainly her apparent deviation from the Marxist path. The foreign press is always alert to the suggestion that Marx is dead in China, always ready to use the word 'capitalist' of any sign that the marketplace is gaining. 'Will China Go "Capitalist"?' asks a paper written in 1982 by Steven N. S. Cheung, the professor of economics at the University of Hong Kong. Officially she may never, the professor concludes, but she may 'eventually adopt a structure of property rights which resembles, or functions in the manner of, a capitalist economy'. Others conclude a little differently, using political criteria: China may have abandoned Stalin, they say, she may have abandoned Marx, but by the one remaining measure, Lenin's, China will continue to be a communist State, where the true power lies in a single Party organised in the Leninist image, headed by a self-selecting group of men who make decisions for the vast majority of the people and who would wish to maintain the political status quo indefinitely.

China is not alone among socialist nations in adopting what Deng calls 'useful things from the capitalist system' in the avowed belief that 'socialism does not mean pauperism'. In her attempt to modify her economic system, she has before her the example of the East European countries. Most countries that adopted Soviet-style central planning have attempted economic reforms since the early 1950s, so they are naturally interested to see how China fares. Even the Russians, though they prefer not to recognise the fact, find the Chinese experiment intriguing: the Soviet leader Mikhail Gorbachev has not only expressed a curiosity about her joint-venture deals with foreign companies, but is also supposed to have written on a memorandum about the Chinese economy sent to him by a Soviet economist, 'Stop carping about their reform; study it instead.'

A Romanian sociologist, Silviu Brucan, even went so far as to suggest that the prospect of China succeeding in her endeavour should concentrate the Kremlin's mind: it will then, *Time* magazine quotes him as saying, 'be confronted with a dramatic choice: to cling to the old ways and rely more and more on military power to exert its influence, or to take the bull by the horns and proceed with a radical change in both economic policy and global strategy. The issue of leadership in the communist movement will depend on that choice.'

There is another reason why China's 'second revolution' attracts so much attention, and that is its impact on the countries of the Third World. As Henry Kissinger put it in an article in the *Observer* in January, 1986: 'The modernisation of China will produce a new model for growth in the developing world, somewhere between unrestrained private enterprise, of which many new nations are afraid, and Soviet-style economics, which cannot work.' As one of the world's poorest countries—her per capita income of $260 puts her on a par with Pakistan and Zaïre—China has to find the means of economic change and development, perhaps replicating the basic steps through which Western societies have passed, but skipping a number of stages. The Chinese may not know what the recipe for success is, but they have recognised the perils of a do-it-yourself strategy. The insight turns out to be not theirs originally. Many developing nations which once opted out of the world economy, the better to build up their own industries and domestic markets, have re-entered it. And yet what China has done remains historically unique. It is true that other poor countries have sought to be transformed by the golden touch of foreign investment, have been persuaded by experts in development economics that the best way forward was 'export-led industrialisation'. It is also true that China was only about the eightieth country to set up a Special Economic Zone to attract foreign money and customs-free manufacturing. And yet her example still excites people. Leslie Sklair, a British scholar who has made a study of such zones—including the one China has established at Shenzhen, just across the border from Hong Kong—tells us why: 'Never before,' he writes, 'has a sovereign communist State so wholeheartedly set out to attract the exponents of capitalist industrial, commercial and management practices, and never before have such clear and unfettered opportunities for profit-making been provided by a communist State to capitalist entrepreneurs.' There is simply no precedent for what has happened in Shenzhen, and the events of its brief history and the plans for its future 'go far beyond the sporadic and relatively random connections that have been made between capitalism and communism in Eastern Europe over the past few decades'.

Another focus into which China has dramatically swung in recent years is that of the Western businessman. 'She is the last frontier,' one of them told me, 'a hitherto unopened field for capitalist expansion, now that that has had its day in Africa and South America.' The first attraction of China to the Western businessman is of course the size of the potential Chinese market: China has 22 per cent of the world's population, and even if only a small proportion of her people were to become spenders, it would mean many more millions of potential consumers in the global marketplace. So far only the Japanese have had much of a look-in, with their Toyotas and colour television sets, but though the tantalising untapped 'China market' remains more of a promise than a reality, more and more foreign firms are opening offices in Peking.

As a sub-continental economy China is more self-sufficient than almost any country in the world, and she will trade far less than smaller countries (at present her trade is only 1 per cent of the world total). Were she to seal herself off completely, she would still not be greatly missed. Yet while foreign trade is not going to be important to China quantitatively speaking, it will be so qualitatively. In 1793, the Emperor Qianlong announced to King George III, in reply to a request for the extension of trade: 'We possess all things. I set no value on objects strange or ingenious, and have no use for your country's manufactures.' On one level, the emperor's claim continues to hold good; but on another, it is quite untrue. To industrialise at the pace she has set herself, China has to look to the world outside for essential new technology, and to pay for it she has to expand her exports and develop other sources of foreign exchange. All this means in effect a deeper engagement in the world economy.

When China first came into vogue in the West, through the medium of enthusiastic Jesuit reportage during the seventeenth century, her claim on European interest had lain in her ideas, institutions and in *chinoiserie*. You do not nowadays look to China for original thinking or to widen your aesthetic horizons. Her creative culture has been at a low ebb since 1949, and what new art forms she boasts are hardly inspiring. Yet she is not so easily dismissed. She is heir to a long and brilliant tradition, and, despite all odds, astonishing examples of creativity have lately begun to emerge. Culturally China is full of anomalies, sterile yet rich, gagged by censorship one minute, bursting out like steam from a boiler the next. Few old cultures can cherish their heritage less, yet few are more intensely obsessed by their history. No nation on earth has done more in recent times to obliterate its past, yet no nation is closer to its roots. Collectively the Chinese have execrable taste; individually they can be very discriminating. There is mass illiteracy. There is prodigious scholarship. One man devotes ten years of his life lovingly rendering James Joyce's *Ulysses* into Chinese; another has never opened a book in his life. Such contrasts are perhaps to be found in many countries, but they are more extreme in China than most.

China is the place of plumbing that leaks, machines made to thirty-year-old designs, shops that are permanently out of things, and mind-boggling inefficiencies. No country, you feel, can be further from the electronic age, or more of a stranger to the microchip. Yet just as it was once said of the Soviet Union, China is the 'Middle Ages plus intercontinental missiles'. For all her laggardliness in the race towards the new technologies, China is an up-and-coming space power. Not only has she successfully tested ballistic missiles, she has broken into the commercial satellite launching market, delightedly cashing in on the void left by the failures of the American space shuttle and the West European Ariane. With her Long March III rocket, she has won orders to launch American communications satellites; and although the Chinese have received no external help since 1960, their American and European customers in the satellite launch business are impressed by their expertise. In their space programme the Chinese aspire not only to prestige, but to a good slice of hard currency.

No matter how one sees China—as a Marxist heresy; as a model for Third World development; as a vast, untapped market and field for Western enterprise; or as a cultural oddity—it is the impulse to modernity which underpins all her changes. Will it work this time? Modernisation in China has run aground before. It is true that the West under-estimated the capacity for change in China, but still it is very difficult to do anything novel in this country: the new seems always tinged with the immemorial. What shadows does the past continue to throw? We must look at her earlier efforts to modernise, the better to understand her present endeavours.

Under the watchword of the Four Modernisations—the upgrading of agriculture, industry, science and technology, and defence—the Chinese have undertaken what looks, at first glance, suspiciously like a repeat of the Self-Strengthening movement which took place as an experimentation with Western techniques in the second half of the nineteenth century. The historical parallel has not escaped Chinese minds, and of late there has been a good deal of debate among historians in China as to how that episode is to be best viewed.

To see it in perspective, one must go back to the eighteenth century. Then China was the greatest empire on earth. She had survived Rome, the Byzantine empire and Egypt of the Pharaohs, and was the only ancient empire to have lasted into modern times. What had ensured the empire's unique continuity was the imperial order, a remarkable political invention which combined great stability with the famous 'right of rebellion'. At the very summit was the emperor, ruling autocratically by the Mandate of Heaven. Below him was the imperial government, manned by scholar-officials recruited through competitive literary examinations based on the Confucian classics. These Confucian men upheld the ideal of 'government by goodness', emphasing right conduct and moral behaviour as the ethical sanction for a dynasty's claim to rule. The ultimate source of imperial authority was Heaven, whose Mandate could be withdrawn from an errant dynasty and given to whoever revolted against it successfully. It was a foregone conclusion that for the rebel to ensure the preservation of *his* newly founded dynasty, he had to honour the good precedents of the past and to conduct himself properly. If he was ever in any doubt, there were always the learned officials to advise him. These men had a vivid sense of history, and an unshakeable faith in the past as a guide to the present.

Throughout the empire they embodied the role of the State as nanny, superintending, down to the last finicky detail, every step its peasant subjects took from cradle to grave. The State was a tyranny, rigidly centralised and frequently stifling, but that was the price paid for the homogeneity and the phenomenal duration of Chinese civilisation. The feared alternative was anarchy, and such were China's geographic and social realities that not to maintain an iron grip on imperial unity was to give dangerous regionalism its opportunity. As a system of State and society, the Chinese empire was staggeringly successful, meeting the fundamental needs of human life on a scale achieved by no other civilisation. It is hardly surprising that the Chinese thought it better than any conceivable substitute.

But by the standards of nineteenth-century European civilisation, it had become obsolete. Europe had been infatuated with China in the eighteenth century. But now its technological lead had enormously widened, and it held China in contempt. John Stuart Mill was expressing a not uncommon view when he said, in 1859, 'We have a warning example in China.' Here was a people stagnating in immobility—'they have become stationary—have remained so for thousands of years; and if they are ever to be farther improved, it must be by foreigners.'

And the foreigners were there, as missionaries, merchants, and opium runners. The concessions which George III had failed to win by diplomatic representation were eventually wrested from the Manchus by an expedition-ary force. By the 1840s, no Briton was likely to question his right to trade in China: the Opium War had been fought, and the Manchu government had had the Treaty of Nanking imposed upon it at gunpoint. Among other things, this provided for the cession of Hong Kong and the opening of Chinese ports—the so-called treaty ports—to British trade and residence. The foreigners who lived in these cities—more and more of which opened as time went by—were subject to the legal jurisdiction of their own consuls rather than the laws of the Chinese empire. They honoured their own standards, maintained their own lifestyles, and they flattered themselves that they were introducing modern methods of commerce to a less advanced people. One could not really claim it to be a colonial system, but one easily detected its resemblance to those bases which expanding European colonial regimes had established in India and southeast Asia. China was to remain unconquered politically and economically, but culturally the treaty ports made a difference. Against the immensity of China the westernised Chinese they bred were a tiny minority, but if they did not actually change China, they left so deep a wound in her sensitive national psyche that to this day, Chinese minds find it hard to dissociate cities from detestable colonialism.

With her defeat in the Opium War, China's fate was sealed, for thereafter the tide of Western penetration could no longer be stayed. There followed a series of humiliations by which foreign powers won more and more privileges from the Manchus. Troubled by threats without, China was rocked by rebellions within. The largest and most devastating of the internal convulsions was the Taiping Rebellion of 1850, which lasted for fourteen years and spurred a steepening of the decline which had already set in. When it was finally put down, the Chinese government at last realised a painful truth. Something was needed to keep the structure of empire standing, and that something was 'Western learning', the kind of technical skill which produced 'ships and guns'.

This was the thrust of the Self-Strengthening movement, launched in 1861 as part of a bid to revive the traditional order. The more conservative Confucian officials declared themselves against it, but others more enterprising got busy. They built defence industries, they created institutions for foreign relations. When they were not opening new schools and translation bureaus they were despatching Chinese students abroad to study. The leading spirit of the movement was that greatest of the imperial ministers, Li Hongzhang, who said: 'China's chronic weakness stems from poverty.' The answer was seen to lie in modern industry, and under his general direction shipbuilding, mining, textiles and cotton enterprises were started or boosted.

But as a modernisation programme the Self-Strengthening movement did not go far enough. Bold as it was, it was also quixotic. And it did nothing to affect that in-built drag against progress in Chinese society—the deep conservatism of the Confucian order of things. Enthusiastically though Li Hongzhang and his kind might pursue the techniques of the West, as a class the officials were still staunch Confucianists, who would not for long support an enterprise that went against the Chinese tradition. Why was it necessary to learn from the barbarians? they asked. As one of them put it, 'If we sought trifling arts, and respected barbarians as teachers regardless of the possibility that the cunning barbarians might withhold from us their essential techniques—even if the teachers were to teach sincerely and the students to follow them faithfully, all that can be accomplished is the training of mathematicians.' And one has never heard of an empire being rescued from decline by mathematicians. (This was a voice from another age, but replace the words 'withhold from us their essential techniques' with 'refuse to transfer their technology', and you have a statement which might have come from the mouth of one of today's more conservative Chinese leaders.)

Even if they conceded that Western techniques were useful, they could not believe that anything else was. A distinction was made between substance and application: 'Chinese learning for substance (or *ti* in Chinese), Western learning for practical application (or *yong*).' This, the *ti-yong* formula, was to underlie the Chinese approach to modernisation in the decades to come, and to persist even into our own times, in the guise of an unresolved ambivalence about things Western—whoever says foreign technology is all right but not foreign bourgeois lifestyles is voicing sentiments very similar to those felt by the Confucians of the nineteenth century. There was no moment when the Chinese thought, if we take techniques from the foreigners, why not political and philosophical ideas too?

Thirty-five years later, it was painfully brought home to the Chinese that mastery of a few Western weapons did not win them much advantage. In their war against the Japanese, historians say, the degree to which each nation had succeeded in modernising itself was dramatically demonstrated. Japan, which had reached out eagerly to new ideas, offered a dazzling example of success. China, defeated, offered only a woeful pattern of failure.

Never was a nation's composure quite so shaken, and never again was the Chinese empire to be quite so certain that it need change only within its own tradition. Another modernisation effort was mounted, this time with the aim broadened to encompass political reform. Again there were people to argue for the status quo, but a more cosmopolitan minority— reformers, intellectuals, men of opinion—saw that for China to survive she must compete: she must become modern. If their political system did this for the Westerners, they asked, why not for us too?

The most compelling of the characters to be caught up in the reform movement of 1898 was Kang Youwei, a figure of evangelical style and confidence. He based his case upon a wide-ranging study of Western institutions, and urged that the young Emperor Guangxu instituted reforms of the kind adopted by Peter the Great and the Japanese leaders of the Meiji Restoration. 'The prerequisites of reform,' he told the emperor, 'are that all the laws and political and social systems be changed and decided anew, before it may be called a reform.' Guangxu was an inconsequential kind of monarch, put on the throne when he was three by his powerful aunt, the terrible Empress Dowager Cixi. But he was extremely taken with Kang Youwei's views, and in a succession of decrees issued over a period of about 100 days, pushed through a programme to modernise the Confucian administrative structure. This programme, one day to be called the Hundred Day Reform, ordered changes in government administration, law, education, international affairs, and industry.

But decreeing these changes was one thing, getting officials in the central and provincial administrations to implement them was quite another matter. Not all of the reforms went instantly to seed, but formidable opposition cropped up on every side. The days that followed showed to what extent they had encroached upon vested interests. The Empress Dowager emerged from her 'retirement' to announce to the public that a serious illness had incapacitated the emperor. Orders were issued to arrest Kang Youwei and his fellow reformers. Kang escaped to Japan, but others were executed, imprisoned or banished.

This chronicle of wasted efforts and dashed hopes suggested to many minds that progressive reform from the top down would not work in China. In these minds, the conception of change had shifted its emphasis, and now carried undertones of revolution. The regeneration of China, it was thought, was only possible with the complete overthrow of the Manchu dynasty.

We know, as they could not, that the sweeping away of the old empire and its replacement by a republic did not accomplish this purpose. Far from ushering in a period of peace and order, the 1911 revolution merely unleashed chaos, as though it were no more than a fall of dynasty, with all the disorder that that event commonly brought. Something more fundamental was needed, and the question of what that was caused much searching of heart among the young. Debates raged, magazines were founded. Between the years 1917 to 1923 there spread across the cities an intellectual movement of tremendous fervour, seizing in its surge teachers, students, merchants, or simply patriots. It began life under the rubric of the New Culture Movement. It climaxed in a huge wave of student protest on May 4, 1919. This was like May '68 in France, though more profound and thoroughgoing. Some historians call it an intellectual awakening, some deem it proto-revolutionary. It was the nearest the Chinese came to experiencing an identity crisis, and through it they moved a stage further in their painful pursuit of modernity.

At the heart of the movement lay a sense of nationalism deeper than anything which had been felt before. Four years earlier, Japan had imposed the infamous Twenty-one Demands, calling for Japanese control of large parts of Chinese territory and for the employment of Japanese advisers in Chinese administrations. And now, at the Versailles Peace Conference which settled the issues of the First World War, the Western allied powers supported the Japanese bid to inherit the German rights to Shandong, coldly brushing aside the Chinese plea that that province, the birthplace of Confucius and Mencius and the Holy Land of China, must remain theirs. The Chinese public received the news of this decision with a stinging sense of betrayal. Its anger flamed into riots, strikes and demonstrations in the cities; and it is to these, lumped together as the May Fourth Movement, that historians date the origins of the social revolution to which the Chinese Communist Party was eventually to lay claim.

The mood which the movement expressed was one of rebellion. There was a profound questioning of inherited values. China was sliding into political partition by the Western powers, and for the movement's spokes-men, her survival was no longer a matter of mastering mechanical skills or introducing political reform; so long as Confucian values prevailed, the Chinese could not be brought to save themselves from foreign domination. Only an all-out assault upon the evils of custom and traditional morality—the very 'national essence'—could clear the decks for a new and vigorous China. The Babylonians were no more, said Chen Duxiu, one of the most vehement of the movement's iconoclasts, of what good was their civilisation to them now? The leading lights of the movement were concerned above all to develop a new culture, and one of their successes was the introduction of a new literature based on the spoken language. This was a momentous change, not unlike the European switch from Latin to the national vernacular.

It was only to be expected that in their rejection of Chinese tradition, the movement's spokesmen should become pro-Western. Many had studied abroad, in England, France, Japan and the United States, and they were influenced by European and American notions. 'Science and Democracy' became one of their grand themes.

Yet though there was talk of a need for out-and-out Westernisation, it was not (is still not) in the Chinese nature to relinquish Chineseness. An ambivalence towards the West was understandable, when there were the treaty ports to remind them of Western aggression and Chinese humiliation. As a group the voices were cosmopolitan in tone, individually there were arguments for indigenous solutions. In the 1920s both the Western liberal and Chinese traditionalist causes found an audience, but in the last analysis neither won the toss. It was left to Marxism, a creed both internationalist and anti-imperialist, to dictate the final character of the Chinese regeneration.

The example of the Bolshevik victory in Russia proved potent. More and more educated Chinese began to think that only a social revolution would restore their country to her lost dignity. Those of liberal persuasion continued to argue that China's purpose could best be achieved by incremental change, by piecemeal reforms and universal education. But Chinese reality made no place for them. Their view of State and culture as separable spheres—the one public, the other private—found no cultural resonance in a country where, for 2000 years, the two had been one. Confucianism had imbued the whole of life, from government to personal relations; in Marxism the Chinese found another orthodoxy, and they took to it, with one feels a flash of recognition.

In all this, the presence on their coast of the foreigner, admired yet resented, was a goad. To this day the thought of treaty ports nags at Chinese pride. A story told of Mao Zedong as a young man in Shanghai in 1924 illustrates how deep it went with the Chinese. Coming across a former schoolmate in Western garb, Mao, dressed in old Chinese clothes himself, told the man to change his suit. When asked why, Mao said, 'I'll show you', and led his friend to the infamous sign in a nearby park which read, 'Chinese and dogs not allowed.' In fact, though Chinese citizens were indeed barred from the Public Gardens, no such sign carrying precisely these words existed in Shanghai, but the Chinese believe it did and, more to the point, the thought of it brings out the xenophobe in them.

The modernisation which first got underway in the treaty ports might have extended to inland China had their foreign residents been less resented, or had the traditional pattern of social and economic life seemed less adequate. More than other Asian countries faced with European might and expansion in that age of imperialism, China retained her cultural sense. Perhaps it would have been better if she hadn't. For she would scarcely be agonising over the open door now if the historical issues of Westernisation and modernisation had been resolved at an earlier date. And perhaps she would not have remained the anachronism she is if, instead of starting the race in the 'eighties to catch up with the West, she had thought it worth the price in cultural dilution to have done so in the early decades of this century.


China's communist leaders in 1949 were masters of their own house as the Self-Strengtheners of the 1860s, propping up a crumbling political authority, were not. Yet the circumstances in which they found themselves were hardly less dispiriting: a country vast and impoverished, a people half-starved and exhausted by war. Socialism, and even more so communism, presupposes a level of social wealth sufficient to satisfy every citizen's material and cultural needs and to leave him free to develop his own potentialities. It was obvious to everyone that China was very far from having reached that happy level, and that the first of her purposes was to rehabilitate her national economy. The question which faced the revolutionary victors was how.

They started by securing control over the 'commanding heights' of the economy, taking over banking, railways, steel and other important industries. At the same time they completed the land reform which they had already begun before 1949. But as the estates of landlords and rich peasants were being redistributed and industry nationalised, the question in the minds of all remained: how to build a modern economy, without which they could not begin to meet the needs of 500 million Chinese, in a country of peasants?

Luckily for the Chinese revolutionaries, they did not have to work in the dark: they could look to what Stalin had done in the USSR. There a heavy industrial base had been considered a first necessity, and to finance it money had come from investment and saving. This had meant holding down immediate consumption, squeezing harvests out of peasants, and coercion. To the accompaniment of the slogan 'Learn from the Soviet Union', China's First Five Year Plan went the whole hog of Stalinist planning, with heavy industry, in particular producer goods manufacturing, receiving the bulk of the State's capital outlay, at the expense of light industry and agriculture. It went in for giant industrial plants and engineering works in the true Stalin tradition.

It was not until much later that China had second thoughts about central planning. None of its failings mattered much in the early years of her industrialisation, when economic growth was a case of producing steel and more steel. These were the years of infrastructural building. There was a sense of conquering the vast hinterland for the use of industrial man, and whole new manufacturing centres sprang up in the undeveloped inland regions. Of the large schemes set out in the First Five Year Plan, five out of every ten were located in the interior.

Thus was set the pattern of China's regional development for the 'fifties, 'sixties and early 'seventies; for all the later talk of regional self-sufficiency and devolution of administrative authority, the State never wavered from its policy of making the rich areas pay for the poor. Regional equality is of course a proper ideal of socialist planning, but there were also strategic reasons for shifting resources away from the coastal regions. In the days of friendly Sino–Soviet relations the military threats were seen to come most probably from the sea, from the United States, from Japan and Taiwan. These motives were reinforced by an old antipathy towards the coastal cities, traditionally the preserve of Western capitalists and imperialists.

Much of this industrial expansion depended on the State receiving a steady supply of grain from the countryside to feed the towns. China's agricultural policy was perhaps not so extreme as Stalin's, but one cannot claim it was sympathetic to the peasantry: compulsory delivery quotas were used to extract the peasant's harvests; and grain prices, centrally fixed, were kept low in relation to everything that he had to buy from the urban sector, from tractors to chemical fertilisers.

It was against this kind of background that Mao evolved his economic principles, if such they may be called. Mao was no economist really, though it was he who dictated the character of China's development in the ensuing decades. He saw the whole grand process in cyclical terms. Each cycle, in his view, would be set off by an upsurge of activity, a rapid advance to a higher socialist form with targets pushed up, the populace mobilised, a fever of speed and output washing in a High Tide over the whole country. But the moment this produced disaffection and a deterioration in economic performance—as it was bound to sooner or later—the phase of rapid socialist transformation would be brought to an end by a liberalisation of policy. A big push followed by retrenchment, each wave leaving the economy in a better state than before—that was the Maoist notion of advance, a matter of moving 'two steps forward and one step back'.

The very epitome of the Maoist method was the Great Leap Forward of 1958–60, an exercise which, so its enthusiasts believed, would catapult China from socialism to communism in one short sprint. Relations with the Soviet Union having already deteriorated, it was to be the supreme example of what China could achieve when she went it alone. Mao had come to believe that China might not need as much time as previously thought to catch up with the big capitalist countries in industrial and agricultural production. He had become obsessed with the idea of overtaking Britain in steel production in only fifteen years (not so extravagant an aspiration, as it turned out, because China very nearly achieved it fifteen years later, though this may say as much about British productivity as Chinese).

Under the slogan 'More, faster, better and more economically', everything happened at fever pitch. Backyard furnaces, the most emblematic of the Great Leap's enterprises, appeared where no furnace had ever been, suggesting for a thrilling moment the triumph of native make-do-and-mend over scientific technique—and then dissolved into mud and brick after a few showers. There was grand euphoria, as production figures soared. So intoxicated was everyone by it that scarcely anyone in the top leadership stopped to wonder if the statistics were perhaps false, or if the cadres were reporting the true state of affairs. Deng Xiaoping was as taken in as any of the others, and did not question the fantastic yields that many communes were claiming. China was on the brink of plenty, they thought, envisaging an immediate transition to communism.

The consequences of the Leap were catastrophic. The backyard furnaces consumed all the coal but produced unusable steel. The very existence of industry was at stake, as over-extended machines ground to a halt and whole factories closed down. Millions of peasants had made for the cities in response to the industrial boom, but now there was no work for them, and they had to be forcibly evicted. There was no food either, as natural calamities exacerbated the crop failures. About 30 million people died of starvation and related ailments, and those who lived were so hungry that they were reduced to eating wild plants and leaves.

Wild as many of Mao's ideas may seem, they inspired his followers. For they were not all without reason. China abounded in human labour, and mustering that as a substitute for the modern technology that she lacked must have seemed quite logical. But this recognition of Chinese realities burgeoned into patently misguided manifestations, and the notion that a whole country could industrialise in the twentieth century on the basis of native improvisation could never stand up to the test of history. In some ways the Great Leap Forward was yet another episode in the century-long struggle of the Chinese to modernise on their own terms, without sacrificing their 'national essence'. In that perspective, Mao stands in the line of the Self-Strengtheners.

It was left to Liu Shaoqi, in whose favour Mao was forced to relinquish his position as head of State, to repair the damage the Leap had left in its wake. Liu was helped by Deng Xiaoping, and together they laid the ground for a phase of economic liberalisation. The strategies which emerged reminded Western leftists uncomfortably of Lenin's New Economic Policy. In China the policy was a breathing space, lasting only a few years, from 1961 to 1964, but many of Deng Xiaoping's current economic reforms are widely seen to have had their origins in this period of economic recovery.

Mao was implacably opposed to the new economic course. He was a man made for revolution, but now he was condemned to live in a period of creeping capitalism. To this he could never reconcile himself, for the last thing he wanted was to see his revolution sputter out in Yugo-slavian-style market socialism. He decided that a new cataclysm was neces-sary, and to trigger it off he launched the Great Proletarian Cultural Revolution.

The name was new, but it was an old idea. Ever since they took power the Chinese communists have advanced their revolution through a series of intensive mass movements or campaigns. These are, not to put too fine a point on it, terror campaigns. They are directed from the top and carefully orchestrated. They involve large-scale persecutions, with the masses of people whipped up to 'struggle against' designated target groups, be they landlords, the bourgeoisie, the intelligentsia, or proponents of liberal policy. They are emotional binges on a mob scale, mixing fear, hatred and frus-tration to release spasms of extreme violence and cruelty. They are often linked in their rhythms to the ebb and flow of economic High Tides and grace periods, and they spring partly out of the Marxist view that it is the relationship between classes that acts as the dynamo of change, and partly out of Mao's conception of historical progress through protracted class struggle.

The Cultural Revolution was more extreme than any of the earlier campaigns, more long-lasting and more profound in its implications. It was also a more genuine struggle, in that the young Red Guards Mao used and inflamed into action came up against real opposition. Clashes of rebel against authority, of faction against faction, reached a peak of bloody armed fighting. The primary targets were Mao's rivals in the Party—Liu Shaoqi, Deng Xiaoping and their supporters—but as the movement advanced the hit list was expanded to include writers, artists, the academic community, and anyone who had overseas connections. Fear and destruction followed the Red Guards, who rampaged about the country assailing the educational system, the bureaucracy, the Four Olds (old ideas, old culture, old custom, and old habits). Unlike the intellectual attacks of the May Fourth iconoclasts, these were physical operations, leaving temples desecrated, homes raided, persons bodily harmed.

Higher up, there was a purge of the upper ranks of Party and government organs on an unprecedented scale. Whole layers of the urban bureaucracy were removed to the country, for 'reform through labour' on farms or re-education in the so-called May Seventh Cadre Schools. Huge numbers of young people were urged to leave their 'soft' city existences for new lives in the villages. Earlier campaigns had seen the forced migration of large contingents of city dwellers to the country, but the mass 'sending-down' movement reached new heights in the Cultural Revolution.

A power vacuum having been created, the military was sucked in. Court politics came fully into being, and within the ambit of Mao—a single leader in absolute or near-absolute control—followers and personal representatives conspired. The chief of these representatives, Mao's own wife Jiang Qing, exploited the opportunity to settle old scores and, supported by her three allies in what people were to call the Gang of Four, determined policies in the name of an increasingly doddering Mao.

For many of its victims, the Cultural Revolution was only the latest episode in a story which began in 1956. That was the year the intelligentsia had their say, encouraged by Mao's liberal call to 'Let a hundred flowers bloom, let a hundred schools of thought contend.' But when it became apparent that they were not so unanimous in their support of him as he had thought—that they were, indeed, deeply critical of the Party—Mao retaliated by starting the Anti-Rightist movement the following year. Perhaps half a million people were affected by this campaign—denounced, banished, or driven to suicide. And to be labelled a Rightist was to head the hit list in the next round of persecutions.

The Cultural Revolution was the Anti-Rightist campaign magnified many times. But it spawned a happier result: in the opinion of most thinking Chinese I have talked to, the Cultural Revolution made the 'second revolution' inevitable. Without those 'ten calamitous years', they say, there would have been no sea change in Chinese policy. If it had not been for the trauma of those years, Deng Xiaoping could not have turned Chinese policies around so sharply. The Cultural Revolution took radical policies as far as they would go, and once it was over, and people saw the appalling costs that it exacted, there was no going back to how things were before it started. 'Who knows,' one Chinese said to me, 'instead of breaking with the Soviet path, we might still be trundling down it if there hadn't been a Cultural Revolution to make us think twice about everything?' The Cultural Revolution had tried to create a blank out of which a fresh start might be made; perhaps, in some longer historical perspective, we may see it as part of China's century-long struggle against her past, in her painful and still uncertain quest for modernity.

Mao Zedong died in September 1976, and shortly afterwards the Gang of Four were arrested by his successor, Hua Guofeng. Deng Xiaoping's hour came two years later, at the Third Plenum of the Party's Eleventh Central Committee in December 1978. The meeting inaugurated the policies that would set China on a new course. As the apologists of Deng Xiaoping's regime would have us see it, the plenum was when the Chinese revolution, put on the skids by the Gang of Four and the Cultural Revolution, was snatched from the brink of disaster by a decision to shift the focus of the

Party's energies. Academic analysts will want to see it in a more complex light, to disparage so simple a view of history. Yet, whatever their objections, there is no doubt that the plenum was a turning point.

One of the first undertakings of the new regime was to repudiate the Cultural Revolution, and to set its face against 'class struggle'. This is not to say that it will abandon the stop–go approach to the execution of policies, only that the Maoist dimensions will be taken out of it. But that is already change enough.

# 2

# FARM AND VILLAGE

So immense is China's territory that when the sun rises over the Ussuri River in the northeast, the Pamirs in the west are still dark; and when all is cold and grey in the north, coconut palms sway in the green tropical humidity of the south. In area, China is about the size of the United States including Alaska. In character, she is divided into north and south by the Yangtze River. The north is the country of wheat, maize and millet; of houses made of yellow-grey pounded earth; of the mule, sheep, and camel; and somewhat dour people; the south is the land of green paddy fields and tea, brick houses surrounded by bamboo thickets, streams and canals spanned by elegant hump-backed stone bridges, the water buffalo and ducks, and considerably livelier people.

Physically and economically, China may be divided into east and west, with the relief low in the one and high in the other. It is in the east, in a coastal belt which largely abuts the Pacific, that the most prosperous and developed plains of China are to be found. Running from the northern provinces of what used to be called Manchuria, the zone includes 'the land of fish and rice' (or, to translate this into English, of milk and honey), as well as Guangdong, the richly endowed province bordering Hong Kong and home to Cantonese immigrants in Chinatowns across the world. It is in this eastern belt too, that Peking, Shanghai and Tianjin, the three metropolises governed directly by the central government and placed on an equal administrative footing with the provinces, are located. Except for Sichuan, Deng Xiaoping's home province and China's largest rice bowl, the west summons up images of mountains and plateaux, of nomadic herdsmen rather than tillers. The northern slab of it is the thinly populated Chinese Wild West, where between one settlement and the next there extend immense emptinesses, sometimes of sandy or gravelly deserts, sometimes of steppes and forests.

For all her territorial grandeur, China is not rich farming country: compared to the United States (and to Europe), she has more land that is rugged, mountainous, or extremely arid. Only about a tenth of her total area is any good to the farmer, whose kind makes up eight-tenths of the population of China. Indeed, the country's tillable land per head is among the lowest on earth, less than a third of the world average. Yet with only 10 per cent of the world's arable land, China has to feed a fifth of the world's people.

Little wonder, then, that the Chinese peasant has to plough every bit of land that can possibly be cultivated, however unyielding or far. I was made unforgettably aware of this when, travelling by coach towards northern Shaanxi province one day, I found myself in one of the world's most astonishing regions, the Loess Plateau. Since loess is a soft, friable soil whose proneness to vertical fissuring is its most notable characteristic, the landscape is a unique reticulation of crevasses, some as deep as several hundred feet. Grand as it was, the sight of that strange and dramatic plateau gave me a chilling sensation. Coming upon it as the coach snaked up a ridge, I saw the plateau falling grey and yellow below me, with its great stern folds of impassable slope snatched from utter desolation by assiduous terracing. Everywhere the land is split, and where I looked, the only paths were the narrow tracks which wound up the steep walls of the cleavages. Along one track, across the lunar emptiness, the ageless figure of a Chinese peasant, dot-sized in the distance, doggedly trudged. The terraces showed strips of green: the wheat that he had coaxed out of the earth by back-breaking labour.

If China's agriculture is bedevilled by the shortage of workable land, it is also greatly hampered by climate. With a monsoon climate, China has very little rainfall in winter and often too much in July and August. The pattern would not spell trouble for agriculture if it were stable; but it is not, and there is great variability in rainfall from year to year, both in total amount and seasonal incidence. Travelling in north China, I have been caught in violent excessive downpours, the sort which causes disastrous floods and yet still leaves much of the growing season overly dry. It is no wonder that, since the earliest times, the most compelling of the questions faced by China's agriculturalists and rulers (including Mao in his time) was how to beat the floods and reap the rewards of irrigation.

Today, no matter where you look, there seems little room for tillable land to extend; the only way in which agriculture can grow seems to be by increasing yields. Western experts, surveying the scene in 1979, suggested more water, more fertilisation, higher yielding varieties of grain: in a combination of these, they suggested, lay nearly all of China's potential for increasing agricultural output. But they had not thought to consider the human factor. In the year in which they spoke, a movement to change the face of Chinese countryside was started. Following an about-face in the government's agricultural policy, the fields flourished, the production surged, the harvests broke records, and China was turned from a grain-deficit and cotton-deficit country into a net exporter of these commodities. We shall look in detail at these changes; but first, a little history.

For more than a quarter of a century, Chinese agriculture was collectivised into a three-tiered structure. At the lowest end was the production team, which corresponded to a hamlet, consisting of thirty to forty families. Each team was part of a production brigade, each brigade part of a people's commune. Communes were simultaneously an agricultural, defence, social and local government grouping, embracing farms and small-scale industries like iron, fertiliser, and food processing.

For as long as Mao dictated policies, the degree of public ownership and the size of the economic unit were altogether at the mercy of whatever phase of his economic cycle was prevalent. During a more radical phase, the team would go over to ownership by the brigade so that the economic disparities between individual teams might be evened out. At other times land, machinery and livestock would be owned and used collectively by the team, which would form the basic accounting unit of the commune, responsible for distributing income to its members. The peasants would express their opposition to being moved up to a higher level of collectivisation by slaughtering their pigs and sheep and chopping down their fruit trees, and not a few teams would surreptitiously divide up their property and sell off all their assets whenever rumours of super-socialisation were in the air.

Accustomed to difficult times, Mao Zedong, the ex-guerrilla turned national ruler, wanted the granaries full and a modern iron and steel industry in every province. His obsession with grain, the guarantor of life throughout the ages, from dynastic times to the years of guerrilla warfare, was made to fall upon all Chinese no less fanatically, and turning as much land as possible to growing basic food crops became a dominant feature of agricultural policy. This meant trees being cut down, pastures being ploughed, grasslands being destroyed; it meant that not the best use was made of land, wheat and rice planted in areas better suited to cash crops or animal husbandry.

Although, under a system called 'small freedoms within the big collective', peasant households were allowed to engage in sidelines like chicken raising and handicrafts, and to cultivate small private plots of their own, the radical phases of Maoist policy saw the eradication or severe limitation of such privileges. When the Cultural Revolution was at its most extreme, these activities came under attack as 'tails of capitalism' which had to be 'cut off'. In some places they were altogether abolished; in others, it was decreed that the number of chickens must not exceed three—any more than that number was capitalism (in some villages, such chickens came to be ruefully called 'revolutionary chickens'). In places where limited private plots were allowed, a local leader might come and measure their sizes, and if they turned out to be larger than what was permitted, he would pull out the crops. Of course not all peasants took this lying down, and one heard of brigade members retaliating by tearing the clothes of the cadres who destroyed their crops.

Traditionally the peasants sold the produce of their sideline activities at country fairs, but during radical phases these were either banned or subjected to repressive official regulation. It was common, for example, to allow peasants to market only what they could transport under their own power, whether this was by wheelbarrow, bicycle, or the immemorial carrying pole; the use of trucks and tractors by production teams was condemned as a vehicle for reviving capitalism. In any case, the conveyance of farm products between distant markets was forbidden, and goods and services had to flow to an official pattern, along the administrative channels of the State network.

One of the most compelling images to have come out of the Cultural Revolution was of massed ranks of peasants working with little more than their bare hands to terrace mountain slopes, dig irrigation canals, and build dams against floods. The image exactly fits the Maoist conception of the mammoth strength released by collective effort; but though it is genuine enough—peasants really did work like that in those days—in some ways it is a deceptive picture. It masks the fact that although overall agricultural output grew over the years, in the twenty-odd years since the commune was established productivity per farmer did not improve at all. One didn't have to be a specialist to see that what agriculture required was investment and a better incentive system. This was the state of affairs which Deng Xiaoping's regime faced when it began charting a new course for China's development in 1978.

The slogan might have been 'The Commune is Dead! Long Live the Household!' The policy-makers began by substantially increasing the purchase price of a whole range of farm and subsidiary products. The largest price rise to have occurred since 1949, the move did more to break the exploitation of the peasantry than had a quarter of a century of people's communes.

Simultaneously, the organisation of agriculture was transformed. The collective had been the bedrock of the whole rural structure, affecting the life of every peasant; but in five to six years, from 1979 to 1984, the familiar three-tiered system—the tens of thousands of communes, the millions of brigades and production teams—was all swept away. The decollectivisation was gradual, but throughgoing; and at the end of it nearly the whole of the Chinese countryside had gone over to family farming under an arrangement called the responsibility system.

Under this system, parcels of the production team's land are contracted (that is, leased) out to individual households, work groups, or families in partnership. The type of contract varies from family to family, from a simple arrangement, in which the peasant household pays the government a fixed sum for collective investment and welfare, sells an agreed amount of grain to the State, meets State taxes, and keeps everything it earns after these deductions for itself; to a more complex one in which the household earns work points with the grain it delivers to the government, and receives income for it when cash is distributed at the end of the year. The brigade became simply the village, whereas the commune was converted, and sometimes subdivided, into *xiang*, a township administration.

Revolutionary as it may seem, household contracting is not new to the Chinese rural economy; it had appeared briefly in 1956–57 as a result of the peasant's opposition to collectivisation, and also in 1959–62, as an emergency measure to get agriculture back on its feet after it had fallen to famine levels following the establishment of the communes. The story is now told of a seventy-year-old peasant who started it in Anhui province. His son having been put out of action by tuberculosis, this now legendary peasant was told by his commune to enter an old people's home. But the old man had a better idea: what if his production team let him take his sick son up into the mountains where he could care for him and at the same time farm some land for himself? Any extra grain he reaped, he promised, would be turned over to the State, but if his yields should fall short of his needs, he wouldn't ask the State for relief either. It was poor soil up there in the mountains, but the old man did well enough to be able to turn a surplus over to the commune in the very first year. Why didn't the commune, the old man then suggested, contract all its land to its members: wouldn't that stimulate the individual's sense of responsibility? The commune leadership brightened at the idea, and put the matter to the peasants. When the peasants declared themselves to be in hearty agreement with the proposal, the system was adopted across the province under the name of 'fixing output for each piece of land and responsibility for each person', or 'responsibility system' for short.

Its Chinese apologists say that the new system replaces the dead weight of 'everybody eating from the common pot' with the vigour which comes of 'linking output more directly to labour and initiative', under the socialist principle of 'to each according to his work'. But all it is really is the injection of material incentives into production, with the admission that people work harder if they are doing it for their own private gain than if they are doing it for the good of all.

When first adopted, the contracts were meant to be temporary and indefinite in term. But no peasant was going to put much money into his land unless he could be sure it would be his for some time. So the term was set at three years; then at fifteen (or up to fifty years for horticulture), with even the provision that if the farmer should die before the term was up, he could bequeath his contract to his descendants. Nearer and nearer, it seemed, the peasant's rights to his land approached those of possession, or ownership of the means of production. The State continues to own the land, but for all practical purposes it has, somewhat unsocialistically, offered the Chinese peasant the chance to realise a dream, to farm a patch of land he could call his own.

Many a prosperous peasant, taking matters into his own hands, contracts for more land than he could possibly farm himself, and either takes on hired labour to help work it, or sub-contracts it to others so as to free himself for more profitable pursuits. This amounts to the transfer of contracts—a grey-market deal to begin with, but a perfectly above-board practice today. As for the hire of labour, this was restricted to seven, as befits a socialist economy; but the authorities wink at farms which employ as many as 100 labourers apiece.

This smacks of landlordism, and socialist observers at home and abroad are right to be indignant. The regime, though, draws a distinction between the right to own land and the right to use it; and maintains that since the State retains ownership of the land, the responsibility system remains within the bounds of socialism. But does it? Hong Kong University's Professor Steven Cheung, to whom I addressed this question, explains it this way: 'From the standpoint of economics, an "ownership" right need not be a criterion of private property; for example, all lands in Hong Kong are "owned" by the Crown. ... The responsibility system, if reduced to its simplest and therefore most perfect form, is equivalent to the granting of private property rights via a State lease of land. ... Various dues exacted by the State may be lumped together in the form of a fixed rent, and since this rent is paid to the State, it becomes a property tax. ... In ancient China, as in medieval Europe, there was no distinction between the meanings of "rent" and "tax". A feudal lord who collected "rent" became a collector of "tax" when he assumed the role of a "government" in providing services such as justice and protection. From this point of view, the evolution of the responsibility system in China has come close to replicating in three astonishing years the course of several centuries of development in medieval Europe.'

'They are an adjunct to the socialist economy' is how the regime justifies private plots, family sideline activities, and rural markets. Along with the decollectivisation has gone the easing of restrictions on private plots, though under most forms of contracting there is no practical difference between these and the contracted land farmed by the household. As for the sideline occupations, they now thrive as never before, unfettered by the restrictions which once bound them. Similarly, rural marketing has seen a dramatic revival. Though none of these reforms are new to the rural scene, the boldness with which they were launched, and the length of period for which they have been sustained, are altogether unique in the history of China since 1949.

What has been their impact upon China's agricultural production? The results were so spectacular that they were reported all over the world. Grain production grew impressively, with bumper harvests in 1982 and 1983. In 1984, a record 407 million tons were harvested, a target China had originally planned to reach over three decades; and in the summer of 1985 the commercial attaché of the Australian Embassy in Peking told the foreign press that China's exports of rice, maize and soybeans had exceeded her imports of wheat, making her a net exporter of grain for the first time in living memory. Cultivation patterns have greatly shifted, now that farmers are no longer forced to grow grain, and acreages have been diversified to other crops according to the principle of comparative advantage. One of these is cotton, of which the yields have been so sensational in recent years that where there used to be an acute shortage, there is now a surplus. Rural incomes per head since 1981 have gone up at an annual rate of 14 per cent: a rapid increase, even allowing for the concurrent rise in the cost of living. The various growth figures are unprecedented in China; and Janos Kornai, the renowned Hungarian economist, was so impressed with what he saw when he visited the country in 1985 that he pronounced the changes in the Chinese countryside to be of importance to world history. 'The events in China,' he said at a symposium of economists in Boston the following year, 'make necessary an overall rethinking of the theory and practice of farm policy and agricultural development in the world.'

The glut of grain, though, was not without its problems. In absolute terms China does not have too much grain, but instead of using their harvest of coarse grains for feed, the peasants have always sold it as food to the government, which was obliged to buy as much grain as the peasant had to sell. But its granaries in 1985 were full to overflowing. For years, peasants had schemed through under-reporting and concealment to keep all the grain they could from the government's clutches. Now they were only too keen for the government to take it off their hands. The government found itself in a bind, because on the one hand it wanted to ensure a sufficient supply of grain, while on the other it would like to see the economy diversify to other crops. How to reduce its procurements without dampening the peasant's incentive and causing grain production to drop too sharply was the problem which the government now had to resolve.

The solution, which became effective as the 1985 grain year began, was the ending of the compulsory procurement system and its replacement by a contract system. Under the new system, the government contracts with the individual household before the sowing season for the purchase of a specified amount of grain; the contracts are voluntary, and leave the peasant free to produce for the free market if he so wishes. For the government, the additional potential advantages of the system are that it encourages the diversified use of grain and stimulates the circulation of grain in the economy. What the new scheme will do, if it works in the way intended, is to take the rural economy a step further into a free market system. For the peasant though, the advantages are not so apparent: it is true that the system frees him of the burden of compulsory quotas, but it also leaves him without a secure income. Market mechanisms take some getting used to, and farmers who have never had to adapt to price fluctuations are finding it difficult to gear their production to demand and supply conditions. Grain has always sold in the open market for twice the government purchase price, but now that there is so much of it about, market prices are not what they were. Besides, after decades of growing nothing but grain, many peasants find it hard to switch to other crops. On the other hand, grain production is more costly and less profitable than cash crops, so those who can, do diversify. Meanwhile, to make sure that there continues to be high enough incentives to grow grain, the government offers contracting households attractive procurement prices for the varieties of grain it wants and special subsidies like lower-priced chemical fertilisers.

After successive years of bumper harvests, China's grain production dropped drastically in 1985. This was partly caused by bad weather, and partly by a substantial cut in the acreage sown with grain. The government could hardly complain if peasants had turned to more profitable cash crops, animal husbandry and rural industry, but ever increasing grain yields have always had a powerful symbolic value for the Chinese Communist Party, whose fetishisation of self-sufficiency in grain goes back beyond Mao to imperial days. So there was instant consternation among the leaders, some of whom did not hesitate to make political capital out of it. Chief among them was Chen Yun, who with his dedication to central planning, may be counted on to speak out the moment anything goes wrong with Deng Xiaoping's 'capitalist' experiments. Now he was heard to murmur darkly that 'grain shortages will lead to disorder'.

The word 'disorder' carries emotional undertones for the Chinese, whose entire tradition has been one of putting up with repressive government control as a lesser evil than anarchy. All it takes for the bureaucracy to slap controls back on is a feeling that disorder looms. This has been encapsulated in a popular saying: 'Control spawns stagnation, stagnation prompts liberalisation; liberalisation spawns disorder, disorder prompts control; control spawns. . . .' So when grain figures fell below expectations, the government quickly acted; but instead of over-reacting by reviving restrictive measures, this time it left well alone, choosing to use incentive schemes to stimulate grain production.

For all that it has given Chinese agriculture a shot in the arm, the responsibility system is not without its undesirable side. If, for instance, you visit southern Jiangsu, the most successful of China's provinces and a densely populated region, you can tell at a glance how fragmented the fields have become under the new policy. Some fields are an extraordinary sight, splintered into hundreds of narrow strips just so that each family will get a piece of each quality of land—a piece of the good, a piece of the poor; a strip of the near field, a strip of the far. The officials responsible for the allocation were only trying to be fair, but the effect has been to divide the plots—already absurdly small, at a fifth to a third of a hectare per contract—into even tinier patches. It is just as well that the Chinese farmer still works with the hoe and the carrying pole, because the strips are not wide enough for a cart or a tractor. But farming on so small a scale does not lend itself to the proper arrangement of crops; and how is Chinese agriculture ever going to mechanise when the fields are so fragmented?

This is what William Hinton, the renowned American author and old China hand, has against the household contracting system. He had thought from the very first that family farming would slow down mechanisation, without which the rural economy would be held back. The total tractor-ploughed area, he recently noted, had decreased by nearly 3 million hectares since 1978. The government has been claiming for some time that peasants were buying more tractors, and that the total horsepower had risen greatly; but this is no mechanisation because, as Hinton pointed out, most tractors were small ones used for transport rather than field farming. But the Chinese farmer, who since ancient times has derived his sense of security from the possession of land, is not easily persuaded to give up his contracted plot. That expanding the scale of farming will make for greater efficiency is something his mind may understand, but not his heart. Even as he finds other trades more profitable than farming, he stubbornly hangs on to his plot of contracted land to produce his own food from it.

For centuries China was based on subsistence farming, highly developed in its way but entirely dependent on traditional techniques; it was an agrarian society consisting of countless cells of peasant families existing in self-sufficiency, each an individual entity, each isolated from every other. To those who mourn the passing of the commune, the break-up of collective production into family-based units looks suspiciously like a step backwards, a regression to the historical pattern rather than an advance.

They are reinforced in this view by the resurgence of old customs, old superstitions, and old conflicts among the peasantry. Country life has not been the same since the privatisation of farming. Old habits, surviving the worst that official suppression could do to stamp them out, have sprung back defiantly. When William Hinton spoke on these themes in London in early 1986, and somebody in the audience asked him if he thought foot-binding would come back, his startling answer was yes.

For myself, I do not think that these trends can be blamed on the break-up of collective life. If old habits burst to the surface when the lid of suppression is lifted, it is only for their reappearance, and not their existence, that liberalisation may be held responsible. If what the Chinese call unde-

sirable feudal habits have not died out, it must be because there has been
no fundamental change of values since the communists took power; and I
consider that to be more of an indictment of the Maoist regime than of the
present one. Perhaps only the transformations of economic growth and
modernisation will prise the peasant free of his attachment to old customs,
and not any attempt to advance him towards ever higher forms of socialism.
Indeed, one might even say that the harsher the surrounding reality, the
greater is the need to seek shelter in the past; only let life get better, and
the old customs will lose their strength to become mere ritual.

All the same, there is doubtless less cooperation in the villages than there
used to be; not being part of a whole any more, and no longer so closely
under the eye of the authorities, farmers are not so responsible about
communal property, or so ready to contribute to collective endeavour. The
area of irrigated land has not expanded since 1978, no doubt because private
interests now take precedence over public projects. In their heady pursuit
of personal profit, many villagers behave irresponsibly, helping themselves
to all kinds of public property, from trees to the beams of collective
piggeries. There is more theft, more squabbling over land use and water.
As the new policies give life to economic activity, so they release rapacity.
The process is sometimes disconcerting to watch, but for millions of peasants
there is certainly more material well-being, and there may well be a brighter
future. If one agrees that any policy which raises living standards, and
makes possible the widening of opportunities, is good, then one must
reconcile oneself to the face of the new Chinese countryside.

One change has led to another. As family contracting spread, there
emerged more and more 'specialised households', families which cut down
on farming to earn their livings as self-employed producers, making a
handicraft for the market, say, or providing a much needed service. Livestock
raising, rabbit breeding, horticulture, weaving, beancurd making, carpentry,
brick making—these are some of the trades the specialised households
engage in. The government planners think them a very good thing, because,
as they say, they 'shift the rural economy in the direction of a commodity
economy'. We may simply think of the specialised householders as China's
new budding entrepreneurs, and of their pursuits as small businesses.

Many specialised households combine, pooling their resources to form
larger ventures. Others take on relatives and extra hands as they expand,
becoming employers (a new breed in the People's Republic, where hitherto
the only employer had been the State). New networks of cooperation
evolve, some grounded on family ties, others combining around particular
skills or production processes, and yet others involving the taking out of
equal shares in a joint business. All are voluntary, with the partners deciding
for themselves how best to use their investments and skills. This is a far
cry from the way things were run under the collective, for no household

under that system enjoyed any real degree of self-management, and liaison between household and household, or level and level, was governed by local government and Party officials. Now common business interests and economic advantage link man with man, family with family, family with village or local authority, unconfined by rigid administrative borders, or even by geographical ones.

What the country has seen in the past six years is a restructuring to an entirely different pattern, economically, administratively, and even politically. The consequences for Chinese society are profound; some of the more disapproving observers even go so far as to see them as amounting to a betrayal of socialism, shaking their heads at the widening disparity in incomes, and at the creeping corruptions of prosperity. It is certainly true that under the new policies, some people become much better off than others—because they are luckier in their land or skills, because they work harder, because they happen to be engaged in a particularly lucrative trade, or simply because they are abler or more opportunist. Doesn't this mean a degree of inequality unacceptable to socialist society? Well, of course it does; but one of the most startling slogans to be heard in China in recent years is the exhortation to 'Let some people get rich first.'

The privatization of rural activity has inevitably weakened the authority of the production and team leaders; and the once powerful commune cadres have had to suffer a change in their jurisdiction. But they have by no means stood aside from the new activities. In many villages, a large proportion of specialised householders turn out to be cadres or ex-cadres; this is not surprising, because they are the ones with the necessary managerial skills, the ones who know their way round sales outlets and resource-allocating offices. There is no doubt that it is the better educated people that become entrepreneurs: a large number of specialised householders are 'rusticated' youths from the cities; demobbed soldiers who have learnt special skills in the army; craftsmen; ex-landlords, one-time petty capitalists, and even old Kuomintang officials. Many of these new entrepreneurs would have made it as rural cadres under the Maoist regime, so it seems as if, in some villages at least, the old social ranking remains in place, and it is still the same people who win.

The most successful of China's rural entrepreneurs have got into the papers, glorified as today's new heroes; for, as the new slogan had it, 'To strike it rich is laudable.' The super-heroes are the *wanyuanhu*, the '10,000-yuan householders', a new term which has the same ring in China as 'millionaire' does in our society.

Let us meet a few of them. Wang Zhaomei is an eighteen-year-old girl living in the rural outskirts of a city not far from Peking. The papers wrote her up because she became rich by growing and selling flowers. Soon she was inundated with letters, asking for her money, flowers or love. Not only did the poor girl spend 500 yuan in postage writing back, but she found that each day more than seventy uninvited visitors would drop in—all of whom expected to be richly fed, it being a Chinese habit to be lavishly hospitable to one's guests.

The Chen family, another *wanyuanhu*, discovered they were sitting on a gold-mine when the grandfather flourished his beancurd-making skills. His ability had lain dormant all through the Cultural Revolution, but once he started grinding the beans, it all came back to him. In no time at all, the entire family was making beancurd with him, and selling it in the market for a profit. The Chens are particularly lucky in their enterprising second daughter, who started cultivating tree seedlings on a part of the land contracted to the family, and richly supplemented the family income with the money she made from her nursery.

Often the true entrepreneur of the family is the wife. One woman in northern China, the wife of a demobilised soldier, hit upon the idea of breeding martens for their skins. In 1981, with a loan from the bank, she sent to south China for a pair of baby martens. Though they cost her as much as 80 yuan each, they multiplied after a few years and she sold them to the government for up to 300 yuan apiece. It wasn't all plain sailing though. At first, because of her inexperience, some of them died on her, and there is nothing worse than having one of a pair of martens die, she claims, because martens are so loyal that the bereaved partner won't mate with another.

The rural prosperity has spurred a housing boom, and some of the two- to three-storey villas the prosperous farmers have built for themselves in the countryside around Xiamen and the Yangtze delta are a sight to see. When I was in northern Zhejiang province in the winter of 1984, I heard amazing stories of peasants buying pianos and building swimming pools. I did not find them difficult to believe, because at the time I was staying with a *wanyuanhu* who not only had a Japanese colour TV set and a name-brand refrigerator, but a porcelain bathtub as snazzy as anything made by Jacuzzi. I was given the supreme honour of christening it, and this was the source of some commotion because, although the tub came complete with shiny taps, the house had no running water, and my bath had to be filled with buckets of water from the single tap in the courtyard.

Nor was my host the envy of his neighbours, for they were almost as well-off themselves, the village being in one of China's most prosperous regions. But elsewhere the rich are prey to the malicious gossip and slander of the 'red-eyed' (Chinese for 'green-eyed') and the harassment of local officials, among some of whom there still linger many of the old misgivings about private wealth. If the newly affluent peasants are not, like poor Miss Wang Zhaomei, pressingly imposed upon by grasping supplicants, they are subjected to the extortions of local officials, who make them feel they are either selfish or mean, or that their profits are nothing but ill-gotten gains, if they do not donate large sums (part of which the officials would no doubt divert to their own pockets) to communal projects.

Despite the official call to 'let some people become rich first', there is still enough disapproval of wealth among certain cadres—especially those who do not do well out of the new policies themselves—to keep the newly affluent peasants awake at night. Now and then voices are raised against the widening gap between the haves and the have-nots. A moneyed class is emerging, they warn; and so it is. There exists a potentially exploitative relationship between employer and employee, they say; and so there does. Times have changed, and getting rich quick has begun to supplant collective labour as the high road to socialism in China.

One day in late 1982, shortly after I had arrived in Shandong province, I found myself at the Victory Oilfields, near the estuary of the Yellow River. Not having seen an oilfield before, I had only the vaguest notions of what I would find there. One thing I did not expect was rusticity. But at the oilfield, harvested grain was stacked all round the oil wells, and one crossed from rig to rig by wading through fields of cultivated crops. At the office of a farming collective at Victory, a woman official quoted a saying coined by the late Zhou Enlai during the Cultural Revolution: 'Integrate industry and agriculture, town and country, for the benefit of production, and the convenience of living.'

Here, then, was a good example of the combination of agriculture and manufacturing industries and the gradual abolition of the distinction between town and country urged by the Communist Manifesto. The oilfields reflected a socialist ideal, that of every family having one foot in farming and the other in industry. China would industrialise, the idealists maintained, but she would do so without abandoning the traditional virtues of village life. In much of the Third World, as the *favelas* of Latin America and the shanty towns of Asia attest, the fastest growing type of urban massing has been the slum. Western Marxists, ever eager to find a future that works, were gladdened to find that this has not happened in China: that stock Third World image, the Coca-Cola sign erected on the edge of a blighted urban slum, was cheering by its absence.

The lure of the city, though, is no less strong in China than in other Third World countries. After the communists took over, China experienced urban growth at a rate and on a scale unprecedented in world history. If China managed to achieve impressive industrial growth without the urban squalor which seems to go with the early phases of industrial revolutions, it was not because of any Marxist town planning. The years have seen massive migrations into the cities, but equilibrium of a sort has been achieved with the forcible ejection—the so-called rustication movement— of huge numbers of urban dwellers to the country. These people began returning to the cities in the late 1970s, and one of the first tasks the new leadership had to tackle was how to re-settle them and provide them with jobs.

Nor are these returnees the only people to converge upon the city. A disturbing finding of China's demographers is that by the year 2000, China will not only have 200 million more people added to her population, but a surplus of around 200–225 million rural workers whose labour will not be required in traditional agriculture as arable land per head declines, mechanisation increases, and the structure of the rural economy changes. Already, two farm hands are doing the work it took three to do just a few years back. The pressures which these people will put on urban amenities, already on the point of collapse, will be horrendous. How to deal with this problem is one of the biggest challenges faced by China in the 1980s.

The problem has existed for some time, but agricultural unemployment was masked as underemployment under the old commune system, which allowed every individual, no matter how unproductive, to 'eat out of the common pot'. But there is no room for overmanning in a diversified and privatised rural economy, and once the household contracting system was in place, the labour surplus became only too obvious.

Within a few years of the advent of individual farming in the countryside, there emerged a class of people the Chinese call 'rural inhabitants detached from the land'. Here is a portrait of one such inhabitant. Li Manzhu was born the second of three brothers in a county in Hunan. Life was hard for his widowed mother, and only the eldest boy, Li Yuan, got to go to school. Li Yuan was lucky enough to join the army and to be sent to university in Shanghai. He now lives in Peking, working in an enviable job in government. Li Minzhu, though, had remained in the countryside, where he farmed and supported his wife and children on less than 0·2 hectares of land. On a visit to his brother in Peking, he noticed clusters of young men, most of them country folk like himself, squatting or sitting on the pavement around the intersection at Hujialou. They turned out to be self-employed carpenters, as one might have guessed from the bundles of saws and samples of wood finish that lay around them. Carpenters have been pouring into Peking for some time; in earlier days they went from door to door, but now they all congregate at Hujialou, which has become a sort of carpenters' mart. Li Manzhu decided to go into business too, and leaving his wife and children at the farm, moved in with his brother in Peking. A wardrobe could go for as much as 150 yuan in Peking, so Li Manzhu was soon earning more money than his brother.

Other rural migrants work as private traders, domestics, salesmen or purchasing agents and, above all, as construction workers. So phenomenal has been the growth of this last group that it has become a part of China's economic planning to expand the export of labour services to various parts of the world. But although crews have been despatched to Japan, Africa, South Asia and the Middle East, sending labourers abroad is only a temporary and partial solution to the problem of agricultural unemployment. Urbanisation cannot be staved off in the long run, but in which cities are these hundreds of millions of extra people to be accommodated? This is a matter of regional policy, intensely debated by China's scholars in recent years. Some argue in favour of spatial concentration, drawing upon the experience of European and North American cities, where urbanisation intensified with the growth of per capita manufacturing output, and then, as the economy advanced and the tertiary sector expanded, there was a move away from the city to the surrounding country. These people believe that a strategy of urban concentration would be more appropriate to China's present level of industrial development. But in the first years of the debate, it was another school of thought, one which saw China's road to urbanisation to lie through her small rural towns, which gained the wider support.

The development of small towns is of course dependent on the growth of small-scale industry, something which certain Western economists have dismissed as being misguided attempts to encourage uneconomic cottage industries. But if Japan is anything to go by, small industries can play an important role in the early phases of industrialisation; being labour-intensive, they can mop up excess farm labour and meet the needs of a rural and small-town population with increasing purchasing power.

The development of small community enterprises has been at its most vigorous in southern Jiangsu province, which has been publicised as a model for the rest of the country to follow. Located in the heart of the Yangtze delta, Jiangsu, the most densely populated of all China's provinces, is now the country's highest performer in terms of output value. Jiangsu's prosperity is largely owed to the growth of its rural enterprises, which made up as much as half of the industrial output value by 1986. Brought into being during the Cultural Revolution, when production in city factories was severely disrupted by infighting, and further stimulated by Deng Xiaoping's reforms, these so-called township enterprises have recently enjoyed a veritable boom, revealing the astonishing capabilities and entrepreneurial vigour of the rural sector. For the country as a whole, the growth of their output value surpassed that of urban State and collective enterprises in 1984, and now they account for an astonishing 20 per cent of the total industrial output. By the end of 1984, more than 50 million people were working in township industries; add their families to this figure, Chinese planners say, and you find that 100 million people, a tenth of the nation's population, have been 'detached from the land' and turned into an industrial labour force in a matter of five to six years.

For a picture of a village through which these winds of change have strongly blown, one could settle upon Huaxi in southern Jiangsu province where, above the chirp of insects and other country sounds, the clattter of a textile mill can now be heard. Huaxi is fast becoming a rural town, one which boasts a steel fence plant and a pesticide spraying equipment factory (the parts for the sprayers being distributed to individual households for assembly). Enterprisingly, when the villagers moved out of their country dwellings into new housing in 1983, they converted their old homes into a guesthouse for conferences and foreign tourists; complete with traditional carved, ivory inlaid beds, the guesthouse caters to foreign tourists who want an authentic taste of country living and a closer look at village life than is normally offered by the package tour.

Another fairly typical example is Dongjiang, a village which now bristles with factories in Wuxi county in southern Jiangsu. Its entrepreneurs got started by establishing links with larger business, which helped train staff and upgrade technology. Many rural enterprises have become 'satellite plants' to the large-scale urban factories, which open up small economic niches which they, with their heavy overhead costs, cannot efficiently fill. The factories in southern Jiangsu learn special skills from Shanghai, which they in turn 'transfer' to other areas in exchange for raw materials. In Chinese, the process is known as 'the big fish helping the small fish, the small fish helping the shrimp.'

As elsewhere in the developing world, small-scale industry cannot compete where economies of scale are significant, and in China they are further disadvantaged by the fact that, instead of being allocated raw materials under the State plan, they have to buy their raw materials from the open market, at prices higher than those paid by the State enterprises. And in a country where energy supplies are short, and electricity has to be saved for the big plants, it is the rural factory which has to suffer the frequent power cuts. Yet another constraint is finance: when the government tightened credit control in 1985, many rural factories felt the pinch.

Though the government thinks township enterprises a very good thing, it is nevertheless disturbed by their spread—rampant in some areas—into agricultural land. Inevitably, many rural enterprises are a jumble of the good and the bad, the perfectly legal and the shady: virile they certainly are, and a great way for the peasants to prosper, but they are also extremely polluting, and their health and safety standards simply don't bear looking into. There is a no-holds-barred feeling to many of them; and in their opportunism they often cut corners to produce not only shoddy goods but outright fabrications of name-brand products. Still, for the moment they are seen to be indispensable vehicles of high growth, and the so-called 'southern Jiangsu model', we are frequently told, represents the Chinese path to industrialisation.

Meanwhile, from a far corner of the neighbouring province of Zhejiang, news of a new trail being blazed by rural entrepreneurs reaches us. This other path to Chinese modernisation is called the 'Wenzhou model', after the port in whose environs the way is being carved. Wenzhou lies in the frontline, facing Taiwan, and smuggling of blue jeans and digital watches from that other 'China' had brought its fishermen much prosperity. But Wenzhou is otherwise disadvantaged: it had long been deprived of government investment, and it is woefully inaccessible, with the nearest railway line stopping 250 kilometres short of it. Perhaps because it is so isolated, Wenzhou was chosen as a testbed for some large-scale economic reforms—whose effects, if disruptive, would at least remain confined to a small area. In 1981, the year the reforms were adopted, the rural people around, long noted for their traditional handicrafts, were given the go-ahead to develop cottage industries and family workshops. It was mainly articles which larger units were not interested in manufacturing that these workshops began turning out—shoe laces, elastic bands, school badges, plastic cards, garments and, above all, buttons. (Within a few years, Wenzhou's wholesale button market became the largest in China, doing 80 million yuan of business a year.)

Soon a capital market began to burgeon in Wenzhou, as the Agricultural Bank's rural credit cooperatives adopted floating interest rates to suck in scattered local savings to funnel to the businesses. Various financial institutions sprang up, and money for investment was further raised by the issuing of bonds and the selling of shares. All this has helped to boost the local economy. By 1986, more than half of the rural labour force within Wenzhou's administrative ambit had transferred from the land to private or family business, commerce or trade; and annual average income had shot up from about 60 yuan in 1978 to 447 in 1986.

National leaders, sociologists and economists have come visiting to look at what the *People's Daily* has described as an 'economic miracle'. Zhao Ziyang, one of the visitors, suggested among other things that some 'theoretical work' be done on the Wenzhou experiment with a view to its bearing on nationwide economic reforms. But to fit what has happened in Wenzhou to a theoretical Marxist scheme may prove difficult, because it is more than a niche that private enterprise has found here: already it accounts for a sizeable proportion of the local economy.

To the government, development of the kind Wenzhou and southern Jiangsu illustrate suggests answers to a national problem. Today there is much talk of the peasantry 'leaving the land but not the village'—working in rural township factories or trades by day but returning to their village homes by night, or partly carrying on trades and businesses at home. When national leaders inspect townships in southern Jiangsu, or villages in the countryside around Wenzhou, they tell themselves that the shape of modernisation which they foresee for China as a whole is already discernible in these small parts of the country. Here are families working simultaneously on the land and in industry. Here the population of small market towns is growing. Here cottage industries are thriving. Here, they think, you may find an answer to that big question facing China, how to industrialise but not to over-urbanise.

# 3

# FACTORY AND CITY

Socialism is supposed to provide for people's wants without the inequality and waste of capitalism. One of people's wants in China is for Shanghai's Phoenix and Forever brand bicycles to get them about. Yet there are never enough supplies of these and one waits an age before one's turn comes up on the waiting list, while mountains of inferior makes waste away in warehouses across the country.

A visitor to China in the 1970s might not have known that a distressingly high proportion of people were out of work, but he could certainly see that even among the employed, large numbers were merely idling. Professor Steven Cheung tells how, during a stay of several days in a Canton hotel, he noticed three men repairing a small hole in a wall: one held a tray of plaster, another applied it, and the third merely stood there pointing at the hole. Coming from frenetic Hong Kong, he could scarcely believe that these were Chinese he was watching. How could a people famed for diligence be reduced to such lethargy? he asked himself.

China's industry needs revitalisation as badly as its agricultural economy. And in 1985, after some years of conducting pilot and experimental reforms in selected factories in various parts of the country, the Chinese turned the focus of their reforms from the countryside to the urban and industrial economy. The answer the Party Central Committee came up with to Steven Cheung's question, at an important meeting in the autumn of 1984, was that 'the ardour, initiative and creativity of the urban enterprises for production and operation, as well as their 80 million workers and staff workers' had not been 'brought into full play'. The Central Committee's proclamation of sweeping reforms in industry struck some British journalists as being almost Thatcherite in its enthusiasm for market competition; and one commentator, the British scholar Richard Kirkby, observed that in just four years, China 'moved far closer to a fetishisation of market forces than have the Eastern European nations in two decades of liberalisation.'

Yet there can be few socialists who could contemplate an unmanaged economy, one in which 'blind' market forces fight it out, with anything but anxiety. The national leaders admit that reforms are a great deal more complex in industry than in agriculture; here their progress is no straightforward march along a clearly signposted path, but more the groping and sometimes faltering advance of a scouting party, 'feeling about', as the leaders themselves put it, 'for stepping stones to cross the river.' Although

most countries that adopted Soviet-style economic planning have attempted
to reform their systems, there is no hard evidence that these attempts have
made a significant difference to economic growth rates or other indicators
of economic performance. It is true that Chinese economists have tried to
learn from the East European experience—among books published in the
second half of 1985 were titles like *The Industrial Reforms of Hungary and
Other Countries—With an Appendix on Hungarian State Enterprise Legislation*
and *How the Soviet Union Exploits the Western Economic Crisis*—but the
lacklustre results in these countries can't be all that encouraging. When
Zhao Ziyang was asked by a Yugoslav magazine in the summer of 1986
to comment on the Yugoslavian reforms, he diplomatically observed that,
much as the Chinese admired Tito's pioneering steps, China's historical,
national and geographical circumstances were different, so that reforms in
the two countries were bound to be 'tinted with their own characteristics'.
Privately, though, members of Zhao's think tank believe the Yugoslavian attempts to have been a failure. The Chinese search for inspiration
certainly ranges beyond socialist economies; this is why, on top of those
books on Hungary and the Soviet Union, one finds titles like *The British
Decline: Its Causes and Effects*, and *The Way to Wealth: The Experiences of
Successful American Firms*. One also finds, perhaps to one's surprise, translations of the works of Milton Friedman.

As we saw two chapters back, when China's revolutionary leaders
decided on policies and means in the early 'fifties, they found a precedent
in Stalin's method of rapid industrialisation based on heavy manufacturing.
As they saw whole new industries created, steel factories going up and
gigantic dams raised to produce electric power, the Chinese no doubt felt
that they had managed matters well. And so they had in a way, judging
by the high rates of growth of heavy industry and overall measures of
national product. Judged by other standards though, China's economy had
done less well. Growth rates had been high, yes, but they had only been
achieved at an expanding cost in terms of foregone consumption. For as
long as Mao dominated economic policy, China maintained a high rate of
savings and investment; this had been steadily rising, and a given amount
of investment was producing an ever smaller return, so that to sustain her
high growth rate, China had to devote a higher and higher proportion of
Gross National Product to investment, with a correspondingly lower share
remaining for consumption.

Another source of imbalance in the economy was the way heavy industry
had crowded out agriculture and light industry. This China's new leaders
began correcting when, under the catchphrase 'adjustment', they changed
investment priorities in 1978. One of the methods they used, as we saw in
the last chapter, was a hefty hike in agricultural purchase prices. Also given
a boost was light industry, which has the added advantage of being a

labour-intensive sector offering jobs to the unemployed.

Even within heavy industry, the balance needed adjusting: under Mao, steel was to industry what grain was to agriculture. Other sectors were less favoured, and now China is faced with three serious bottlenecks in her economic development, because her energy, transport and tele-communications industries are simply not up to satisfying the demands which the projected pace of her modernisation is going to place on them. Hardly surprisingly, these sectors became high-priority areas in the Sixth and Seventh Five-Year Plans (1981–85 and 1986–90).

But of all the defects of the Chinese economy, the one which exercises the minds of the policy-makers most is its inefficiency. With their 'adjustment' policies, the Chinese government successfully altered the composition of output, striking a better balance between the various sectors of the economy; but what continues to elude them is the key to improving the operating efficiency of industry. What is termed 'extensive' economic development (that is, achieving growth by adding more capital to the economy) is all very well in the early stages of industrialisation; but now China must grow 'intensively', through technological change and managerial innovation.

The inefficiency of Chinese industry, all Chinese policy-makers are agreed, stemmed from the way it was run. Three phrases sum up its chief charac-teristics: State ownership, Stalinist central planning, and the concentration of power in the hands of the Communist Party. To improve the performance of the economy, some aspects of these features would have to give. It is not, obviously, going to be State ownership first, nor will the Party give up its power without a fight. The first steps the Chinese leaders took were in the direction of reforming the management of industry by giving more autonomy to individual enterprises or factories, but since this entails leaving people to run things for themselves, sooner or later the other two features will be affected.

Before we examine the reforms themselves, we should look in some detail at the complex and unwieldy system they will modify. State enterprises in China belong either to what are called 'line' organisations (central govern-ment departments), or to 'block' ones (local authorities). To put it another way, they exist in two interlocking sets of hierarchies, the departmental and the regional. To complicate matters further, there are several tiers to the regional structure, namely provincial, city, and county. Over the years, the degree of economic devolution has fluctuated, with control over enter-prises remaining in the hands of the central authorities during some periods, and handed over to the provinces at others.

I can best illustrate the confusing and, economically speaking, irrational way in which enterprises are controlled in China by citing the case of the Qingdao Forging Machinery Plant, a State-owned factory studied by the World Bank in the early 1980s. The plant, one of the most important of its kind in China, is named after the city of Qingdao, to whose Machine-Building Bureau it belongs; it is the bureau which determines its annual production and financial plans and evaluates its performance. It is the bureau, too, which approves matters relating to wages; the distribution of bonuses; and the recruitment, training and transfer of all staff save cadres—though the bureau must also send an aggregated report to the City Labour Bureau. But when it comes to the appointment or dismissal of technical and professional cadres in the factory, and cadres in the Party organisations within the factory, it is the Party Committee of the county which has the say. The County Finance and Tax Bureau is entrusted by the City Finance and Tax Bureau with collecting taxes from the plant and with receiving the profits it remits to the State. It is the county branch office of the People's Bank of China which assigns and manages the plant's circulating funds, makes the loans it needs for production development, and supervises its use of funds.

When it comes to the supply of raw materials needed to fulfil production quotas, the central Ministry of Machine Building, the province, the city and the county all share some responsibility, depending on the category of goods and the location of the supplier. For the major raw materials needed to fulfil the quotas set by the City Machine-Building Bureau—materials such as pig iron, steel, non-ferrous metal products, coke, wood and so on—the plant must apply to the Provincial Machine-Building Bureau; the Bureau then assigns a quota to the plant, on the basis of which purchase contracts are signed between the plant and the suppliers. For coal, it is the City Materials Bureau to which it applies for a quota; and when granted, this is supplied by the City Fuel Company. However, for gasoline, diesel fuel and lubricating oil, it is the County Commercial Bureau which sets the plant's quotas, and the petrol supply stations under its control which supply them. It is on the county, too, that the plant depends for its electric power and for local building materials such as bricks, tiles and stones.

As for sales, this is sometimes a matter for the enterprise itself, and sometimes a matter for the city. Export sales are handled by the Ministry of Machine Building and the Provincial Export Corporation. No department exists to coordinate sales with production and supply. Not surprisingly, a balance among these three areas is seldom achieved.

Since the enterprise comes under the authority of both the City Machine-Building Bureau and the local county (in whose annual plans the factory's output value is included), it often receives conflicting targets and is left not knowing which to follow: for example, the county's plans for the factory's output value for 1982 amounted to 19 million yuan, while the quantity and product variety quotas assigned by the bureau came to 13 million yuan. If the plant was to meet the target of the one, it would not be able to fulfil the quota of the other.

Not all enterprises in China are as complexly supervised as the Qingdao Forging Machinery Plant, but they are all over-managed. The Chinese have a graphic way of describing their enterprises: they say that enterprises have 'too many mothers-in-law looking over their shoulders'. The first aim of any reform, then, is to decentralise authority and shift the locus of decision-making down to the factory manager; in effect to strike at the heart of the Stalinist command economy, for instead of receiving orders from above, producing enterprises are to be allowed to decide their own way of doing things.

Of the rights granted the enterprises where the reform was first tried out, one was the retention of part of their profits for expanding production and for paying bonuses to workers. (If the enterprise made a loss, on the other hand, the State would subsidise it.) Another was the right, once the State plan was met, to produce extra goods and sell them on the market. A third, hardly less significant, allowed the enterprises to engage in export trade and to keep a part of their foreign exchange earnings to import new technology and materials. Yet another, the stick to the carrot of bonus payments, was the right to fire their workers (though it was understood that this right was to be exercised sparingly, in only the most serious cases). On top of these measures, there was a change in the role of financial institutions, with bank loans replacing State appropriations for investment in capital construction.

But the profit retention scheme proved unsatisfactory; the rates of retention were based on the growth of profits achieved by each individual enterprise, and it was the poor performer which had the larger potential for increasing profits, and which got to keep a larger proportion of its earnings. Enterprises in China are subject to the notorious 'ratchet effect', a familiar feature of centrally planned economies, created by the fact that targets are constantly revised in the light of actual performance; it doesn't take much intelligence to know that it is better to perform less well than you can because if you make a much higher profit than other factories, the State will raise your target in the future and reduce your profit retention ratio.

A new scheme was tried out in 1980, one which allowed the factory to retain all of its profits and to assume sole responsibility for its profits and losses; instead of turning its profits over to the State, the factory was made to pay a proportion of its earnings as income tax, and if it incurred a loss, its staff would have to suffer for it by having their bonuses or welfare benefits cut. It was hoped that by making individual plant managers and other employees bear a greater risk for investment decisions and performance, efficiency might be improved.

If carried to its logical conclusion, the reform would mean that unless failing State enterprises pulled themselves out of the red, they would go bust and their workers would be laid off. Socialists baulk at the very thought of liquidation, but in the spring of 1986, the government hardened its heart and drafted China's first bankruptcy law. The first city to subject its enterprises to the threat of closure was Shenyang, a northeastern city which the press hailed as a daring trail-blazer in economic reforms. There, three factories running at a loss were told to put their houses in order and to turn over a new leaf; and when one of them had failed to do so by the spring of 1986, it found itself named as China's first official bankrupt company. Considerable heart-searching had preceded Shenyang's audacious action, for bankruptcy had always been seen as a by-product of capitalism and to declare a socialist firm bankrupt and to lay off its workers was to attack a taboo.

To relate productivity to individual incentives, the industrial reforms resorted to the responsibility or contracting system, already tried and found effective in agriculture. But such is the complexity of the industrial production process that contracting arrangements have to come in many more forms in the factory than on the farm, and what you find is not just contracting between the State and the factory manager, but sub-contracting between the manager and shop floor, and sub-sub-contracting between the foreman and individual worker. The success stories got into the newspapers, and the manager who turned a losing business into a profit-making one ranked with the *wanyuanhu* (the 10,000-yuan peasant household) as China's latest hero.

Here is one to relate his own story. He is Ma Shengli, the holder of a responsibility contract in the northern city of Shijiazhuang, where we meet him in the last months of 1984. He works in a paper factory set up during the Great Leap Forward, where the machinery was reasonably advanced by Chinese standards and the performance more than creditable. But that factory's impressive record could not be sustained, and the annual profits started falling, from about 1 million yuan in 1979 to 61,000 yuan in 1981; by 1982, the factory was in deficit by 165,000 yuan.

'This year,' said Mr Ma, 'the State handed down a profit target of only 170,000. Low enough, you'd think, but still the factory wouldn't accept it. Back and forth we argued, insisting they lowered it to 140,000; one thing for which there's never a shortage of verve, I tell you, is the haggling you engage in with the State!'

In March 1984 he put himself up for contracting, sticking up a big red poster on the factory gate, 'Pledging my Determination to the Party.' As for what it said, the main point was that he volunteered to contract with the paper factory, undertaking to make it turn a profit of 1 million yuan within a year, and double the workers' income. Soon, pledges by the workshops had gone up too, and the toilet-paper shop even held a big meeting to express their support for him.

Fearing that a target of 1 million yuan might be too much to ask of him, the provincial and city authorities who approved Ma's draft plans lowered the figure to 700,000. At the signing ceremony, the mayor called Ma's exercise 'the bloom that heralds spring in the reform of Shijiazhuang'. At a meeting of the factory which followed, Ma stipulated the accomplishment of ten good tasks in ten days—tasks like expanding the kindergarten and clinic, and providing a twenty-four-hour canteen service. When everyone had tired of clapping, he announced with a wave of his hand: 'Let's all set our shoulders to the wheel and aim for 170,000 yuan in May. We'll have a Victory Meeting on the 3rd of June, and don't you come without a bigger bag for your bonuses!'

By the early hours of June 1, the factory gates were already hung with bunting. The night shift, the afternoon and midday shift, the day shift who'd come back specially—everyone was waiting for the accounts office to tot up its figures. When Ma at last emerged from the office, and revealed that they had surpassed the target, there was jubilation all round; no sooner had he announced the figure—215,539 yuan—than people were taking out firecrackers.

On June 3, bonuses were issued as promised; the highest was 217 yuan, the lowest 11. Ma didn't go in for hiding the sums in red packets; it was all open, so everyone knew who got rewarded for hard work and who got punished for laziness. By the end of July, the factory had chalked up 700,000 yuan in profits; by the end of October, 1·1 million.

Unfortunately, Ma's story was not to be duplicated everywhere, and the application of the contracting system to industry was found to present insuperable problems. For it is not as though one can physically divide up productive assets such as machines, brand names, skills and know-how as one can divide up land. Unlike land, too, industrial productive assets depreciate; and whereas with land one can draw a distinction between ownership and use rights, one cannot so easily do so in the case of depreciable resources whose values will vanish in time. Moreover, it is difficult to negotiate the terms of the contract and to decide on a fair division of income because neither the contractor nor the sub-contractor has the option of withdrawing and of seeking competitive bidding elsewhere.

According to Professor Steven Cheung, there is only one general solution to the difficulties of applying the responsibility system in industry—and that is for the State to relinquish ownership of the productive resources to the highest bidder or to the staff of the enterprises, and for freely transferable stock shares to be issued and assigned to individual owners. 'If necessary,' says the professor, 'this division of wealth may be done by voting, as baseball players in the United States vote to divide the income from the world series.'

This is of course unthinkable for a socialist government, which, without the public ownership of the means of production, could no longer claim to be a country run on Marxist lines. Moreover, to allow the transferability of shares would be to condone capital gains, the earning of income without labour. A few years ago, the southern city of Foshan was thrust into the limelight when it started to issue 'shares'; but these were really bonds issued to raise capital. However, in a dramatic transformation of the financial system in August, 1986, a stock market dealing in negotiable securities, the first to open in the People's Republic, began trading in Shenyang, home to China's first bankrupt company. There is no doubt that hundreds of million yuan are stashed under mattresses in China's households, and selling shares to workers is a means of tapping all this 'idle' capital. This was a break-through, said the Chinese press, for if the practice was to spread, a profound change would occur in the system of ownership of the means of production. What the Chinese papers said, though not in so many words, was that China had taken another step down the capitalist road.

If having a stake in the company is an incentive to greater productivity, the cradle-to-grave job security of Chinese employees is not. One of the first aims of the economic reforms was to 'smash the iron bowl', in other words to lift the dead weight of lifelong employment. But the experience of Werner Gerich, a retired West German manager whom the Chinese put at the head of a State diesel-engine plant in Wuhan, is illustrative. Finding the plant grossly overstaffed, he thought he could improve efficiency by laying off 700 of its 2,140 employees. But though many workers did nothing but read newspapers and take naps during working hours, the Party officials wouldn't hear of sacking them. The practice of having one's job for life and being paid a fixed wage regardless of performance has proved extremely difficult to shake off; but on October 1, 1986, new employment rules came into force to introduce work contracts throughout the country, and to enable factories to sack unsatisfactory workers—in effect to subject labour to market forces.

What also needs to be smashed, the Chinese have been saying for years, is 'the common pot'—the habit of income levelling. Unlike Ma Shengli, all too many managers still baulk at using their powers to the full, dividing bonuses equally among their staff rather than differentiating between the deserving and undeserving. Wealth and income disparities have been ana-thema for so long that even now, the Chinese find it difficult to live with them. Many factory directors have not even taken the bonuses due to them, for fear that this would arouse criticism or envy; one hears countless stories of managers who, instead of pocketing the huge bonuses they made under their responsibility contracts, donated them all to the factory school or nursery. Though the political pendulum has swung the other way, they are still not altogether sure that it will not swing back and hit them; so although their new autonomy is supposed to encourage innovative decision-making, they would rather let the grass grow under the feet.

Nor are their fears misplaced: there really are people to report them to higher-ups if they do anything out of the ordinary, or if they appear too bent on making money. There is the case, famous in Shanghai, of a factory director who was pulled up short by the authorities for turning out a new line in men's shirts; being in bright designs, these were immensely popular, but Chinese men had seldom worn brightly coloured shirts before, and the authorities took the innovator to task for 'encouraging bohemianism', and decreed that men's shirts should only be in white, blue or grey. Later, yet another brush with the authorities occurred when the factory produced a line of shirts which sold extemely well but which were declared 'politically questionable' and banned; the reason was that the design featured stars and stripes.

Another well known case concerned the woman director of the Chong-qing rubber belt factory. She managed to turn the floundering firm into a thriving one, but was attacked in the press and put under investigation by various discipline and financial inspection teams for 'having gone too far with the reforms'. What was her crime? It turned out to have been the use of some soft-sell marketing techniques, a sales promotion conference she had organised to which certain popular singers had been invited to entertain the potential buyers.

Most members of the top leadership are keen enough to see the flowering of what they used euphemistically to call a 'socialist commodity economy', and which some of them now unabashedly term a 'market-oriented economy'. So, apparently, are the rank and file. But the cadres in the middle are a stumbling block. Giving managers more authority means taking power away from the political cadres, and their antagonism to the reforms may be imagined. The Chinese, as always, have an expression for this state of affairs—it is to be 'hot at two ends and cold in the middle.'

The Chinese say that their economic reforms are now straddling two boats, one old and one new. Because reforms are tried out in batches in some cities (the testbeds) and not in others, different systems of management and banking now prevail. This is difficult for many people to digest; and as the scope of reforms widens, so political pressures from those they affect adversely will become more intense. Every European socialist country, the Soviet Union included, has taken steps to decentralise economic decision-making and expand the use of market mechanisms; but except for Yugoslavia and Hungary, all have turned back. We have not seen any fundamental backsliding in China, and many Western onlookers believe that the reforms have reached the point of no return, and will not be aborted. But there can be no doubt that more and more problems militating against a smooth transition will crop up as the reforms proceed.

For the man in the street, the most unpalatable consequence of the reforms is inflation. The key to the reform of China is the adjustment of prices to reflect demand relative to scarcity. Enterprises might be encouraged to lower production costs and raise profitability, but if some factories lose money simply because the State prices their raw materials at an artificially high level, rather than because they are inefficient, no amount of freedom in deciding their own inputs and outputs will improve their performance. Nor is there any incentive to raise quality or increase variety when, instead of producers bidding prices up or down to market clearing levels, they are frozen by the State. All light bulbs, for instance, sell for the same price, though some brands have a longer life than others. Besides, in China as in other centrally planned economies, a seller's market exists for many goods, so that manufacturers are seldom persuaded to compete by making their products cheaper or more enticing. Because the Chinese had not seen a price rise for thirty years, the immediate effects of decontrol were very disturbing, even though wage increases have outpaced price rises over the past five years. So the introduction of price reforms has had to be piecemeal, and what has been adopted is a dual price structure, with different costs for the same commodity. Coal, for example, comes either at a price fixed by the government, or as a commodity subject to market fluctuation. Similarly, a factory may have to buy raw materials at fluctuating prices but can only sell at prices decreed by the State.

For the government, the immediate consequences of the reforms were very disagreeable. By the start of 1985, the money supply had gone almost completely out of control. The retained profits, the bloated bank loans, the extra money in workers' pockets from bonuses and rises—all these had contributed to a surge of money and credit, not brought under control until the beginning of 1986. Millions of Chinese, their appetites grown insatiable with all those years of austerity, went on a buying spree, and enormous sums were spent to import coveted consumer goods like colour television sets, fridges and washing machines. These did sop up the excess money, but the imports swelled the expenditure of precious foreign exchange, and contributed to China's trade deficit. Inflation was further fuelled by unauthorised price rises and the upsurge of speculation in raw materials.

All too many enterprises, going full steam ahead to expand, invested heavily in capital construction at a time when the government's 'adjustment' policies were trying to moderate it. The huge industrial growth—an incredible 23 per cent in the first half of 1985 instead of the targeted 8 per cent—made for an overheated economy, straining transport systems and the supply of raw materials and energy. Much of it came, as we saw, from the village and township factories, a sector lying almost entirely outside the State planning and allocation system. All of a sudden, China's leaders found themselves presiding over one of the most extraordinary periods of economic growth the world had ever seen.

Through a tightening of controls on credit and money supply, the breakneck expansion was finally curbed in early 1986, with the growth dropping to just under 5 per cent in the first half of that year. All this happened when the banking system, whose weaknesses had contributed to the runaway boom, was itself in the process of being overhauled. Though the figure fell short of the 7·5 per cent industrial growth projected by the Seventh Five Year Plan, it was a not unwelcome sign that the Chinese economy was off the boil. Politically, the hyper-growth put the reform process at risk, for it gave political forces opposed to it an opportunity to reassert themselves. But China's reformist leaders withstood the test, and showed how dedicated they were to their policies by moderating, but not abandoning, the bold experiments they had started.

Success will not come easily, if only because, on top of their opponents in the central leadership, reformers find themselves thwarted in the provinces where their orders are sometimes outrightly ignored. China's industrial enterprises, as I earlier suggested, are distributed among 'lines' of central government departments and 'blocks' of local authorities. The system has fostered administrative fiefdoms all doing their utmost to expand their authority over the enterprises which come under their sway, and to command their output and profits. Clearly, they are not going to take kindly to external incursions into their interests.

They care little for what other 'lines' or 'blocks' do, and lack of coordination and duplication of effort have become routine features of China's economic system. Bruce Reynolds, an American specialist, has remarked that Chinese provinces today are less economically integrated than the nations of the European Economic Community. Stories of local protectionism abound. A commune in Anhui, instead of buying its tractors from the backward county tractor factory, imported better and cheaper models from another province; in a fit of pique the local county government declared, 'Those tractors will never run,' and refused to allocate the diesel fuel for them. Another example illustrates the walls that separate 'line' from 'line': a thermal power plant cannot use the coal from a mine next door because the two concerns fall under different administrations.

In an attempt to break these barriers, the Chinese government has tried to lump enterprises together by economic rather than administrative means. To that end, many enterprises have been encouraged to combine. This has been successful in a number of cases, and many large industrial and commercial consortia straddling administrative boundaries have been set up. But it soon emerged that some of these 'corporations' were not economic entities at all, but only government offices under another name. These so-called corporations have interposed themselves between the local governments and the individual enterprises, and not only have they retained the power that was supposed to have gone down to the enterprises, but they have intercepted the raw materials allocated by the State and siphoned off the profits of the enterprises for such 'administrative expenses' as new office buildings, fancy cars and banquets. When the press reported these undesirable trends, it quoted the comment of the director of one of the factories they affected: 'The government's regulations are like a piece of soap in a shop window—it looks good all right, but you can't get at it.'

The administrative fetters are not to be so easily broken after all, but China presses on with schemes to make the bureaucratic order abdicate in favour of an economic one. One of these, thought up a few years ago, required a rethinking of regional policy. Might it not be wise, the planners wondered, to create a new kind of spatial order, one based on a different logic, a different set of priorities? Might it not be a good idea to create economic macro-regions for coordinated development, and to make the most of the specialities of different cities? Instead of the administrative pyramid rising to a peak in the provincial governor, it was suggested that planning be turned over to the cities. Zhao Ziyang was all for it, and in 1982 the call went out to 'rely on the big cities, create economic centres at every level, and rationalise the economic network'. So far, so good. But how far can the big cities be relied on without an improvement in their amenities? Reconciling their fine intentions with practical realities has presented the planners with enormous problems, as we shall see when we look at the chief exemplar of China's urban woes, Shanghai, more closely.

One of the most famous of pre-communist Shanghai characters was Cassia Ma, who made her fortune from nightsoil collection, and was known to all as the Nightsoil Queen. Shanghai in those days was a city of contrasts, Chinese in one neighbourhood, French in another, and as British as they come in a third. The contrast was strikingly borne out by the plumbing. While homes in the better parts of the foreign concessions often boasted porcelain flush toilets by Doulton of Lambeth and Paisley, many more made do with commodes. This was where Cassia Ma came in. Her carts used to call every morning.

Though it is no longer a private business, the service which Cassia Ma provided for more than twenty years continues to be performed in Shanghai today, where it is said that 10,000 tons of nightsoil are carted away each day. There are 705,000 homes still using commodes in the city, and when I was there in December 1984, their owners were faced with a tiresome problem.

It had come of Deng Xiaoping's urban reforms. There used to be more than twenty repair shops in the city, to which you could take your commodes and washtubs whenever they needed mending. The shops used to be under the jurisdiction of the Jiangnan Wooden Tub Factory, but they have been turned over to a neighbourhood bureau for organising urban collectives. These collectives, small neighbourhood workshops or service trades, come somewhere between State-run enterprises and private businesses; reviving them was part of the move to replace State monopoly with a greater variety of business organisation, and to provide jobs for the 400,000 young people who have returned to Shanghai from the country.

All of a sudden, instead of twenty repair shops, there was only one. This made life difficult for enormous numbers of people, and a customer living near the North Railway Station complained that she had to change trams twice to get to the one repair shop in south Shanghai. The administrative change had been made on the understanding that the newly constituted collectives would continue to provide the same service; but it was not long before they started branching out into more agreeable kinds of business, from making paper flowers to selling dumplings.

The incident is a homely illustration of how difficult and complex it is to introduce economic reforms in a Chinese city. It is on the backs of industrially developed cities like Shanghai that the Chinese economy is supposed to make the great leap into the twenty-first century, but how is this to be done when the urban facilities have not been renewed for thirty years? Almost two million more people live in inner Shanghai than when it fell to communist administration; yet what is true for plumbing is true for every other amenity of life in the city. Things have simply stood still.

A traveller to Shanghai today visits a revolution that is more than three and a half decades old. Ageing and decay apart, he sees a city little changed physically from what it was when the communists came to power in 1949; or from a generation before that, when the Communist Party was secretly founded at 106 Rue Wantz. Shanghai was China's pre-eminent port, her most modern and cosmopolitan industrial city. Yet looking for signs of modernity today, the visitor sees only smoky factory stacks reminiscent of the 1930s. It is apparent from the moment one sets eyes on Shanghai that the city has been run into the ground, its housing dilapidated, its waters befouled, its traffic a torment, and its resources milked to the point of exhaustion.

When the hinterland and the outside world began to converge upon Shanghai in the wake of the open door, the effects of its neglect, accreting over the decades, began to show themselves in every sphere. They showed in the two-month layover for berthing space by the numerous ships which call at Shanghai's port, China's pre-eminent Pacific gateway. They showed in the stink emanating from the liquid dump for Shanghai's toxic industrial waste, the Suzhou Creek—once a city waterway, now the city's cloaca. They showed in the crippling congestion (at peak hour eleven people have to stand in each square metre of bus space, a physical impossibility), the number of deaths on the roads (548 in the first ten months of 1985). The pressures on space and services are appalling, and it is a miracle that the citizens survive in decency.

'Only when ... consumer cities are transformed into producer cities, can the people's political power be consolidated.' So said Mao Zedong in 1949, in an utterance destined to provide the slogan for China's urban policy. For an example of a 'consumer city', one guesses he had in mind an emporium like Shanghai where, in the communist view, a profligate bourgeoisie squandered the wealth yielded by the labour of the proletariat and the peasantry. For a 'producer' city, he probably envisaged a place like Lanzhou, the beneficiary of Soviet technical aid in the 'fifties—all fractionating columns and chemical works. Like a disease stimulating the antibodies needed to overcome it, Shanghai's earlier capitalism and cupidity had probably engendered the central bureaucratic dampening to which it has been subjected down the years.

The decay of the physical fabric of Shanghai, and of other cities in China, is a legacy of the Maoist tendency to regard the purpose of production as enhanced future production. Money spent on housing, heating, domestic electricity, transport, cultural facilities and so forth was, in the Maoist view, non-productive investment. Little wonder, then, that China now has some of the most polluted cities on earth, and that millions of urban Chinese have to live in overcrowded and squalid conditions.

The 'adjustment' policy of the post-Mao regime tried to rectify this, and one of the most dramatic changes to have occurred since 1978 was the surge in investment in housing. The accumulated problems of China's cities were tackled head on, after two decades of studied neglect, and by 1985 there was more housing completed than in all the years from 1950 to 1977. This extraordinary increase has much to do with the reforms in enterprise management: a very high proportion of the new dwellings was financed out of the profits the State factories were allowed to retain.

When the First Five Year Plan was launched in 1953, and economic priority given to developing the interior, Shanghai and other coastal cities had to surrender their revenues, including even their depreciation funds, to the central government in Peking. Since that time the proportion of earnings Shanghai has been allowed to keep has varied with whatever economic policy is prevalent in Peking, from about 14·5 per cent of profits in some years to a niggardly 8·7 per cent in others. If its citizens feel a sense of deprivation, they have good reason to. There is no doubt that Shanghai has been hard done by, and even in 1985 its rate of industrial profit retention was still among the lowest in the country.

Yet, for all that, Shanghai became the ultimate socialist city, China's pre-eminent industrial powerhouse and the citadel of central planning. If its

State-owned industries were left with little money to renew their technical equipment, they were given enough raw materials for their manufacturing. Shanghai was a great success, its extraordinary productivity matched by no other place in the country.

Because it did so well out of central planning, Shanghai is finding it harder than most to embrace Deng Xiaoping's reforms. Though the order to allow State enterprises to look after their own affairs has long been in force, an investigation of 113 Shanghai factories in early 1985 found that only 15 per cent had carried it out. There is some truth in the Chinese joke, current in early 1986, that the last two places to adopt economic reforms in China will be Shanghai and Taipei.

With the system of State allocation giving way to a proto-market, Shanghai's industries have found they have had to develop new links with the providers of their resources. The city's industrial output fell in 1985, and the chief reasons cited were lack of funds, lack of raw materials and the shortfalls in energy supplies. The establishment of 'lateral linkages' with the hinterland, said the city's newly appointed Party boss Rui Xingwen in early 1986, was absolutely essential to its future expansion. Administrative walls had for a long time served as trade envelopes, confining the flow of goods to narrow channels. Now these routes were to be unclogged, and Shanghai must think regionally. To that end, new economic entities have been defined, focused in large centres like Shanghai and Canton. One of these, the Pearl River delta, has Canton as its hub; another, the Yangtze River delta, revolves round Shanghai.

Nobody in China doubts that Shanghai's unclogging is essential to the forward movement of the whole nation. But it is also upon a redefinition of its role that Shanghai's fortunes depend. One school of thought believes that it is not upon manufacturing that the city should be focusing its energies, but upon financial services and trading. Yet it is difficult for Chinese socialists to revise their conception of cities, and to imagine them as stepping stones in the march of goods and services rather than as industrial hives, busily clanking, screeching and smoking.

Listing Shanghai's assets, the new mayor Jiang Zemin names the celebrated astuteness of the Shanghainese, the technical strength of its workforce, and its historical familiarity with the outside world. Certainly Shanghai's human resources are considerable: the city has always stood for sophisticated skill and experience. But since 1949 it has been part of Shanghai's business to provide technicians and professionals for China's more backward places, and over the years their ranks have diminished. A recent report reveals some alarming figures. One set shows Shanghai to be at the bottom of the list for per capita investment in capital construction for educational, scientific and cultural purposes. Yet the picture is not so gloomy as these figures suggest. In absolute terms Shanghai is still the nation's biggest repository of skills and knowledge. For the neighbouring provinces, Shanghai is still the place to go for technical help or know-how, and the Shanghainese are right to pride themselves on their keen business sense. I once observed to an American China-trade consultant that the reason Shanghai was not getting as much foreign investment as one might expect was that the Shanghainese drove such a hard bargain. His comment was that this was putting it mildly; 'in Shanghai the foreign investor gets screwed'.

How crucial human capital is to China's future is at last beginning to be understood, the economic reforms having exposed existing shortages of skills throughout China, both by stepping up the demand for these skills and by presenting new and unfamiliar challenges to the country's managers and workers. With the economic reforms has come a fuller appreciation of the importance of human assets to the country's well-being. Nor are human assets, it is now realised, merely a question of know-how. Values, habits of mind, how scholarship might be harnessed to economic purposes—of late all these matters have come in for a reappraisal.

The American business guru, John Naisbitt, author of the number-one bestseller, *Megatrends: Ten New Directions Transforming Our Lives*, is better known in China than in Britain. This seems odd: one would think his ideas on the information age would have greater applicability here. In China his book has sold a million and a half copies, and I have yet to meet a university student there who hasn't read it or heard of it. The Chinese read avidly the aphorisms with which his book is studded: 'The gee-whiz futurists are always wrong because they believe technological innovation travels in a straight line. It doesn't. It weaves and bobs and lurches and sputters'; 'Computer buying will never replace the serendipidity and high touch of shopping for what we want to be surprised about', and the like. Though their sententiousness sparks some memory of the gnomic utterances of Chairman Mao, it is not this that made Naisbitt so popular; it is that his book has been cited with approval by Zhao Ziyang.

Zhao's interest is understandable. The book arms those who espouse economic reforms with one of their best arguments. The whole world is becoming more interdependent, and in an increasingly competitive world, no national economy can any more remain isolated or self-reliant. China, these people say, is caught in a powerful change, one which, to quote Naisbitt, is 'transforming the planet into a global economic village'. Furthermore, in a country where the entrepreneur has suddenly become the hero, an American business guru easily catches the fancy.

Another bestseller in China is Alvin Toffler's *The Third Wave*, which has also been recommended by Zhao Ziyang. It is not surprising that Toffler's book, with its division of the course of human civilisation into agricultural, industrial and information ages, should go down so well in China, a country which believes its vast agricultural labour force to be on the threshold of metamorphosis into an industrial workforce. The book offers exciting visions of the future, to the imagination of a people consciously headed for the year 2000. When the video of Alvin Toffler's book first became available in China, in early 1984, people watched it a little furtively, not altogether sure if it was politically kosher. By the summer, though, you would find it openly viewed in the smallest county town in the interior.

As an in-phrase among China's educated circles, 'the third wave' is rivalled by 'systems engineering'. Zhao Ziyang gave the approach his imprimatur when he said, in the course of presenting the draft of the 1986–90 economic and social development plan to the Party, that Chinese economic reforms were a gigantic project of society's 'systems engineering'. Now it enjoys a great vogue among China's academicians, who are said to be all trying to integrate at least some systems theory into their research. Even Chinese journalists these days like to let drop the fact that they have studied systems theory—as indeed they have, at a crash course in Peking at which theorists and policy-makers of China's development strategies lectured.

Megatrends, the third wave, systems engineering—these buzzwords are very much part of the vocabulary of Zhao Ziyang's think tank and supporters. To use them is to declare oneself to be with the reformers. This is certainly true of Wen Yuankai, the head of the Applied Chemistry Department of the China University of Science and Technology at Hefei. Born in 1946, Wen studied quantum biology in France in the early 1980s. Upon his return to China, he addressed a proposal to the government on how one should set about reforming the organisation of Chinese scientific research. One of Wen's most controversial suggestions was to make it possible for lecturers to offer their services as paid consultants to industry. Wen saw the possibility of a fruitful relationship between scholarship and business. He spoke approvingly of the recognition accorded to scientists in the West by the business community, and the practice of engaging them as consultants at enormous fees. It may seem strange for a scientist in a socialist country to suggest that a proportion of that country's scientists and technical experts become entrepreneurs, but this was more or less what Wen Yuankai did. Peking gave the go-ahead for this and other of his proposals to be tried out at one of the departments at his university. By setting up a couple of consultancy services which offered technical know-how to scores of enterprises and rural specialised households, he made a great deal of money for the university. Nowadays the potential of scientific research findings for China's economic well-being is widely recognised, but it was Wen Yuankai who pointed it out and demonstrated it.

Wen is an enthusiastic reformist, and when he talks publicly, his subject-matter ranges freely, from the changes needed in the organisation of science and technology to those necessary in society. A selection of his talks were later brought together in a book, called, with a nod to John Naisbitt, *China's Megatrends*. What faces China, he points out, is the challenge posed by the 'third wave' and the new information age. The first places in China to meet these challenges, he says, are the coastal areas abutting the Pacific Basin, that most dynamic of the earth's regions, seen by many people in the West as taking over the focal role played by the Mediterranean in the sixteenth century and by the Atlantic throughout the Industrial Revolution.

It is not enough, he argues, that China compares her performance with that of her past: 'Our whole system of coordinates revolves round our past ... instead we should take our bearings from an international framework. It is only by this means that a sense of urgency will be created in us, a sense of crisis even. This is extremely important. How different are we from the Japanese, who have always maintained a sense of crisis.'

What stands in the way of the reforms' success, Wen maintains, is the conservative national character, dominated still by the Confucian doctrine of the golden mean: rather than striking out in new directions, all too many Chinese prefer to tread the middle way. Conspicuousness, many Chinese believe, invites trouble and envy, so they 'fear fame as much as pigs fear getting fat'. They would say, quoting one of their innumerable saws, 'A tall tree catches the wind'; and it is true that a person in an elevated position is more liable to calumny. Like almost every other Chinese, Wen considers envy and the destructiveness it breeds to be a deep national susceptibility. 'In another nation,' Wen says, 'jealousy may spark competition; in China the reaction is more likely to be, if I don't make it, you mustn't either.'

Wen shares the view of many of his countrymen that convention holds the Chinese in a tighter grip than it does most other peoples, and that this greatly hampers their response to the reforms. For whatever they do they want to know that there is a precedent, that an example of it exists in some book. Unless we break free of these manacles on our thinking, Wen tells his listeners, we will have a hard time adopting new styles and theories.

Another inherited condition they must repudiate, Wen tells his fellow-countrymen, is their isolationist attitude to the outside world. 'We used to think of Europe and the United States that their technology, their science, and even a little of their management experience would repay study. But in actual fact culture and science are inseparable: you can't have one without the other ... When Japan first opened up to the West, it was the whole of the West's industrial culture that she absorbed, whereas to this day we in China still cling to the old *ti-yong* idea'—the hundred-year-old idea of grafting Western modern techniques onto a Chinese base.

When Wen Yuankai published his book, the problems which Chinese habits posed to modernisation were not yet a hotly debated issue. But within a few short years, all his themes would be taken up by scholars working in the social sciences, in history and philosophy, and intensely discussed in the media and at academic gatherings. This did not happen without design, for the Party had started the ball rolling by interpreting the Cultural Revolution in terms of the dark forces of China's feudal survivals.

The issues were seen to revolve around two questions. One, what are the elements of the Chinese national character which hamper China's modernisation? And two, why didn't capitalism, which might have propelled the Chinese economy out of its stagnation, take root in China (or, to put it in another way, why did the old imperial order last so long)? Slavish ways of thinking, the petty farmer's belief in economic levelling, the political tradition of the wise ruler to whom all men owed absolute allegiance—all these were seen to be long-standing drags on Chinese progress. As for why industrial capitalism, whose economic productivity is tacitly acknowledged, did not develop in China, every young Chinese intellectual I spoke to in 1986 told me to read *Behind the Idea of History*. Written by Jin Guantao, a member, I am told, of Zhao Ziyang's think tank, this influential book fashionably adopts a systems approach to 'feudal' Chinese society, analysing its structure of power, economy and ideology. It portrays the old imperial order as a super-stable system with a very special regulating mechanism— the disorders to which peasant uprisings subjected it every two to three hundred years. Not only did these cyclical cataclysms sweep away the stresses impinging on the superseded system, and pave the way for a new system to be reconstituted in the image of the old, they more or less brought the economy back to square one, thereby contributing to the empire's material decline.

The recent debate on Chinese culture must be understood against the background of certain ideas which Western thinkers have advanced, ideas relating to the question of the social, cultural, and even psychological concomitants of economic growth. Starting from Max Weber's famous theory that the Protestant ethic, with its values of hard work and discipline, lay behind the genesis of capitalism in Europe, Western historians and social scientists have looked for 'functional equivalents' of this ethic in the developing world. When the economies of Taiwan, South Korea, Hong Kong and Singapore began to grow as impressively as Japan's, some thought they found it in certain post- or neo-Confucian values, for a Confucian heritage is what these industrial upstarts (Japan included) have in common. They argue, for example, that the industrial success of Hong Kong is largely owed to its citizens' Chineseness. In this they differ from Chinese theorists, who believe (or perhaps are obliged to believe) that Confucian hangovers hamper rather than help their country's modernisation.

But the two views are perhaps not as irreconcilable as they may seem at first sight: it is true that Confucianism did inhibit China's modernisation, but if it seems to spur it in other countries, it may be that it has to die first—and in China herself it is still alive and kicking.

Wen Yuankai had a point when he said that Chinese reformers were up against the Confucian disparagement of the profit motive and the ancient prejudice that trading was an unworthy way to make a living. Merchants have always ranked lowest among the classes in traditional society—and socialism heightened this disdain of money-making. Yet, Wen keeps saying, the times demand businessmen and managers, not Confucian-style swots. Today enough people in government agree with him for management studies centres run by trainers from foreign capitalist countries to be set up in several cities: the European Economic Community at Peking, the West Germans at Shanghai, the Americans at Dalian, the Canadians at Chengdu, and the Japanese at Tianjin. In the 1950s a number of Chinese management trainers and enterprise directors were sent to study in the Soviet Union. Today China looks to the West, although, said an EEC paper in 1983, 'Faced with an unprecedented challenge to modernise in a very short time, the country has, as yet, no clear idea of how this managerial resource might best be used. In other words it lacks a model to follow.'

If the Canadian course (funded by the Canadian International Development Agency) at the Sichuan Management Institute at Chengdu is anything to go by, it has not been easy for either side to get over the cultural gap. Chinese trainees are much more accustomed to being lectured at than being asked to participate actively in class; but despite all the odds against it—the language barrier, the unfamiliarity of Western styles of thought and teaching to the Chinese mind, the rigidities of the system from which the trainees are recruited and to which they have become accustomed—the project seems to be a success. I sat in on a couple of lectures when I visited the centre in the spring of 1986. The classes were enormous and the ages and experience of the trainees varied very widely. I could only marvel at the way the Canadian teachers coped.

One of the aims of the programme is to train Chinese teachers to take over from the Canadians eventually. To that end, Chinese management trainers are 'apprenticed' to the Canadian ones, and also sent to study at Canadian colleges or universities. The EEC project, too, trains indigenous faculty; their members spend four months at the Manchester Business School. The American centre is even more ambitious. There a selection of Chinese trainees study for American Master of Business Administration degrees at Dalian and at the New York State University.

Muffled these foreign influences may be, limited they certainly are (the corps of Chinese managers receiving training is only a tiny part of the whole), but these transfers of Western manners of thinking will nevertheless contribute to a widening of Chinese horizons. To aid-giving countries, it is doubtless important to upgrade China's managerial resources so that they can be harnessed more effectively to the purposes of her economic reforms; but how much more important to impart the styles of thought that will make her economic system respond more appropriately to foreign demands in a rapidly changing international economic environment.

In Deng's 'second revolution' China has been made to accelerate her rhythm to try and catch up with the world; what is done at home has always to be related to what happens abroad. This demands an altogether new style of intercourse with the world.

# PART TWO

\*

# THE OPEN DOOR

If there is to be any change in the policy of opening to the world, it will be that China's doors will be opened even wider.

Deng Xiaoping, 1985

He who builds his cart behind closed gates will find it not suited to the tracks outside the gates.

A Chinese proverb

# 4

# MAO'S HEIRS

In a picture in the November 22, 1985 issue of *The Economist*, a large man in a hat is to be seen, explaining things to a group of workers. The headline, 'Russia under Gorbachev', leaves the reader in no doubt as to his identity. This is just as well, for the man is not named in the caption accompanying his picture—which simply reads 'Deng-minus, or Deng-plus?'

This is a kind of tribute to Deng Xiaoping, who is seen to have set a standard by which to judge other reformers. Since Gorbachev himself has claimed that the changes he envisages for the Soviet Union amount to a revolution, it seems proper to compare him with Deng Xiaoping, the progenitor of 'the second revolution' in China. *The Economist*'s verdict is that he is 'Deng-minus', for while the Chinese leader is a reformer in deeds, Gorbachev has so far proved to be only a reformer in words.

If *The Economist*'s tribute is indirect, *Time* magazine's could not be more explicit. Looking around in 1986 for the person, people or thing that, for better or for worse, had most significantly influenced the course of world events in the preceding twelve months, *Time* magazine alighted on Deng Xiaoping, choosing him for their Man of the Year out of a company which included Mikhail Gorbachev, Nelson Mandela and Bob Geldof. The magazine, which had made Deng Man of the Year once before, in 1978, strikes a high note, describing him as having 'changed the daily lives of his nation's citizens to a greater extent than any other world leader', and his reforms as holding 'more promise for changing the course of history than anything else that occurred during 1985'.

There is truth in these statements, for all their American amplitude. The Chinese themselves would tell much the same story. Wherever I went in China, I found enthusiasm for the leader. Asked how Deng would weigh in the scales of history, many Chinese I spoke to said, 'More than Chairman Mao, for sure.'

If Deng Xiaoping's reputation now stands higher than the late chairman's, it is partly because, by undoing almost everything that his predecessor had stood for, he has cut Mao's down to size. On his visit to Moscow in 1957, Mao drew Nikita Khrushchev aside and said, pointing to Deng, 'See that little man there? He's highly intelligent and has a great future ahead of him.' Little did he guess how far that great future would be at his own expense. Deng was a capable if refractory colleague: Mao once said of him—he had lost the hearing in his right ear—'The fellow's deaf [yet] whenever we are at a meeting together he sits far away from me.' Later Deng did to Mao what Khrushchev did to Stalin with his Secret Speech of 1956: he demolished Mao's myth.

Under a communist regime the evaluation of a historical figure goes deeper than judgment on a dead man, because it is subjected to the interpretation (and if necessary the falsification) of the past in the service of the present. We may be sure that it was only after prolonged and intricate discussion that agreement was reached on the assessment of the Cultural Revolution—and Mao's role in it—for the historical record. In June 1981, at the sixth plenum of the eleventh Central Committee, a resolution was issued which pronounced the Cultural Revolution to have been responsible for 'the most severe setback and the heaviest losses suffered by the Party since the founding of the People's Republic'. These words were followed by the statement that it was 'initiated and led by Chairman Mao Zedong', and that 'the erroneous "left" theses on which he based himself . . . conformed neither to Marxism–Leninism nor to Chinese reality'. And just as Khrushchev had made a distinction between Stalin's actions before 1934 (when what he did was praiseworthy) and afterwards (when megalomania got the better of him), so Mao's 'errors' were deemed to date only from 1955.

It was important to conclude that Mao's 'leftist' errors were not Marxist–Leninist, to refute any suggestion of a natural progression from Party dictatorship to Maoist despotism. To forestall the argument that there was something wrong with a system that could throw up a Mao and a Cultural Revolution, the Party said that the Cultural Revolution had behind it complex social and historical causes. Its roots, explained Mao's heirs, lay deeper, in the centuries of 'feudal autocracy' from which China had yet to extricate herself.

Tearing down the edifice of Maoism cleared the way for new purposes and a new structuring of power. But the large question which now faced Deng was: 'With what will you replace Maoism?' This is how he had justified liberalising economic policy on an earlier occasion: 'It doesn't matter if a cat is black or white, so long as it catches mice it's a good cat.' Celebrated as it is, the saying hardly amounts to a credo. Time magazine recorded a joke he made about liberalisation in 1985: 'Marx sits up in heaven, and he is very powerful. He sees what we are doing, and he doesn't like it. So he has punished me by making me deaf.' But this is an opportunist remark, made by one who knows how well it will go down with a Western audience. In the leadership there continues to be serious debate over what is and what is not proper socialist policy. While many applaud Deng's approach as the replacement of terror and unworkable utopianism by sensible, practical policies, others oppose it, seeing it as the betrayal of early revolutionary ideals. Deng rationalises it all into a creed he calls 'socialism with Chinese characteristics'. Whatever that is, it is what is proper for China at her present stage of development. There is not yet wealth enough in China, it is argued, to provide the basis for a communist society, so 'building socialism' there is a matter of 'expanding the country's productive forces and economy'. Marxist theory should be applied all right, but not without regard to time, place and circumstance—this is the vein in which Deng the realist (or 'pragmatist', as Western commentators like to portray him) talks.

This means improvising as one goes along, and much of 'socialism with Chinese characteristics' is actually trial and error. The patriarchs are no guide. Marx, Deng is said to have observed, had never travelled by air, nor had Stalin ever worn Dacron. Socialism Chinese-style has no very definable limits, no precise economic formulae. Deng himself has admitted as much when he said, 'I'm a layman when it comes to economic matters. True, I have spoken on the subject, but only from a political point of view. For example, it was I who proposed the opening of China to the outside world; but with what goes with this policy, the details and the specifics, I can't say that I am altogether *au fait*.'

His task is not made any easier by the opposition he sometimes faces in the Central Committee, whose members may agree with his overall purpose but not necessarily with his methods or the speed with which he applies them. His open-door policy, its sheen tarnished by scandals like the Hainan Island affair,* is particularly contentious among people who, even now, hold the Western world in a Chinese mixture of admiration and suspicion.

Of all the critics of Deng's economic policies, the most formidable is unquestionably the octogenarian Chen Yun. Chen sees more dangers in the opening to the West than Deng and his followers, and it is against opinions like his that the latter say, 'We shouldn't shut the window just because a few dirty flies come in; that would be like giving up eating for fear of choking.' Chen once ranked higher in the politburo than Deng Xiaoping, and no one dominated economic policy in the early years of the People's Republic as much as he. Chen was the one person who did not hesitate to say just what he thought of the Great Leap Forward (and to pay for it with years of political decline); and he would not wish China to repeat the sad history of that mad sprint towards instant industralisation by rushing to modernise with a market economy and with wide open doors. As he was then, so he is now: cautious, conservative, disapproving of precipitate policies. He hates the idea of a budget in the red, and sees trade deficits as a signal of financial adventurism. 'We are communists,' he likes to remind his colleagues, 'who believe in planning.'

Since the 1950s he has expressed a preference for combining planning with a degree of market regulation. 'Birdcage economics' is how Hong Kong periodicals describe Chen Yun's approach, because he has likened the

* See Chapter 5.

relationship between market and plan to that of a bird to its cage: if the cage is too tight, the bird will suffocate; but without the cage, the bird will fly away.

His image seems to be consciously upright; he is generally thought of as an example of socialist rectitude, the last to be enthralled by the capitalist West and the first to speak out against Party privilege and corruption. But his critics abroad say that this is hypocritical of him, citing the fact that he seems happy enough to have his son Chen Zhongying, his daughter Chen Weili and his granddaughter Chen Qian study or live in the United States.

Chen Yun, though, is held back by his frail health, and at the start of 1987, when those in the leadership who wanted to push the reforms forward and those who wanted to pull back found themselves in a deadlock, it was the octogenarian Peng Zhen, the head of the National People's Congress, who emerged most forcefully to challenge the power of Deng Xiaoping. Once known as the 'smiling tiger', this ex-mayor of Peking speaks as if the political values of the 1950s were still in vogue. His taste for power sharpened by the slippage Deng Xiaoping and the reformists suffered in 1987, he lost no time in stoking the fires of repression in the higher leadership.

There is a strong tendency among observers of the Chinese scene to see personal and policy schisms in the higher reaches of political power, with Chen Yun, Peng Zhen, and Party idealogues like Hu Qiaomu and Deng Liqun heading the conservative (or 'leftist') faction, and Deng Xiaoping and Zhao Ziyang heading the reformist one. It cannot be denied that the truly dynamic politics of a socialist system is to be found in the politburo and the Central Committee, and that behind the appearance of uniformity can lie intense conflict over policy. But it is difficult to know how deep the dissension really goes, or how far down the hierarchy the factions and alliances penetrate. The picture often blurs, with the reform-minded espousing liberal policies one minute and back-pedalling the next. To read some of the commentaries, one would think that the reformers would be going full steam ahead if it weren't for the conservatives. But is that how it is? Are the reformers' periodic hardening of policies forced upon them by the opposition of the conservatives, or is there, at bottom, not really all that great a conflict between the two camps? We simply cannot know for sure.

Yet conflict there certainly is, be it a difference of opinion about a policy, or a clash between older and younger generations (or more pertinently between old-style and new-style socialists). Seeing Chen Yun as the rallying point for the critics of Deng's reforms, many outside observers wonder what would happen if he were to gain the upper hand. On the face of it Deng's reforms seem safe enough, but they have only to falter, and their critics will want to have their say. There is endless speculation about how the story will end. 'What if Chen Yun were to outlive Deng Xiaoping?' asks *China Spring*, a magazine published by Chinese living abroad. For all his insistence that he has retired to the 'second line' and left the running of China to his younger lieutenants, nobody doubts for a moment that Deng is still number one. It is especially hard to imagine the military taking orders from anyone else. He is 83 this year, and it is unlikely to be very long before he goes, as he himself puts it, 'to see Marx'. So it was natural that when he disappeared from public view for three months in early 1985 (popping up only at a lunar New Year gathering in his home province of Sichuan), jittery rumours about the state of his health suddenly started up. In Hong Kong, where the stock market suffered a slide, a China-watching magazine lifted the veil from the whole mysterious matter by saying that Deng had been recovering from a minor kidney ailment at a spa in southern Guangdong province. But before further rumours could fly, Deng reappeared—chuckling heartily, it is said, over the speculations. Meeting New Zealand's prime minister, he joked about the virtues of smoking and cold baths. He was concerned to show that China could carry on without him, it was claimed; yet the event demonstrated how much the world thinks the reforms depend on him. When, in the summer of 1986, floods and earth tremors plagued certain parts of China, rumours were rife that these heavenly portents of dynastic collapse signalled the death of Deng Xiaoping.

So the question which seeps into most discussions of China is the question of succession, the question of what will happen when the old man goes. It is a question which Deng Xiaoping himself has long anticipated.

The Chinese have been at pains to assure the world that the current policies would endure unaffected by leadership changes into the twenty-first century, and that Hu Yaobang and Zhao Ziyang had been running most things already. But it is the fate of these two men to live under a system in which appointments are made—and unmade—from the top. By naming him general secretary of the Party, Deng had Hu in mind for a successor, but when, in a power struggle with his antagonists in January 1987, Deng found it necessary to sacrifice Hu, he did. Before his luck turned, though, Hu was the man everyone assumed would take Deng's place one day.

For years Deng had been getting him ready. The task was made easier by the fact that Hu had grown up under the wing of the Communist Party. The son of a poorish Hunan peasant, Hu had run off as a boy of fourteen to join the communists in neighbouring Jiangxi. He became one of those Little Red Devils that one frequently saw in the revolutionary base areas, children of the communist Young Vanguard who served the Red Army as errand boys, buglers, propagandists and spies. He continued his political apprenticeship on the Long March, surviving the epic trek to add it to his revolutionary credentials. He remained close to the crux of the revolutionary struggle in Yanan, where he attended the Red Army War of Resistance University and heard Mao Zedong's lectures on dialectics and philosophy.

His launching pad though was the Youth League, that Party auxiliary which Lenin termed the 'transmission belt of the communist system'. By the time the Long March began, he was already secretary of the Jiangxi soviet's Youth League. Afterwards there was no holding him: in 1952 he became ranking secretary of the Youth League in Peking, in 1954 he doubled its membership; in 1955 he won a seat on the Central Committee, at forty-one the youngest person to rise to that august body.

If he was nurtured by the Party, he was raised ever upwards by Deng. Mentor and prodigy met in 1941, when Hu was assigned to work under Deng in the Taihang Mountains, where the older man had set up a soviet with the celebrated General Liu Bocheng. Hu's job was to run the organisation section of the First Group Army's political department. Later, when Deng was Party boss in the southwestern provinces around the time of the communist victory, Hu was one of his four immediate subordinates. What Deng thought of his protégé then may be seen from the nickname he gave him—Broadsword Guan Sheng, a stout-hearted martial character out of that well-known tale of bandit heroes, *Water Margin*. Though it may not be the most obvious qualification for the top job in China, Hu is not deficient in another important respect—notably a taste and gift for bridge. Deng, a bridge fanatic who was voted Bridge Player of the Year by the World Bridge Federation in Switzerland in 1986, regularly relaxes by playing with Hu and other Chinese leaders; and it is widely believed that it is around the bridge table that many of China's affairs are decided.

Deng's political ups and downs in the 1960s and 1970s were exactly mirrored by Hu's. Hu's fate during the Cultural Revolution was the familiar one of humiliation, house arrest, and 're-education' through manual labour. Though he resurfaced for a while in 1975, it was with Deng's final comeback in 1977 that Hu Yaobang truly got into his stride. The job which Deng had for him was the all-important one of overseeing Party appointments as head of the organisation department. Putting him there was sheer political brilliance, for at a stroke Deng achieved the condition for his capture of power from Hua Guofeng and for the consolidation of his own position. A man who had it in his mind to launch China on a new path had to start by making sure that he had absolute command and the right people. What better way to start than by rehabilitating those who, like himself, lost their all in the Cultural Revolution, and who were anything but nostalgic for the past?

Hu was the one who saw to it; he too could see that the key to Deng's ascendancy lay in the creation of supporters, and he worked energetically to swell their numbers. Deng watched his opportunity, and then, when the moment came, stepped forward firmly to brush his rivals aside. As the mantle of Mao fell on his shoulders, Hu Yaobang by his side stepped into Party chairman Hua Guofeng's shoes. (The post of chairman was abolished in 1982, but Hu stayed on at the summit of the Party pecking order as general secretary.)

Zhao Ziyang, also handpicked for his job by Deng Xiaoping, displaced Hua as prime minister. Deng liked what Zhao did in his own native province of Sichuan where, by introducing reforms of the kind that were later to sweep the Chinese countryside, Zhao had impressively boosted grain production and given rise to a popular peasant saying: 'Want to eat grain? Go get Zhao Ziyang.'

Zhao brought to his appointment a lifetime of experience as a professional Party functionary. After six years in the Youth League, he joined the Party in 1938, when he was nineteen. He began his career as a county Party secretary in his home province of Henan, but he made his early reputation in Guangdong, the southern province just over the border from Hong Kong. There he found a patron in Tao Zhu, the regional Party boss; when Tao was brought to Peking as vice-premier, Zhao was to succeed him, at forty-six the country's youngest provincial first Party secretary. But because of his enthusiasm for the liberal agricultural policies of the early 1960s, he found himself in bad odour with Mao. He was not above offering his loyalty, for tactical and opportunist reasons, to the winning side, whether it be Liu Shaoqi's or Mao's, but still he could not save himself from the purges of the Cultural Revolution, or from being paraded through the streets of Canton wearing a dunce's cap. By 1971 he was past the worst of his ignominy; a spell in inner Mongolia ensued, followed by the resumption of old duties in Guangdong province. In Sichuan, to which he presently transferred, he was confirmed in his belief that the raising of agricultural output depended on workable policies and the application of scientific and technical know-how.

Such is the man who, with Hu Yaobang, set the style of the Chinese leadership in the early and mid-1980s. They are both reformers in the public mind, both new-style socialists. Their outward appearance is the index of their inward convictions. Certainly the two men's penchant for lounge suits—something Western journalists love to describe—is not to be seen as merely personal preference, but an indication that they are men of their times, outward-looking and open-minded. It is a pity that Hu did not, as these same journalists keep reporting, tell the Chinese people to swap their unhygienic chopsticks for knives and forks, because that makes such a good story. But what he did say was mould-breaking enough: 'We could do with some reform in our eating habits as well,' he said to villagers in Shandong province in 1984, 'and get rid of our worst practices; we should discard our unhygienic way of taking a meal; instead we should promote the Western style of each person eating from his own plate. That way we will reduce the risk of infectious diseases.'

Remarks like these add to Hu's reputation for speaking rather too freely. It was a speech of his that contained the startling statement, picked up in a matter of days by newspapers across the world, that 'We can't expect the works of Marx and Lenin to solve our present problems.' Although the *People's Daily*, the Party paper in which the speech was quoted, made an editorial correction, to the effect that '*all* our present problems' was how the sentence should have ended, the damage had been done. Yet Hu Yaobang's carelessness is only another side of his directness, and one thing he cannot be accused of is irresoluteness. It is perhaps the source of his authority, his willingness to stick his neck out.

Many of his countrymen think that there is something faintly uncouth about him; set beside the nattily turned-out Zhao, the scion of a well-off landowning family, Hu bears the marks of his peasant pedigree. This is perhaps just as well, because it makes it easier for the rank and file of his Party, country men mostly, to identify with him. Where Hu's appeal is to the common man, Zhao's is to the intelligentsia. It is among white-collar, urban and educated Chinese that Zhao is above all respected. They like him for his nice sense of realpolitik, and for the way he interests himself in high-tech, in business, and in the challenge to China of global technological change.

His image is that of an exceptionally able executive, a doer rather than an intriguer. He is often compared to the late Premier Zhou Enlai—good at playing what appears to be a secondary role and getting on with the job. Of all China's leaders, he is seen by his fellow-countrymen to be the most cosmopolitan—well-travelled, businesslike, and not liable to let the nation down with a gaffe in front of the world's politicians. As for entrepreneurial activity, he seems to be all for it. Two of his four sons are known to be engaging in business down south, the place to be for pursuing commercial opportunities. And one of his pet projects is Everbright industries in Hong Kong, a $600 million private business set up with his blessing to swing deals with foreign firms for products and projects for China—and to make money while it's at it. The man Zhao put in charge is a Wang Guangying, a Red Capitalist after his own heart. Wang thinks so well of the premier that at first, so gossip has it, he wanted to take a syllable from each of their names and call the business Ziguang.

Of course not everything one hears about Zhao Ziyang in China is favourable. His reputation has been tainted by an improper romantic attachment he is said to have formed during his time in Guangdong, and dark rumours of his sons' unexplained business dealings percolate periodically down from Canton and Shenzhen to Hong Kong. All the same, the opinions held of him by professionals and intellectuals are generally admiring. One of these is worth quoting: 'There is no doubt that, if he had lived in America, and if his experience had lain, not among farmers in Sichuan and Guangdong, but among business circles in New York, he'd have become president of IBM, at the very least.

For a man in Deng's position, of his age and conviction, the sense that his legacy will not be squandered becomes crucial. If Mao was concerned, in the face of inevitable biological death, to render his revolutionary works eternal, Deng is no less anxious to maintain the continuity of what he has started and what will go on after his own individual existence. If his 'second revolution' is to endure, he knows that he must get the next generation of leaders ready.

Looking around him, he must have noted that today's seventy- and eighty-year-olds were yesterday's eager young revolutionaries. The generation which, came to power in 1949 has stayed in power—a sluggish gerontocracy which a Chinese peasant saying has aptly described as 'the four cadres with the five teeth among them'. What made it worse was that the professional experience of these ageing leaders had lain largely in guerrilla warfare, not the best kind of qualification for directing a modernisation drive, to whose future the importance of human capital is recognised to be central. In the days of revolutionary war it did not much matter that one's leaders were semi-illiterates. It is when one starts modernising that their deficiencies become glaring.

Deng had had it in mind to start a grand shake-out for a long time, both to put younger and better qualified people in charge, and to instal allies and enthusiasts for reform in positions that matter. But it took several rounds of changes to sweep the old lot aside. The matter was complicated by the fact that, before he could do anything else to the bureaucracy, he had to bring back those who had been purged in the Cultural Revolution. With Hu Yaobang's help, he reinstated no fewer than 2·9 million of these— all of them potential allies, as we saw, in his bid to dethrone Mao and dispose of Hua Guofeng.

That was the first big change. Next he turned his attention, in a move which combined political boldness with masterly organisational skill, to the superannuated officials. He devised a compulsory retirement scheme, and under it nearly 1·1 million cadres recruited before 1949 were pensioned off between 1980 and 1985. The beguiling terms Deng offered them did much to soften the blow. They could draw a pension that was higher than their normal salary; they could still have access to internal information; they could keep their house or flat; and if they liked, they could continue to serve in an off-stage advisory capacity. All the same, Deng's attempt to weed them out affected many of the old guard most disagreeably. Nobody wants to be a has-been, especially not in China, where power and perks go with position rather than with money or other advantages.

But Deng had his way, and though it took a few years, the old revolutionary generation has unquestionably passed from the scene. This occurred throughout the political and administrative hierarchy, from national level to provincial. It was an astonishing feat of political and administrative manoeuvring, quite unprecedented in the history of the People's Republic. For at no other time since 1949 has the leadership changed so much or so dramatically; even the Cultural Revolution, with its mass purges, did not see as high a turnover of officialdom as has occurred under Deng in recent years. It is difficult for the uninstructed outsider to grasp the scale of the change; but David Goodman, a British scholar who has been making a study of the Chinese provincial leadership, tells us that it has been colossal. 'For the first time since 1949,' he writes, 'the generation which became China's leaders at that time have ceased to be in the numerical majority.' He offers some impressive statistics. Only seventy-five of the 656 cadres in the civilian provincial leadership of September 1983, he reports, were still provincial leaders of any kind in any province by September 1985. And the index of annual leadership turnover—that is, the proportion of the sum of appointments, retirements, dismissals and deaths to the total number of posts in existence at the start of a twelve-month period—approached 200 per cent in 1983 and 1985. From other figures one may also see the inexorable way in which the shake-out proceeded. In February 1983 the average age of provincial Party secretaries was sixty-three, and some 53 per cent of all provincial leaders had been appointed as leading cadres before the Cultural Revolution; following changes in March and April 1983, these figures fell to fifty-seven and 27; since August 1985, they have become fifty-three and 1·5.

Nor is it only the scale that is remarkable; what strikes one with equal force is the dramatic change in the leadership's profile. This had remained constant throughout the years from 1949 to 1984, and even the upheavals of the Cultural Revolution had done little to change it. The old profile is that of a male born before 1919 in an area of early communist activity, and recruited to the Chinese Communist Party before 1949; he has had little formal education (or, if he has, it was from a military academy), and has become an administrator when young almost incidentally. But his successor is noticeably different: younger certainly, and on the whole better fitted by his education and experience to respond to the needs of a rapidly changing society. He may not be a technocrat, but he will know a thing or two about modern methods and planning.

What Deng had also to effect was a layering of generations among the power-holders, with the tiers following one after the other in uninterrupted succession. In early 1985, as part of a Party rectification movement, a talent-scouting exercise was undertaken. There were to be three leadership echelons, the Chinese public learnt, with seventy-year-olds in the first, sixty-year-olds in the second, and thirty-five- to forty-five-year-olds in the third. The exercise, aimed at finding the right people for the third echelon, was to be carried out in two stages. Beginning with the selection of 1000 young and middle-aged cadres for jobs at the provincial and ministerial levels—

these to be groomed as a 'strategic reserve' to replace the first and second echelons when the time came—it was to proceed to the appointment of 130,000 cadres to positions lower down the regional scale. The exercise completed, Deng turned his attention to the leadership of the provinces and the State Council; here he saw to it that those who managed to survive the shake-out of 1982–83 made way for 126 younger men, 63 per cent of whom were under fifty and 80 per cent educated up to university level.

Then came the army's turn. The People's Liberation Army (PLA) could see it coming; already, in December 1984, forty old warriors were pensioned off, the largest top-level 'voluntary' group retirement in the PLA's history. He hoped 'to see more open-minded people in the army', said Deng in an interview accompanying the announcement; on another occasion, he described the PLA's senior officer corps as 'undisciplined, arrogant, extravagant and lazy'. There would follow further pruning: 10 per cent of the officer corps to be retired by the end of 1986, and another 20,000 to 30,000 to have done so by 1990. I shall be discussing the restructuring of regional commands in another chapter, so suffice it to say that the moves were the work of a supremo: there was a hovering, a swoop, and then the stuff of which Deng is made did the rest.

Following these achievements, widely publicised in China as 'the greening of the Chinese leadership', Deng wrought the last of his great reshuffles, the rejuvenation of the inner Communist Party elite. This took place in September 1985, around a special national Party conference. Reported by newspapers across the world, the clear-out was dramatic: the politburo, the Party's ruling core, lost ten of its members, nearly half its strength, and the Central Committee sixty-four of its 341 members. Of those who resigned from the politburo, the most prominent was the ailing Marshal Ye Jianying, venerated warrior of the revolution. As Ye was a member of the politburo's six-man standing committee, his retirement gave the triumvirate of Deng Xiaoping, Hu Yaobang and Zhao Ziyang a clear, if slim, 3–2 majority over their more conservative-minded colleagues (Chen Yun and the State president Li Xiannian) in that most exclusive of ruling bodies.

Into the vacated seats stepped appointees at least one generation younger, if not two. Among the sixty-four replacements on the Central Committee, it is not easy to miss the third echelon. But age and education were not always decisive, as China-watchers were quick to point out; Deng had also hoped, they said, to group around himself individuals who thought as he did, pointing to the fact that there was a higher proportion of resignations among those who managed to hold on to their seats all through the Cultural Revolution (because they did not, presumably, resist Mao's policies) than among those who, like Deng Xiaoping and Hu Yaobang, were thrown out of their jobs during that upheaval. But if the reshuffle was partly calculated to rid Deng of his most exasperating critics, it was a qualified success. It did not escape the same China-watchers that though Deng managed to remove the doctrinally hostile Deng Liqun (no relation) from his post as propaganda chief two months earlier, he failed to dislodge him from the Party secretariat. One guesses this to have been a concession Deng made to the conservative opposition, part of the constant horse-trading that goes on behind the scenes.

What also struck seasoned observers of the Chinese scene was the orderliness of the change; it was not a blood-letting. 'I cannot think of an example in modern world history,' the American expert Doak Barnett told the press approvingly, 'that is comparable to what is happening in China.' Under Deng, changes befell the machinery gradually. One is struck by the contrast between his approach and Mao's: instead of the wholesale purges of the Cultural Revolution, Deng took things one at a time, going for the ministries first, tackling the central Party authorities only after he had diluted the opposition of the army. That way, observed the Yale University analyst Hong Yung Lee, he could 'prevent his potential adversaries from forming a grand coalition against him'. Also, he wielded the carrot more than the stick, enticing the old guard into retiring at the same time as he chivvied them into it. This was no easy matter; just preparing the ground for the reshuffle of the Central Committee took four months. The task was under-taken by Hu Yaobang, heading a seven-man team.

Six newcomers, nicknamed 'Deng's yuppie corps' by the American scholar Richard Baum, were named to the politburo, including two, Li Peng and Hu Qili, who were to be groomed to succeed Zhao Ziyang and Hu Yaobang, as premier and general secretary.

It was understood that the thirteenth congress of the Communist Party, which was scheduled for the autumn of 1987 and which was to fix China's course and leadership for years to come, would set the seal on these appointments. But the transition of power from the old guard to the new generation of leaders suffered a setback as 1987 began, with the old men reasserting their power against that of those who presumed to brush them aside. A wave of student demonstrations (see chapter 9), seen by those nostalgic for the simpler certainties of the 1950s as an unruly manifestation of 'bourgeois liberalism', gave these men the ammunition for striking back at Deng Xiaoping.

There had been much talk of opening the Party to new, more liberal ideas, but this, to the gerontocrats, spelt the doom of the Party's monopoly of authority. They saw Hu Yaobang as the source of these unwelcome new ideas, and in January 1987, they forced him to resign from the job of Party general secretary. This threw the leadership succession into disarray, and obfuscated for a time the transfer of power at the top of the Party.

The battle between the so-called liberals and conservatives was fought in the guise of a nationwide campaign against 'bourgeois liberalization', an attack against Western and unorthodox ideas. Three celebrated critics of China's political system were expelled from the Party, and it was reasonable of Western observers to suppose, as Peng Zhen, Deng Liqun and other old-fashioned Marxist leaders became increasingly vocal, that the conservatives would fight the economic reforms to a standstill.

But when the Party congress opened in October, it was clear from the outset that China was to press ahead with outward-looking reform policies: instead of the stirring communist anthems of early Party gatherings, those Chinese citizens who could be bothered to follow the proceedings on television were eased into the event by a selection of American pop tunes and an animated rendering of Joseph Haydn's *Surprise* symphony. The surprise of what the audiences next heard, which was a bold two-and-a-half hour speech by Zhao Ziyang, was that it told the Party, which has always stood at the government official's elbow, to loosen its grip on those whose proper job it was to make administrative decisions. It has always been hard to say where a Party cadre's power ended and his responsibilities as a civil servant or factory manager began, but Zhao now proposed to define this: 'The State regulates the market,' he said in summary, 'and the market guides enterprises.' Let government govern, he was saying in effect, and managers manage.

This was all very well, the sceptics among our television viewers would say, but it was one thing to declare a policy and quite another to translate it into action. What about the millions of Party functionaries who would lose their jobs if the Party cells in government departments were abolished, as was proposed? It is obvious that getting the Party out of government is not going to happen overnight.

The man in the street finds it hard to summon up much interest in the Party, which, with its constant changes of policy has lost not just his sympathy but any ideological credibility. But if he has not already switched off his TV set he will learn that the policies of the past decade—the concessions made to the market, the private farming of land, the various economic practices normally associated with capitalism—have now been given Theory. With her backward economy, our viewer learns, China was in a 'preliminary stage of socialism', one which justified the mixing of private with public ownership. This primary stage of socialism is seen to last at least a hundred years, stretching from the 1950s to the middle of the twenty-first century. Of course it hardly matters to our man in the street whether the reforms are really socialist or not, but in order not to lay themselves open to the accusation that they have no Marxist rationale for their policies, China's reformist leaders, however much they may depart from Marxism in practice, still have to doff their caps dutifully to doctrinal authority.

The personnel changes at the top reflected a reformist triumph and took the rejuvenation of the highest organs of power a stage further. Zhao Ziyang was confirmed as Party chief, and given military muscle by being named as Deng's number two in the Military Affairs Commission. Deng himself, by retiring from all posts other than that of chairmanship of the Military Affairs Commission, made it difficult for the other octogenarians, Chen Yun and Li Xiannian and Peng Zhen, to remain in the politburo, although as long as these men are alive they may continue to influence events obliquely, either outside the formal system, or through the Central Advisory Commission, the semi-retirement home for elderly leaders who have handed on other powers, and of which Chen Yun was made the head at the congress.

Nevertheless, those who lost out in the power struggle earlier in the year were no doubt delighted that Peng Zhen did not get any of the Party jobs that count, and that Deng Liqun was voted out of the Central Committee altogether. It was with great finesse and adroitness that Deng Xiaoping stage-managed the congress. Who would have thought, only a few months ago, that Hu Yaobang would keep his seat in the politburo— and yet here he was, voted once more onto that august body.

The new politburo is on average five years younger than its predecessor, and shows a balance between high-speed reformers and moderate-speed ones. As for the political postures of the four men who joined Zhao Ziyang in that holy of holies, the standing committee—Hu Qili, Li Peng, Yao Yilin and Qiao Shi—they, too, are a mix of semi-liberal and middle-of-the road. Of the four, two in particular are thought to be headed for bigger things: Li Peng and Hu Qili.

Li Peng is expected to succeed Zhao Ziyang as premier. Though his official biography describes him as a native of Chengdu, the provincial capital of Sichuan (the province of Deng Xiaoping's birth), Li was actually born in 1928 in Shanghai. However, there is no doubt that his parents, both communist activists, were from Sichuan. His father was a political commissar in the 25th division of the forces which, under the overall command of Zhou Enlai, staged the famous Nanchang uprising of August 1927, the uprising from which dates the official birth of the Chinese communists' armed forces. Li Peng never really knew his father, who died before he was three. Part of Li Peng's early childhood was spent in Hong Kong, where his mother worked in the communist underground. Although presumed dead by some Hong Kong reporters (Li is always described as an orphan of revolutionary martyrs in Chinese write-ups), his mother was still alive in the 1970s, though inexplicably we hear nothing of her, and it is as if she ceased to exist from 1939. It was in that year that the eleven-year-old Li Peng, then living with his parents' relatives in Chengdu, was adopted by Zhou Enlai and his wife, who were themselves childless. In 1941 he was taken to the communists' wartime stronghold of Yanan, where he attended the Yanan Institute of the Natural Sciences. Later he worked as an electrical technician; still later he was sent to the Soviet Union, where, as a student of the Moscow Power Institute, he is said to have distinguished himself by getting an A in every one of his subjects.

It was as the director and chief engineer of a large power station in northeast China that Li Peng worked upon his return to China. His career advanced; he came to play an important part in Communist Party affairs. The Cultural Revolution appears not to have affected him, either personally or professionally. The way to eminence was opened by the retirement of his superior, the power industry minister Liu Lanbo, who had been impressed by Li during visits to the USSR in the 1950s, and who had long had him in mind for a successor.

It is hardly surprising, given his knowledge of Russian and his early Moscow connections, that Li Peng was the one whom the Chinese sent to Chernenko's funeral in 1985. Then and later, he had a chance to talk to Mikhail Gorbachev, a leader to whom he has not infrequently been compared. He accompanied Hu Yaobang on the general secretary's first visit to Britain in June 1986, and seemed to have stood out in the big entourage. Here is how he struck one journalist: 'Unlike his other senior colleagues who looked straight ahead while he spoke, nodding and laughing on cue, Li frequently interrupted the general secretary, who is notorious for his unpredictable slips. Once when Hu was answering questions about the leading critic of Deng's reforms, Chen Yun, and referred to him merely as a great thinker, Li leaned over and whispered, 'Say he's a leader.'

Li Peng's American hosts, during his trip to the US in the summer of 1985, saw less the Party man than the inquiring technocrat with a keen appetite for information on nuclear power stations, hydro-electric power dams and the Silicon Valley. 'On a boat trip around the Rock Island area of the Mississippi River,' reported a Chinese newsman with awe, 'the vice-premier barely glanced at the beautiful scenery. He was too busy asking questions and taking notes. . . .'

But it has been said that, had Zhao Ziyang had his way he would have picked Hu Qili, a contender for Hu Yaobang's job in the Party the last time round. Hu the younger is not related to Hu the elder, but one may detect certain similarities, the most important of which is that they both rose through the Youth League. As a teenager Hu Qili was active in youth affairs in Yanan, which is not far from Yulin, the place of his birth in northern Shaanxi. In the 1950s he was a student at the famous Peking University, but although his official biography describes him as a graduate in mechanical engineering, we can't be certain that he really completed his course, for he is chiefly remembered by some of his contemporaries as a representative of the Youth League, working harder for the communist cause than he did for any academic degree.

If there were two things he was thoroughly familiar with, they were student unions and youth federations. It was as a student and youth representative that he travelled frequently abroad in the 1950s and 1960s—to Czechoslovakia, North Korea, Cuba, and a number of north African countries. With so much familiarity with the student world, he must have seemed the perfect man for the vice-presidency of the prestigious Qinghua University, when he was appointed to that post in 1973. This was after some rough treatment at the hands of the Red Guards and a spell of 're-education' at a Cadre School down in the country, an experience which gave him something in common with Hu Yaobang, who, according to one source, did time at the same school. With Hu the elder giving him a leg up, Hu the younger soon shot up the political hierarchy. He became the youngest of China's mayors when, at the age of fifty-one, he was made responsible for the important northern metropolis of Tianjin.

It is not only in their relative youthfulness and educational qualifications that Li Peng and Hu Qili exemplify the new generation of leaders. To many analysts in Hong Kong, Li and Hu are proof that two of the commonest routes to the top lie through nepotism and the Youth League. As the adopted son of a revolutionary luminary, Li belongs to the group they call 'the dauphins'; these are the offspring of Party bigwigs on the Central Committee, the beneficiaries of the best educational opportunities. They are the elite stream in whose favour the system is most heavily weighted, not only because they are well connected but because the third echelon stresses higher or specialist education in its intake, and this is the very thing they can offer.

How far will it continue to be true that who you know counts more than what you know in China? It is hard not to think of a small, privileged class of those with higher education perpetuating itself. There is certainly no lack of precedent for such a state of affairs: one may recall that the supreme privilege enjoyed by the mandarins of the empire was the privilege of reproducing themselves through their monopoly on education. Today, with a system in which posts are filled from above, there continues to be plenty of scope for nepotism and favouritism.

If personal ties matter so much, how far will individual personalities affect future policies? If we are to find the key to the shape of the future, should we follow certain Western journalists and begin by slotting the new men into 'reformist' or 'conservative' categories? Pekinology, the study of China's top leadership, certainly has its uses; but I would not like to try and predict how 'hard' or 'soft', how bold or cautious China's future policies will be on the basis of what we know about the past careers and experiences of the leading lights of the younger generation of leaders. What can one really say about Li Peng and Hu Qili, for instance, other than that the first is a specialist in a crucially important policy area and the other is an apparatchik? In any case, however much one or more individuals may dominate the leadership, one needn't always think of it as a body where power is concentrated in the hands of one man. It is true that the despot is a recurrent figure in Chinese history; also true that what we see in China today overwhelmingly bears the marks of a single personality, that of Deng Xiaoping. But then the dead man's shoes of a dictator like Mao would ill fit a less authoritative ruler. The period over which Deng presides is one of transition, a period offering greater scope than usual for change and new directions—and so for personal initiative and action. Future historians may well say that an era ended with Deng, in whom we see a last display of the power of the emperors. For the period which follows, Deng's own imagination appears to favour a collective leadership.

# 5

# FOREIGN RELATIONS

In 1972, a year after China was readmitted to the United Nations, I was living in Geneva and working on a book on international narcotics control. As part of my research, I sat in on many public meetings of the UN. At one of those meetings, I noticed the Chinese delegates in their places. But I was no longer a citizen of the People's Republic, I had not spoken to anyone from China for a decade, and I did not think for a moment that they would recognise me for one of their own.

So I was surprised to find them walking up to me one day and, after ascertaining that I did indeed speak Chinese, inviting me for a cup of tea. No sooner had we sat down in the United Nations lounge than they were expressing their utter bafflement at the proceedings. They then told me that they had observed me for some days, and wondered what special interests I had in the meeting. I explained to them what I was doing, whereupon they told me that I was just the person they needed. It was plain that they were completely at sea. How UN business was really conducted—the vested interests which lay behind the rhetoric, the horse-trading between nations behind the scenes—was quite beyond them. I did what I could to clarify matters, and it was touching to see their looks of relief and trust as they took it in.

Just as it was generally assumed that the Soviet bureaucrats working in the United Nations secretariat were all KGB agents, give or take a few, it might be supposed that what the Chinese did next was recruit me. But my relationship with this or any other delegation from the People's Republic never progressed beyond a friendly nod as we passed each other in the corridors.

The reason I relate this incident is that it helps to understand Chinese international behaviour just by standing by their side, and seeing the world from their eyes. My encounter at the UN showed how perplexed the Chinese were when they rejoined the international community. The Chinese representatives knew only that in her foreign policy China was opposed to superpower hegemony, and that her strategic objective was to set herself against the menace of Soviet power in Asia. But as to her stand on the countless smaller issues which concerned the international community, to judge by those delegates' blank incomprehension China harboured all the uncertainties of a novice. Many Western observers think only of the self-assurance and urbanity of Zhou Enlai when they think of the Chinese conduct of diplomacy; they do not remember the inexperience of the thousands of Chinese who suddenly found themselves having to practise international power politics on the ground. Many a Western participant at those UN meetings yawned at the way the Chinese would, at the drop of a hat, noisily rant at Soviet 'social imperialism' and 'revisionism'; but perhaps few of them paused to wonder if behind the crudeness of their diplomatic style lay diffidence and immaturity.

The way those delegates sought my advice in Geneva was also indicative, I thought, of the inherited Chinese habit of trusting only those they see as their own kind. It did not matter to them that the people I worked for were European, or that the passport I held was foreign; by birth and descent I was Chinese, and this was enough reason for them to trust me. A Chinese weakness is that they are not naturally at ease with foreigners. It is an old weakness, manifesting itself sometimes in haughtiness, sometimes in the xenophobia and inwardness of their foreign policy (as when they befriended almost no nation except Albania). They are ready enough to discover instant affinity with Chinese émigrés of even antagonistic political persuasions, but people of non-Chinese descent are all too seldom seen for their human qualities, as opposed to their racial or national-political ones.

More than sixty years ago, the great Chinese writer Lu Xun wrote: 'Throughout the ages the Chinese had had only two ways of looking at foreigners: up to them as superior beings or down on them as wild animals. They have never been able to treat them as friends, to consider them as people like themselves.' If this generalisation still stands, it is partly because, for every Chinese disarmed by prolonged and intimate contact with people from other shores, there are thousands who, even today, have yet to clap eyes on a foreigner. Given a glimpse of the world by the open door, many Chinese consider the foreigner warily, with a mixture of fascination, fear and indifference. All nations see others through the distorting lens of their own cultural values, but there can be few people as fixed in their stereotypes as the Chinese.

Personally they are subject to inherited biases. Politically, too, their perceptions are coloured by the experiences of their history. If, as Western commentators observe, China plays the role of the aggrieved party in the international power game a little too readily, it has not been for lack of reason. Her first exercise in the open door had been forced upon her, following her humiliating defeat in the Opium War, and for more than a century afterwards she felt herself to be in a position of inferiority to the West. Some Western commentators think the experience not nearly as unpleasant as the Chinese themselves make out, but imagination is far more persuasive than level-headed analysis, and the experience was traumatic because it was perceived by the Chinese as traumatic.

In the twentieth century they have had little reason to revise their opinion of the outside world. No sooner had the communists established control than they found the force of American military power on their very doorstep, forcing them to intervene on behalf of North Korea. American propaganda portrayed China as fearful and aggressive, yet it was the Americans who ringed her with military bases, who imposed against her a full economic blockade, and who provided the rival Kuomintang government in Taiwan with weapons and economic aid. Later, as relations with Moscow deteriorated, she felt the pressure of massive Soviet forces on her borders, as well as an encircling Soviet military presence in Afghanistan, Outer Mongolia and Vietnam. Summing up China's feelings of insecurity, the American specialist Harry Harding puts it thus: 'Few other major powers have felt as threatened, for such a long period of time, and by such powerful adversaries, as China has.'

Until very recently China has behaved in the international scene—now displaying deadly opposition, now wary amity—essentially in reaction to the two superpowers, the United States and the Soviet Union. Were it not for the global strategic balance, it is difficult to see why China should figure so importantly, with so much American attention lavished upon her. It is true that her armed forces are forbiddingly large, and that she is one of the world's five nuclear powers. Yet she is one of the world's poorest countries, and the high cost of her attack on Vietnam in 1979 revealed to all the world how much her army needed revamping. By herself, China is no superpower; and it is chiefly as the key component in the rivalry between the United States and the Soviet Union, and the calculations which these two countries make about war and peace, that China wields the international influence she does—an influence well beyond either her economic or military strength. The Chinese have become masters of the game of playing off one foreign power against another, as a way of strengthening their own position.

No nation in the world has had to adopt as many different positions to the two superpowers as China. In a comment on Sino-Soviet relations in 1964, Mao Zedong quoted the summary of history with which the old historical novel *The Romance of the Three Kingdoms* opens: 'Empires wax and wane; states cleave asunder and coalesce.' Such was the nature of things, the making of alliances and their severance, in a world not of one's making, where one's security was felt to be at stake.

Looking at the international scene in the mid-1980s, one is tempted to the same view of history, the same view of the ebb and flow of shifting foreign relations—for here was the Bolshoi Ballet, not seen for twenty years, performing with Shanghai dancers in the Peking Exhibition Hall Theatre, a gigantic complex built with the help of the Russians in the 1950s. The appearance of the troupe was of course an expression of improving Sino-Soviet relations, a development which would have been outside the range of most people's imagination not all that long ago, but which is what Mikhail Gorbachev wants. If political relations between Moscow and Peking could be still better, commercial relations, both long-distance and frontier, can scarcely be sweeter. Indeed, the two sides have agreed to a doubling of trade between 1985 and 1990, and to the opening of consulates in Leningrad and Shanghai. The internal logic of developments in Chinese economic policy demanded that some at least of the quarrels be buried. For one thing, to continue to accuse Moscow of revisionism would simply be a case of the pot calling the kettle black. For another, the Chinese want independence of action, and to keep their options open. Against their need for capital and technology to realise their ambitious development plans, ideological differences are secondary.

All this is clear from a briefing given by the then Party general secretary Hu Yaobang to Chinese cadres in the autumn of 1984, in the course of an inspection tour in Inner Mongolia. Because it is one of those restricted documents rarely seen by the man in the street in China, let alone the foreigner, it is a great deal more direct and reliable than what one normally reads from China. It is worth quoting the transcript of the talk at some length, because Hu Yaobang was after all one of the makers of Chinese foreign policy.

'You must make it clear to our comrades in the army,' he said, 'that to open up is to strengthen national defence; the wider the opening, the more beneficial to the strengthening of our defence. This is dialectics.

'In July this year,' he went on to say, 'the USSR sent us a trade order for 3·5 billion Swiss francs; we responded by sending them one for 4·8 billion. Our doing this pleased them. Developing trade with the Soviet Union is killing two birds with one stone: it eases tension, and it provides a new market for our goods. ... All this can only be to our benefit, as well as ease world conflict; besides, our being friendly with the Russians will do nothing to reassure the Americans.

'Our trade with the USSR will recover next year to a level higher than at any time in our history. ... You must make a success of the borderlands. ... All along these frontiers, the policy we adopt must be one which makes for prosperity. ... Don't be alarmed if a few people defect. What is there to be alarmed about? If there's one thing we don't lack, it's people. Of course it would be better if they didn't leave; they won't, in any case, if you make a success of things.'

I am surprised, talking to educated Chinese old and young, how little emotional barrier there is to a renewing of links with the Soviet Union. One would not suppose there to be many points of true sympathy between the Chinese and the Soviets, after twenty years of bitter invective and enmity. Yet there are large numbers of Chinese who remember the Soviets with warmth and admiration, and whose potential influence on future

Chinese policy may well be considerable. The 11,000 students and thousands of mid-career scientists, technicians and administrators who were sent for training to the Soviet Union in the 1950s, and the thousands more Chinese who worked closely with the 10,000 Soviet advisers despatched to China by Moscow, have not disappeared. Indeed they are more important than ever. It is from the ranks of their generation that many power-holders are recruited, and it is by such skills as theirs that China's modernisation will proceed.

China-watchers in Hong Kong have even gone so far as to identify a faction of 'returned students' from the Soviet Union among China's candidate leaders, seeing the figure of Li Peng as its great star. To have studied in Moscow is not necessarily to have absorbed Soviet ways and values, but the prospect of a ruling establishment dominated by Soviet-educated technocrats does disconcert the very many young men and women who have gone for further education in the United States and Europe, and who have voiced their anxieties in no uncertain terms. Yet their anxieties may be misplaced. 'We are not about to see a return to the Soviet path,' said a Chinese mathematician studying at a British university, whose views are perhaps more sanguine than those of his peers. 'The careers and interests of these cadres are tied to the success of the reforms,' he explained to me, 'which makes it less than likely that they will stand for Soviet ways of doing things.'

One would do well to hesitate before one makes any predictions about foreign political practice. When, in the course of a televised speech in the far eastern Soviet city of Vladivostok in July, 1986, Gorbachev announced that the USSR would withdraw half a dozen regiments from Afghanistan, and also consider a reduction of Soviet troops in Mongolia, even the Chinese were taken by surprise. It was something new that Gorbachev was offering China; and better still, the concession was accompanied by the proposal that the Amur River, where many border skirmishes between the two countries had taken place, should be the happy scene of mutually beneficial projects. The last thing one expects from the Soviet Union is a willingness to yield a portion of its territory, however small, and yet was Gorbachev not suggesting the handover of some river islands to China? Of course the Chinese want Vietnam out of Kampuchea before they will really warm to the Soviet Union, and of course there is little chance of a revival of the old intimacy, as between an older and younger brother; but still there has been a breakthrough in Sino-Soviet relations.

Just as Peking has re-evaluated its relationship to Moscow, so it has tempered its ties to Washington. 'After the honeymoon' is how a specialist in Sino-American affairs at the Chinese Academy of Social Sciences characterised the mood in early 1986. Chinese leaders are affronted by what seems to them to be a bland American presumption that China could be taken for granted, by American trade barriers, by the American refusal to get off the fence over Taiwan, and by a string of aggravations which, while niggling in themselves, cumulatively detract from the Chinese view of American reliability. The Chinese approach to America is not sentimental. Anything like a state of dependency would be absolutely abhorred.

Now it is the Chinese themselves who bring into definition a new relationship with the two superpowers—still only partially disengaged from their global rivalry perhaps, but not aligned with or strategically dependent on either. They have entered a new phase of foreign policy, more confident, less trammelled by dogma, and freer to consider their options. A moment of reflection on the Chinese past suggests that if one looks back to the Han (206 BC–AD 220) and Tang (AD 618–907) dynasties, one finds China reaching out to the wider world at times of Chinese assurance and power, and one wonders if—as Hu Yaobang believed—extroversion, domestic self-confidence and security go together.

The Chinese have discarded the Maoist position that war is inevitable and that the Chinese must be prepared to fight it at any time. China greeted the UN International Year of Peace with the declaration that she would conduct no more nuclear tests in the atmosphere, after twenty years of insisting that she had the right to do so. She used to have no time for the Western peace movement or any call for disarmament, but there has been a detectable change in attitude. To champion world peace is of course to urge a stable international environment, one in which she may get on with modernising herself without outside distractions.

Parts of the massive network of tunnels and underground shelters which Mao ordered to be dug in every important city as a safeguard against nuclear attack have been converted into factories, hotels, shops and warehouses. In Peking, for example, an army underground shooting range has been turned into a skating rink, while sections of the air-raid shelters house restaurants and dining halls with names like Cave Heaven, Plum Blossom and Chrysanthemum. In Chengdu I recently spent a bizarre evening in the bosom of a former underground shelter, listening to a Chinese cabaret star croon 'Will you cry for me?' to the clangorous accompaniment of an electric organ, drums and a saxophone—upon all of which pink and green electric light bulbs cast a sleazy glow. The whole tunnel seemed to have been turned into a pleasure haunt for the new rich: as well as cafes and restaurants, I glimpsed parlours with sofas and reproductions of Gustav Klimt's pictures, each displaying a sensually stretched female body.

The upgrading of national defence is one of the Four Modernisations, but the other three—agriculture, industry, and science and technology—clearly take precedence over it. Defence spending has been severely cut in successive years, and the money has gone to modernising the People's Liberation Army (PLA) rather than into updating weaponry. Western observers put the share of China's GNP going to military spending at only 6 to 8 per cent, while that of the Soviet Union is estimated to be between 12 and 14 per cent.

Though Chinese military equipment appears outdated when compared with that of the two superpowers (much of it is of obsolete Soviet design), the answer is not to import state-of-the-art technology, before the industrial base and science and technology sector are up to scratch. Though China has window-shopped for technologically advanced military equipment in the United States, Britain and France, she has so far not bought much. In the course of a public address in London in 1986, Hu Yaobang told his audience with a laugh, 'If any of you are looking for huge arms deals with China, I'd better tell you frankly that you will be disappointed.' China would be happy to spend less money on guns and soldiers, and it is in the tightening-up of the army's organisation that she has largely invested her resources. To Deng Xiaoping, the brain behind it all, this is chiefly a matter of training the younger officers to high professional standards and weeding out the old ones.

I used to think that, to look at, PLA men were the most thoroughly unmartial of creatures, fresh-faced country lads in baggy olive-green cotton fatigues. But now they are being girded for new requirements, and their uniforms have changed too. Complete with gold braiding and peaked caps, there is now a suggestion of spit and polish to them, and they look more like regular soldiers, more like members of a professional service.

In the Memorial Museum of Revolution in Yanan, the town which Mao and the Red Army established as the communist capital after they completed the fabled Long March in 1935, the visitor sees an exhibit displaying a rifle and a sack of millet. The symbolism of these objects is very powerful, because it was believed that to conduct a 'people's war', the Red guerrilla soldier needed little more. Today the PLA is reconciling itself with the electronic age, and rather than picturing its soldiers with sacks of millet over their shoulders, one must imagine them sitting in front of computers.

It will be an altogether leaner army. Between 1985 and 1987, the PLA will be reduced by more than a million soldiers, to whose resettlement the government has devoted sizeable resources. The Air Force has had to hand over many of its airports, and scores of the army's special railway lines have been converted to civilian use. Armament factories, ordered to switch part of their capacity to civilian production, now make motorcycles and cassette tapes for the growing consumer market, and it is planned that by the year 2000, half of the defence industry's total production will be of consumer goods.

The military has suffered a sea change at the hands of Deng Xiaoping who, by assuming the post of chairman of the Military Affairs Commission, has ensured that he personally holds the reins of military power. Earlier he saw to it that other top jobs went to his supporters, men like Yang Shangkun, executive deputy director of the Military Affairs Commission; Yang Dezhi, PLA Chief of Staff; and Yu Qiuli, director of the army's political department. Later, by persuading the military to agree to Zhao Ziyang's appointment as his number two on the Military Affairs Commission, he ensured that the way was paved for the Party general secretary to succeed himself as head of the army. After a reshuffle of senior military officers, the number of military regional commands was cut from the original eleven to seven, and the number of commanding officers in these regions reduced by half.

The PLA's heyday appears to be over. It has been the guardian of Maoist ideology, and now that almost everything Maoism stood for is being thrown out of the window, its image is bound to be diminished too. Perhaps its heroic quality would have faded anyway, with passing time and the dimming of revolutionary memory. And it cannot but be affected by the changes in the economy; now that farming and rural trades offer so much better prospects than soldiering, to be conscripted no longer fires the mass of the nation's young manhood, and recruits with the right qualifications cannot be had for the asking. From being a largely volunteer force, the army has been switched to a conscripted one; and now each area except the very poorest ones will have to fill an annual quota of recruits.

The People's Liberation Army has outgrown its guerrilla Red Army origins, and is being trained and transformed to defend a nation which is itself shifting its conception of its security and its place in the world.

Between 1978 and 1985 figures show a near trebling of China's foreign trade, from $20 billion to $59 billion. Such has been the scale of imports that in 1985, the Chinese customs administration announced a trade deficit of almost $14 billion.

This news comes as a bombshell to a country which has customarily traded thriftily, and whose trade philosophy had been 'import whatever is needed to reduce imports, and export only what is needed to pay for imports.' Like other developing countries trying to industrialise, China at the start adopted an import-substituting policy, manufacturing the goods she needed at home instead of buying them abroad. Self-reliance had been an article of faith.

Following the Korean War, Western technology and markets were barred to China by the trade embargo imposed on her by the United States and the United Nations, and it was to the Soviet Union and the East European countries that China had to turn to purchase her plant and equipment. However, since the mid-1970s China has been doing more and more of her shopping in the capitalist West. The pattern of technology imports today, though, is very different from what it was in the 1970s. In those days the Chinese went in for lavish purchases of whole plants, whereas the more recent emphasis has been on supplementing and updating what already exists.

The Chinese have imported a great deal of technology which turns out to be unsuited to their needs or to the technical level of their workforce; and it has been argued by some Western observers that they would have done better to look to the USSR and Eastern Europe, if for no other reason than that the plant designs in these fellow-socialist countries were geared to an unsophisticated, even peasant labour force. But China is in love with state-of-the-art technology, and this infatuation is not without cost, as the notorious Baoshan Iron and Steel Complex, a predominantly Japanese installation, will remind them for many years to come.

Baoshan was fulsomely described by Zhao Ziyang, who cut a ribbon and pushed a button to start it up in November 1985, as the 'crystallisation of the concerted effects of Chinese workers and foreign specialists' and 'the fruitful result of the policy of opening to the outside world and importing advanced foreign technology'. Others might call it a spectacular white elephant, a monument to mammoth miscalculation. The Japanese feasibility studies on which the project based its design have proved to be inadequate. The location, near the banks of the Yangtze River, seemed sensible enough at first, offering water transport of the raw materials and products. But the swampy ground could not bear the weight of the huge blast furnaces and other heavy installations, and enormous amounts of precious foreign exchange had to be spent importing steel pilings to reinforce the foundations. The Japanese blast furnaces were found to require a higher grade of iron ore than China produces, so Australian ore has had to be imported, gobbling up more foreign exchange. And as if these extra costs were not enough, it was found that the 100,000-ton carriers bringing the ore from Australia were blocked from the Yangtze pier by a sand bar in the estuary, and the only solution was to build a new port and storage facilities 130 miles to the south. Here, at Beilun Harbour, off the coast of Ningbo, the Australian ships offload half their cargoes into smaller vessels, and enter the river mouth at high tide. Huge cost overruns have resulted.

Though China is already the world's fourth biggest producer of steel, the Chinese market for the metal will remain a bonanza for foreign suppliers (who have been suffering from a prolonged worldwide steel slump) for many years to come. The chief beneficiary of China's huge demand for steel has been Japan, and China's trade deficit in 1985 was preponderantly with that country. Besides steel, a flood of Japanese consumer goods streamed through China's open door, as an orgy of spending overtook the Chinese in the wake of the economic reforms.

Many Chinese felt themselves being groomed to become a vast market for the products of the Japanese economy, and discontent with this soon manifested itself. Japanese politicians were alarmed to hear of anti-Japanese student demonstrations in Peking and Chengdu in the autumn of 1985, guessing them to be officially inspired (though actually the Chinese authorities wanted such protests no more than the Japanese). When the then Japanese Premier Yasuhiro Nakasone made an official visit to the Yasukuni Shrine in Tokyo—the Valhalla of the souls of the Japanese war dead, among them those sentenced and hanged for war crimes against China—Peking lodged formal protests, and had the Japanese Foreign Minister come to China to receive them. The Chinese point was taken, and Mr Nakasone refrained from another planned visit to the shrine. At the other end, Peking found it expedient to take down a number of large billboards advertising Japanese products in the centre of the city, before popular resentment flared into another demonstration.

A more recent chapter in the story of worsening Sino-Japanese trade relations revolves round China's attack upon what she claimed was a whitewash of Japan's invasion of Chinese territory in Japanese school history books. This was not the first time the Chinese have found it necessary to protest against Japanese history writing, but at bottom China's chief complaint against Japan is one that rings a bell with most nations which trade with that economic juggernaut. The balance of business is simply too much in its favour.

The uncontrolled foreign exchange spending impelled the Chinese into the stop phase of their stop-go cycle, the by-product of which was a slowdown in imports of consumer and inessential goods. Meanwhile, China tried to step up her exports to set off against her imports. Among her East Asian neighbours, import-substitution policy had long given way to a different development strategy. It was in the expansion of exports that South Korea, Taiwan and Hong Kong found the mainspring to rapid growth. With these economies—the world's fastest growing—on her very doorstep, China scarcely lacks example.

China exports largely raw materials, foodstuffs, textiles, machinery, and arms. Because one of her chief exports is petroleum, and she hoped to find as much offshore oil as the North Sea produces in as short a time as possible, foreign oil companies were invited to bid for drilling contracts in the South China Sea, the Yellow Sea and the Bo Gulf. The list of bidders ran the gamut of the world's biggest oil companies, from Shell and BP to Elf and Chevron. Hopes were high when the foreign companies went in, but the initial results have been muted, and the firms were manifestly less enthusiastic about the second round of bidding. The likelihood of finding truly giant fields has been greatly reduced. Besides, no sector of Chinese exports can be more vulnerable to the fluctuations in international prices, and the slump in oil prices in 1986 was a great blow to her trade plans.

As for China's other areas of export expansion, she suffers like other trading nations from declining world trade and growing protectionism. All three of her main areas of export expansion—energy (oil and coal), textiles and machinery—are vulnerable, one way or another. Consider textiles, which make up a sizeable share of the exports of her closest neighbours (such as Hong Kong and Thailand). As China's export sectors change with industrialisation and per capita income growth (in the way that those of other developing countries have done and that economic theory would predict), from labour-intensive raw materials to labour-intensive manufactures to capital-intensive products, she is likely to meet stiff competition from her East Asian neighbours.

Neither her oil revenues, reduced by tumbling world prices, nor her textile export earnings, limited by quota restrictions, are likely to be improved by her decision to devalue her currency in July 1986. Still, the adjustment of the exchange rate signified a recognition of practical reality, for the Chinese *renminbi* had been overvalued. Along with adjusting the exchange rate, China's pricing system will have to be reformed if her manufacturers and trading companies are to be encouraged to export: the discrepancy between the domestic administered price and the international price distorts the incentives of these enterprises, and to stimulate the export of certain products, the central government has had to subsidise the manufacturers. The existence of a seller's market for many goods does not help: when producing for the home market brings in profits with less effort, why should manufacturers bother to compete in world markets?

It was also obvious that to deal with the volume and variety of transactions spawned by the open-door policy, the rigid trade bureaucracy would have to be reconstituted. Until 1979, all import and export transactions were monopolised by the nine State Trading Corporations coming directly under the Ministry of Foreign Trade, and all foreign exchange earnings were arrogated to Peking. In 1979 the monopoly was loosened, and the various industrial ministries were allowed to set up their own import and export corporations; such a change provided for greater functional specialisation, and made for a wider pattern of links with trading partners abroad. Over the years, selected State enterprises have also been given permission to handle their foreign trade themselves, and to do business with overseas firms directly.

With the reorganisation of old institutions went the creation of new ones. One of these, set up on the personal order of Deng Xiaoping, was the China International Trust and Investment Corporation (CITIC), a prestigious company with its headquarters in a twenty-nine-storey tower block in Peking and offices in New York, Paris, Tokyo and Hong Kong. CITIC buys, sells and invests abroad (in the US, in Australia and Latin America) without being hamstrung by the massive complexity of a State and Party apparatus. It is headed by the debonair Rong Yiren, one of those former capitalists who had their factories nationalised by the communists in the 1950s and who were made to clean lavatories in the Cultural

Revolution. Rong is a distinguished family name from pre-revolution days, practically synonymous with Shanghai industry. A millionaire in his own right, and someone one can easily imagine presiding over a board meeting or the Chinese stock exchange, Rong Yiren likes to say, 'I'm not a capitalist; you can best describe me as a businessman.'

For all these changes, though, much trading with the Chinese remains a frustrating experience. At the negotiating table China faces the West, strangers to each other, differing widely not only in interests and priorities, but in the style of conducting business. The decades of isolation show in the cultural misconceptions which the Chinese bring to the encounter, and also sometimes in their naïveté. This last trait has been exploited by many bogus Hong Kong businessmen, who simply take their money and run. China simply does not have enough Rong Yirens, and trying to get the hang of the international marketplace is a slow and difficult process for the Chinese. In almost every area they have to start with first things. With names like Peking Number 2 Truck Works confronting him at every corner, Nigel Campbell, visiting professor from the Manchester Business School, felt moved to urge the Chinese to create and support some strong brand names. Wen Yuankai, the reformer of Chinese scientific research, once offered a comic example of how out of touch the Chinese can be in the world marketplace. 'We export an underwear under the brand name of Pansy,' he said. 'We were pleased enough with this name, which is that of a lovely flower. But the product was a flop. Why? Because, as we later discovered, in English the word "pansy" can mean a male homosexual.'

When American managers came to Peking to run the spanking new Great Wall Hotel in Peking, they found that ideas like public relations were a puzzle to their Chinese staff. The American general manager had to go to great lengths to convey the idea of promotion to them. Halfway through his explanation, one Chinese jumped up and said, 'Oh! I get it! You mean propaganda!'

Because China is unlikely to increase her export earnings to any remarkable degree in the next few years, she has sought other sources of foreign capital inflows. For almost three decades, China refused to take on long-term foreign loans, and even today the Chinese imagination flinches from the negative example of Polish indebtedness. But in 1979 the Bank of China began to engage in substantial international borrowing; and while China's hard currency indebtedness remains unremarkable, there is no doubt that it has risen sharply, and that the People's Republic is operating on a larger scale in the world capital market than she ever did in the past.

Overseas bond issues, aid and concessionary credits, increased tourism earnings, direct foreign investment in joint ventures—all these are means China has lately used to maintain her balance of payments. The most talked about of these is the last. The People's Republic is not alone among socialist countries in cooperating with capitalist multinationals—such joint ventures exist also in Hungary—but here as elsewhere, the pace and scale of development put China in a class of her own. Whereas Hungary had forty-five joint ventures by the middle of 1985, China had signed up nearly 1700; and the figure is three times that if one includes other forms of foreign capital participation, such as sole foreign proprietorship, contractual enterprises, compensation trade and offshore oil ventures.

Why would any hard-headed capitalist want to invest in the People's Republic? China was certainly an untested environment, but then a capitalist will invest anywhere as long as he sees the chance of a good return on his money. What weighs predominantly with him is the cost of production, and if he can reduce this significantly by employing the kind of cheap labour which the Third World typically offers, he will consider investing in these countries. Besides, no investor can be entirely immune to the possibility of gaining access to the Chinese domestic market; talking to foreign businessmen, I found the old China trader's dream of 'oil for the lamps of China'—where you only have to give each peasant a free oil lamp to make the paraffin purveyor rich—still far from dead.

There are two types of joint venture, equity and contractual. The equity joint venture involves the incorporation of a limited liability company, with the Chinese and foreign partners sharing risks, profits and losses in proportion to their equity shares. In such partnerships, the foreigner's share commonly includes equipment and technology, while the Chinese party contributes land and buildings. The contractual (or cooperative, as it is sometimes called) joint venture is not generally governed by legislation and, being a looser arrangement, is much the more popular type of foreign investment. It embraces diverse forms of partnership, from manufacturing-under-licence deals to hotel and other tourism projects.

A wholly foreign-owned venture is a separate case which the Chinese have been anxious to confine to the Special Economic Zones (the subject of the next chapter). Here the foreign party contracts to buy or rent Chinese land, labour and services, and has a set tenure before his assets revert to Chinese ownership. As the foreigner proprietor does not have to work in complex, ponderous and often discordant tandem with a Chinese partner, this type of venture possesses a certain appeal for the investor.

Yet another form of Chinese-foreign cooperation is compensation trade, a buy-back arrangement in which the foreigner provides the technology and equipment and is paid off in goods for disposal abroad. A variant of this is counter-trade, which offers the foreign partner the chance to receive goods for sale abroad other than those produced by the machinery he has supplied. These are to be distinguished from barter trade, which are exchanges of goods of equal value conducted mainly with East European countries.

Foreign investors have come in all types. We hear of a contract being signed at the beginning of 1986 between the Peking Research Institute of Food Industry and the French food firm Grands Moulins de Paris to produce French bread for the capital's Chinese and foreign residents with a production line imported from France. Or there is the joint deal with West Germans to produce Volkswagon Santana cars in Shanghai. Of all China's European trading partners, West Germany is the largest. That the Chinese think the world of German quality is shown in their choice of Schloemann–Siemag, the engineering company, to build a new rolling mill at the Baoshan steel complex. Asked why a German firm was picked, Deng Xiaoping is said to have replied, 'Because only German-built plant survived our last earthquake intact.' So it is not surprising that for their first joint venture with a foreign car manufacturer, they should opt for VW. A spanking new factory, bearing in its brightly painted colours the stamp of the VW corporate identity, has arisen in the rural township of Anting, where the indigenous make, the Shanghai, has been produced by almost pre-industrial methods for the last twenty-six years. The first Shanghais were near-reproductions of a 1950s Mercedes 220 which the factory had somehow acquired, taken apart and copied down to the last screw. (The VW staff are keen to open a museum to display the original.) Now the modernised factory assembles Santana kits. Looking on the brightest side, the factory envisages enough Santanas rolling off the line one day to compete with Japanese and South Korean cars in East Asian markets, as well as to satisfy the huge Chinese demand for vehicles.

Businessmen were naturally wary when they first came in; on top of the usual risks there are the risks of political instability. Might the reforms all fizzle out? Might the open door suddenly close? China has promulgated hundreds of commercial laws and regulations to safeguard domestic and foreign companies, and created a legal system where none had existed before, but the framework is far from comprehensive, and many blanks remain. Practical problems abound in the day-to-day running of joint businesses. When McDonnell Douglas, the US aerospace company, began to introduce new-fangled American management methods—with their free and democratic flows of information and authority—can one not imagine the effects on the Chinese staff, long accustomed to orders being passed down a vertical chain of command?

There were problems with a steady and adequate supply of power and raw materials, something the Chinese have perenially found it hard to guarantee. Above all, there were the difficulties over foreign exchange earnings: the Chinese have assumed that joint ventures would achieve a balance in their foreign exchange earnings and expenditures themselves, but this is hard for companies which use up a large amount of hard currency to import kits or components. In response to a rising tide of complaints, the Chinese government authorised swaps of hard currency between enterprises which have a surplus, and those with a shortfall.

On the whole the Chinese are disappointed with the results of their efforts so far, because they have not brought them the kind of investments they prefer. At the start of 1986, it was found that only 20 per cent of the $4·6 billion invested had come from places other than Hong Kong and Macao, and whereas China would much rather they put their money in infrastructure and enterprises with a high technology content, or projects producing exports which could earn her hard currency, foreign businessmen have mostly invested in light industry, textiles and hotels.

The hotel business thrives because China's new extroversion has prompted a thickening flow of tourists. People who visited China only five years ago can scarcely believe the freedom with which visitors travel about China nowadays; though some places remain out-of-bounds, by the beginning of 1986, when China announced the lifting of travel restrictions from yet more cities and counties, sites had been opened to foreign visitors in every province.

Just one set of figures will show how greatly tourism has expanded in recent years: while Peking received a total of 1 million visitors in the twenty-five-years before 1978, after that date the number rose to 2 million within five years. The grandest hotel used to be the Peking, first opened at the beginning of the century, and managed by a Frenchman. A 1972 edition of Fodor's Guide declared it to be 'not much fun since there is neither bar nor lounge'. But within a matter of a few years hotels run on American lines had sprung up, with swimming pools and closed-circuit TVs, and bartenders trained in cocktail mixing by the Jardine Wines and Spirits International of Hong Kong. There is the Fragrant Hills Hotel, designed by the great I. M. Pei and graced at its opening by Jacqueline Onassis. Or there is the Great Wall, fronted by glinting reflective glass, modelled on, of all places, the Dallas Hyatt Regency, and filled, one gets the impression, by the international glitterati.

In her headlong rush to develop the tourist industry, a business involving low investment and high profits, China is adding to the congestion of her cities, the pressures on her transport systems, and the depredations on her countryside. Yet what country so desperately in need of hard currency can resist the foreign exchange income it brings? The authorities have no qualms about charging the foreigner more than the Chinese for the same goods or services; as an internal government memorandum put it: 'Overseas Chinese, Hong Kong–Macao and Taiwan compatriots are our brothers, while ethnic Chinese holding foreign passports are our kinsmen. In the past they contributed to China's revolution and reconstruction; now they have an important role to play in the Four Modernisations and unification of the fatherland. They should be given preferential treatment when they come to China to visit their relatives or to travel; and a distinction must be drawn between them and foreign tourists.' A welter of government instructions cover the pricing of goods to the tourist, some of them quite specific ('increase the price of train tickets to foreign passport holders by 75%'), some vague to the point of inapplicability ('For special kinds of food like kosher meat and suckling pig, charge the foreigner as high a price as he will put up with').

There is no holding back the tide of mass tourism. Every province wants to cash in on it; even remote Qinghai, whose Luxingshe, the Chinese equivalent of the Russian Intourist, was only up to receiving Chinese-born tourists when I went there in 1982, has flung open its doors to all and sundry. I was horrified to read of bird-watching pavilions, roads and Tibetan-style hotels being built on its bird sanctuary, a nature reserve jutting into the magnificently pristine lake from which the province takes its name. 'The influx of tourists has not scared off the birds,' the officials say, but to go by the experience of the nature reserve in Hainan (a tropical island off the coast of southern China), it soon will. There the protected rhesus monkeys, ogled by some 500 tourists a day, have fallen prey to pneumonia, tuber-culosis and even hepatitis. Qinghai's other great attraction, the holy Kumbum lamasery, is fast catching up with Nepal and Indian ashrams, I am told, in its appeal to the travelling youth of the world.

As throngs of sightseers in drip-dry jersey spill from planes, trains, Hino tour buses and Toyota Coasters at excavated tomb or renovated monastery, China's tourist sites in high season are in danger of becoming less and less alluring. Indeed, the most popular places are nothing short of frightful, their approaches clogged with coaches, touts and souvenir stalls, their quiet corners pullulating with humanity. The simile which a British travel writer used for the crowds surging up the steps of the Great Wall, that of 'ants on to a Mars bar', is exact.

'The time of mass travel to China is a long way off, if indeed it ever comes,' says the 1972 edition of Fodor's Guide to Peking. This remark strikes with some irony, set against the advertisements in today's travel brochures: 'The Golden Road to Far Cathay', 'Kublai Khan's Xanadu Revisited' or 'A Commemorative Journey of 7011 Miles along the Silk Road from London (Charing Cross) to Chang'an'.

# 6

# NEW TREATY PORTS?

In recent decades, multinational manufacturers of sophisticated engineering and electronic products have found it convenient, because of the high wages of easily trainable skilled labour in their own countries, to locate parts of their component-producing processes in Third World countries, where a similar kind of labour can be had at sweat-shop wages. China's East Asian neighbours (South Korea, Taiwan and Singapore) have all tried to attract such foreign investment by providing suitably located industrial estates, and tariff and tax concessions.

One of the most revolutionary of the strategies China has adopted as part of her open-door policy is the decision to allow such zones to be implanted in her socialist economy. She calls such 'islands of efficiency' Special Economic Zones (SEZs).

I made my way one day to Shenzhen, a model SEZ which lies just across the border from Hong Kong.

'Look to your money,' said the girl on the bus. 'Always count your change; be careful you don't get diddled.' She was a shop assistant in a department store in Hong Kong, who had passed through the 'Bamboo Curtain' to Shenzhen many times before. Like many Hong Kong residents who find certain things cheaper in Shenzhen than in their home city, this helpful girl was on a shopping expedition. 'One always feels a bit insecure in Shenzhen, where they are all after your money. I always clutch my handbag tightly to me when I am walking about the streets, for fear of pickpockets.' She made me think I was crossing from socialist China into freewheeling Hong Kong, instead of the other way round.

She told me that the East Gate Free Market was worth a look if I wanted to know what made Shenzhen tick. Two to three hundred shoppers from Hong Kong converge there each day. I could tell at a glance what they had come for. The low stalls of pork, beef and lamb along one side of the market; the water-filled troughs and the wicker baskets; live fish and wriggling shrimps; seasonal fruit; the mounds of haw, chestnuts and walnuts; the open sacks of medicinal herbs; the ducks, the birds, the turtles, the partridges, and the gem-faced civets—all had been brought in from the hinterland before first light.

Greed and sleight of hand contribute to the atmosphere of the market. Here the shopper comes up against the whole bag of bazaar tricks: fakes passed off as the genuine article, steelyards with beams hollowed out or scales weighted with magnets. The Hong Kong dollar openly changes hands. Hawkers make themselves fortunes by Chinese standards doing illegal deals such as selling protected species. The con-man or black marketeer cannot be avoided for long.

The heightened appreciation of the value of money is part of the temper not just of East Gate Market, but the whole of Shenzhen. Shenzhen is in many ways the East Gate Market writ large—bustling, crass, frontier-like, riddled with corruption and possessed of a certain latent commercial power, tied umbilically to Hong Kong on the one hand, and to the rest of China on the other.

To look at, Shenzhen is undeniably impressive for a city which has been in existence for not much more than seven years. Nobody who knew it as a sleepy rural town standing amidst paddy fields and fishing villages could fail to marvel at its emblems of modernity: the high-rise buildings, the luxury hotel converted from a French ocean liner, the fifty-four-storey International Trade Centre (China's tallest building), the eighteen-hole golf course, and the amusement park with its double-loop roller coaster and entertainment devices imported from Italy and Japan.

Shenzhen is the largest and most developed of the four Special Economic Zones which China established in 1980. It and two others—Zhuhai (a town adjacent to the Portuguese colony of Macao), and Shantou (which is better known to the West by its old name of Swatow)—are in Guangdong, the province which adjoins Hong Kong and from which the majority of people in the British colony are sprung. The fourth SEZ, Xiamen (or Amoy as it was once called), is in Fujian, the mainland coastal province opposite the island of Taiwan.

There is nothing random about the location of the SEZs. The Chinese admit that they were chosen with an eye to their historical outwardness, and to encourage investment by Chinese émigrés, most of whom originated in these places. What is not so readily and publicly admitted is the political purpose, the easing of the absorption of Hong Kong, Macao and Taiwan by the Chinese body politic. In an internally circulated transcript of a speech by Shenzhen's Party boss Zou Erkang, one reads, 'The Central Committee has told us again and again that the establishment and development of the SEZs must serve the political purpose of our recovery of Hong Kong and the return of Taiwan to the fold. . . .

'In 1997, whether the Hong Kong or British authorities like it or not, we will regain Hong Kong's sovereignty . . . When we regain Hong Kong, we must maintain its prosperity and stability . . . Our success with the SEZ is an important step towards achieving this . . . Economically the SEZ should serve the country's Four Modernisations; politically it should be useful to the recovery of Hong Kong.'

Politics makes Shenzhen a unique kind of SEZ, but the form of it is familiar enough. Western development specialists have seen its like in some seventy of the world's countries. Like many of these special zones, Shenzhen harboured lavish aspirations. In the flush of its early transformation into a boom town, the Chinese saw it as something more than a tariff-free 'export processsing zone'. As an economist at the State Council's Economic Research Centre put it in 1984, 'China's SEZs are quite different ... A major purpose is to introduce technology-intensive, knowledge-intensive and capital-intensive enterprises for China's own benefit.' It was to be a conduit for the world's capital and know-how, a laboratory in which economic and managerial reforms might be tried out, and passed on to the rest of China.

Deng Xiaoping himself found his decision to create the SEZs vindicated when he came on an inspection tour of Shenzhen at the start of 1984. He was so impressed by it that, upon his return to Peking, he decided to open up fourteen other cities to foreign business. It was a bold gesture, for China had not been broken upon by the world in so extensive and sudden a fashion since the nineteenth century.

The wider opening is not to everyone's liking, though. To many Chinese, the term 'open-door policy' has an ominous ring, for it conjures up a humiliating period in Chinese history, when foreign powers scrambled for concessions and carved out spheres of special interest. Then the open door meant something different from what it means today; then it meant an arrangement among the powers for equal commercial opportunity in each other's sphere of influence. But the distinction gives no comfort to many Chinese, who can only think of the open door as an invitation to a foreign assault upon China's independence and self-reliance, and of the SEZ as a modern reincarnation of the treaty port.

In some ways their fears echo those of many developing countries, where foreign investment has long been equated with 'neo-colonialism' and 'exploitation'. But the Chinese have a further psychological difficulty: an SEZ like Shenzhen has simply never been created in a socialist country before. Deng Xiaoping and his men have appealed to the most sordid human motives to start up the economic life of the country again, and all around in Shenzhen one sees the consequences of this. It sticks in the throats of those who remember fondly the heroic days of the revolution. They see the barbed-wire fence, complete with arc lamps and patrols, along Shenzhen's fifty-mile border with the rest of Guangdong province, and they say: 'China managed to expel imperialism and Chiang Kai-shek. But now we've gone and cordoned off an area to invite foreign capital in: aren't we creating a second Hong Kong and a new colony?'

Doubting Thomases are assured, however, that far from provoking disapproval in other socialist countries, it has elicited eager interest. Indeed, these other countries see it as something of a nursery, for what may be done on their own soil. A group of Romanian holiday-makers, every one of them a Party secretary, is said to have pronounced Shenzhen a challenge to outworn theory on socialist reconstruction. Delegations of Party cadres and scholars have come from Poland and Hungary, expressing keen interest in learning more about the SEZ. Hungary is said to take comfort in China's bold reforms—'There is much similarity between what you are doing and what we have been trying to do,' the Hungarians are reported as having said. 'We used to feel terribly isolated, and hard pressed by the USSR. But now that we have seen things for ourselves in China, we realise that in some areas of reform you have taken even larger steps than us, and that we are no longer alone.'

It will come as a surprise to many people in the West to learn that North Korea, that most introverted of communist States, has sent no fewer than ten delegations, one of them led by politburo members, and despatched by Kim Il Sung himself. Shenzhen, it seems, met with their entire approval; indeed, its cadres were told that North Korea was studying the possibility of opening up to the world herself. To those who have set the pace of China's open-door policy, all this adds up to an international trend.

Shenzhen has served as a powerful magnet to people living in inland China, who have been migrating there in considerable numbers in the expectation of finding better employment, more money, and better material conditions of life. Certainly the wages are much higher, averaging $79 a month in early 1986, double the rate in other cities.

Quite apart from the promise of economic opportunity, there is the lure of Hong Kong, to which Shenzhen is seen to be a bridge and a transit stop, as well as China's most open door. To steal into Hong Kong, many illegal immigrants from the provinces first apply to their local governments for an entry permit into Shenzhen. To inland China, Shenzhen is Little Hong Kong, a place where, because of the freer flow of goods across the border, one can acquire foreign imports hard to come by elsewhere. Shenzhen has prospered by re-selling high-priced goods brought in from Hong Kong to customers further inland. Some of these may be consumer products, others may be raw materials and components intended for Shenzhen's processing and assembly plants. It has done well, too, as a place where one can do a roaring trade in illicit currency exchanges. The above-board shades off into the illegal in Shenzhen, where graft is a commonplace, and where everyone knows, if only by reading the papers, that many of the swindles one hears about could only have been perpetrated with the complicity of the cadres.

But this is something different from its intended role. As originally conceived, Shenzhen was to be an economy fuelled predominantly by foreign investment and high-tech, and founded on exports and manu-facturing. Recently it has become very clear that it has not succeeded in this. In the summer of 1985, Deng Xiaoping, who had been so enthusiastic about the SEZs only sixteen months before, seemed far less certain in his conclusions. Since then a barrage of criticism has arisen, both at home and abroad. The zone's dramatic growth, its detractors say, has been made possible not by large injections of foreign capital, but by domestic 'blood transfusions'; and the time has come to pluck out the needle. What is more, the foreign investment it has received has proved not to have been all that foreign either. No less than 70 to 80 per cent has come from Hong Kong; and of this amount some, at least, has been mainland Chinese money, originating in banks and companies the People's Republic has incorporated in Hong Kong. The headlong rush into producing the visible hardware of economic growth in the form of high-rise buildings or modern factories left Shenzhen dangerously short of money, and word came from Peking to cut down on waste and spending. (Shenzhen's high officials responded by giving up their Mercedes Benz's for humbler Toyotas.)

The planners had looked to something beyond a mere processing centre offering cheap labour unencumbered by trades unions or advanced welfare legislation. But technology- and knowledge-intensive industries require substantial skills, not to be easily had in a place which, until just a few short years ago, was largely paddy fields. There is a world of difference between being able to produce a television set from scratch and being able to put it together from imported components. Shenzhen may do the latter adequately enough, but it was the former which Peking had envisaged for it. Once put together, the TV sets went on sale in the domestic market, against the original intentions of Shenzhen's planners, who had decided that export trade, earning hard currency, was to be the SEZ's *raison d'être*.

The discrepancy between what SEZs ought to be, and what they became, was dramatically encapsulated in 1984 by the Hainan scandal.

Hainan is, as the Chinese like to put it, 'China's largest island next to Taiwan'. It lies, lapped by the warm waters of the South China Sea, to the southeast of Guangdong province, from whose capital Canton it took its administrative orders. Palm-fringed and sun-warmed, it is a place of tropical temper, easy-going and unhurried, where a beachcomber might feel at home. Although, in the days of the empire, it was one of those faraway places, inhabited by betel-chewing aborigines and beyond the reach of Chinese civilisation, to which the court banished its disgraced officials, there is much to be said for Hainan. Certainly, a European visitor to the island in the eighteenth century thought it had potential: 'Most of the mountains are covered with old, dense forests. The plains and valleys are well watered and fertile; they usually yield two crops of rice a year ... they also produce sugar, tobacco, cotton, indigo, betel nuts, coconuts, grapefruit, and all the kinds of fruit to be found in south China. Aloes-wood, ebony, rosewood and a sort of wood, said to be incorruptible, are all grown in the mountains.'

Yet when Zhao Ziyang came to visit in 1983, at the conclusion of a tour of ten African countries, he was saddened by what he saw. To Hainan's administrators, he is reported to have observed, 'I had supposed the world's most undeveloped region to be Africa. Now I know it to be Hainan.' The reasons for Hainan's poverty are not immediately apparent. According to one estimate, Hainan's main enterprises, which nowadays include rubber and mining, earn it profits of about a billion yuan a year. But the people of Hainan had seen little of this money, for almost all of it had gone to the coffers of the provincial government of Guangdong. As a local song has it,

> Hainan is a treasure island,
> But they take all its riches away,
> Leaving nothing but weeds.

The quickest way out of Hainan's plight, Peking decided, was through the open door. Deng Xiaoping proposed that the island should be opened for foreign trade and investment, and the man he chose to start things up was one Lei Yu, a Party cadre then working in Guangdong. A bespectacled university graduate in his forties, Lei is a man of purpose, and anyone who saw him take up the reins of power in Hainan would have said he had the full confidence of the top leaders, and that they had given him, if not an entirely free hand, at least plenty of autonomy.

The initial State subsidy was generous but, in the Hainan context, a mere drop in the ocean. Deng Xiaoping is reported to have said, 'See if we can't make Hainan catch up with Taiwan in twenty years' time.' Yet when it came to further funding, Lei Yu was given to understand that Peking could offer 'policy but not money'. Hainan was to be accorded special privileges, and more than this he should not expect. It was not a Special Economic Zone exactly, but it enjoyed certain liberties: the freedom to import seventeen kinds of goods whose entry into China is normally controlled by the central government.

Hainan had been told to gear itself up for economic take-off. The way to accomplish this, Lei was quick to realise, lay in buying and selling cars. Few businesses could be more profitable, because a car imported free of customs duty into Hainan sold on the mainland for three to eight times the purchase price. Though the hard currency with which Hainan paid for the cars could often only be obtained at the black market price, and this reduced the size of the profits, nevertheless the amount of money Hainan skimmed off was considerable. To indicate the size of the sums involved, just two figures will suffice. All told, the amount of foreign exchange Hainan acquired on the mainland by illegal means was $570 million, ten times the amount of foreign exchange which the State allowed the island to keep, while the bank loans it took out to pay for the cars came to 4·2 billion yuan, 100 million more than the value of its entire agricultural and industrial output for 1984.

The permits to import the cars were signed by Lei Yu and Chen Yuyi, a local government official responsible for foreign trade. The applicants, of whom there were 872, ranged from local government bodies down to kindergartens. Within a matter of just over a year, the whole of the Chinese mainland was turned into a great, bottomless market for little Hainan's cars. Across the sea they were shipped, the navy lending a hand. In Shenzhen, to whose currency market came great hessian sacks stuffed full of *renminbi* from Hainan, dealers were bowled over by the scale and frenzy of it all. It was as if a dyke had been breached, and the Chinese entrepreneurial instinct, damned back for so long, was suddenly found to be in full flood.

Profiteering on so massive a scale could not have escaped the notice of Peking for long, but it was not until Lei and Chen had approved the import of 89,000 cars, nearly three million television sets, and hundreds of thousands of video recorders and motorbikes that the leadership acted unequivocally. An investigative committee was despatched to Hainan; Lei and Chen were found guilty of unpardonable misdemeanours and stripped of their government and Party posts. The cars were confiscated. Hainan's brief moment of glory was over. It was the talk of the whole country, the most exciting thing to have happened to Hainan since the founding of the People's Republic.

In the popular imagination, Lei Yu—who did not seem to have taken any money for himself—became something of a folk hero, who only had Hainan's best interests at heart, and exploited its 'open' status simply as a means of enriching its people. Even Peking had turned a blind eye at first, and no one could say for sure where the legal ended and the illegal began. It was a muddle of intentions good and bad, but it had been a sensational year for Hainan. For the leaders in Peking, though, it has left wide open the debate on how far to take off the brake on their economy.

'What is your native place?' is usually the second or third question I am asked when I talk to strangers in China. This can, but does not always, mean one's place of birth: an ethnic Chinese can have been born in Birmingham and still lay claim to a native place in China. One's native place is where one's forbears came from, however far back in ancestry one has to go. It is the place, above all, where one's deepest loyalties are deemed to lie.

The assumption that no Chinese émigré, however estranged from his mother country, or hostile to China's political system, can be immune to an appeal to his native-place loyalty, lies at the heart of the open-door policy. Many of the world's most accomplished Chinese émigrés have come back to visit; and not just to visit, but to teach, to advise, and to offer their

services. Scientists, pianists, dancers, accountants, lawyers, architects—
China could use them all. Even defectors are welcome to return, with the
assurance that all is now forgiven.

We saw earlier that 80 per cent of the direct foreign investments which
China received by 1986 came from Hong Kong and Macao. Geographical
proximity no doubt had something to do with it, but this is not the only
explanation. When a billionaire in Hong Kong donates a school or a library
to his hometown in China, nobody is deceived. Nobody sees it as an act
of pure philanthropy. Yet it would be wrong to think it out-and-out
opportunism. The gesture may certainly advance the billionaire's business
interests in the country, but if the Chinese hail it as an act of patriotism, an
expression of native-place sentiment, at some level it is.

Hong Kong and Macao apart, the largest concentrations of immigrant
Chinese communities are in Southeast Asia—in Singapore, Malaysia,
Indonesia and Thailand. These communities have grown from the great
streams of emigration which flowed out of the ports of Canton, Shantou
and Xiamen in earlier times, after Southeast Asia was opened up by the
British, Dutch and French in the last decades of the nineteenth century, and
opportunities to work on the plantations and in the tin mines were created.

These émigrés, whom Peking regards as *huaqiao*, 'overseas Chinese', as
distinct from *tongbao*, 'compatriots' (a term reserved for Hong Kong, Macao
and Taiwan), have been enormously useful to China before, and may be
expected to be helpful again. It is well known that they helped advance the
cause of the revolution that brought the Manchu dynasty to an end. They
were among Dr Sun Yat-sen's staunchest supporters, and not a little of his
success was owed to the funds they contributed to his cause. Though they
had made a new home for themselves, and taken on the nationality of their
host country, still they had not forgotten their kinsmen, and some of their
new prosperity was fed back into their native place in the form of remittances. The effect which such remittances had on the life of the native place
was far from negligible. Writing of Amoy in the 1910s, an American
missionary observed: 'The benefits of the Amoy emigration have not been
few; the economic advantages alone have been great. Perhaps this alone
explains the prosperity of this district; it is hard to account for it in any
other way.'

Amoy may now just be an SEZ called Xiamen to the prospective European
investor, but to many Chinese settled in Southeast Asia, it is an ancestral
home too. It is no coincidence that one of the largest joint ventures to be
successfully negotiated there, a multi-million hotel project to be completed
by the end of 1988, is with a giant Singaporean developer. Fujian province,
in which the SEZ is located, is the primary source of emigration to Singapore,
to which it is still strongly linked by dialect.

Xiamen's qualifications for open status are apparent. It is an island with a long tradition of trading with the world. Something of its mercantile past may be seen in the two words it has given to the world—the word 'tea', which derives from the Amoy word *te*; and the word 'satin', which has its origin in Zeitun (or Zayton), an ancient emporium near Amoy from which silk was shipped to Manila and thence to Mexico in the second half of the sixteenth century. Declared a treaty port in 1842, Amoy was opened to foreign residence and commerce, and for the introduction of the gospel.

The experience of having Western companies springing up on its soil was not to be repeated until some 120 years later when it re-entered the world of international business as the Xiamen SEZ. It entered that world modestly, attracting very few large foreign investment projects during the first phase of its development, which began in late 1981 with the establishment of the Huli Industrial Estate. Then Deng Xiaoping came to visit, and it was decided to enlarge the estate from two and a half square kilometres to over 130. The first phase of construction completed, things began to look up. Soon more than a hundred projects with foreign investment were in operation. Yesterday's names were Jardine Matheson, Butterfield and Swire, and Standard Oil. Today they are Wang Laboratories, Kodak and Sony.

The pace of Xiamen's infrastructure development has nothing of Shenzhen's breakneck quality. Xiamen can afford to be more relaxed than Shenzhen, because no date has yet been set on its political purpose, the reintegration of Taiwan, where the vast majority of the seventeen million people are descendants of immigrants from Fujian province. It is Peking's fond hope that, as Xiamen develops and the gap in living standards narrows, the two places will become so like each other that the two systems will peacefully merge.

It has been part of the Kuomintang's political mythology to see itself as representing the true China, the place where the Chinese essence has best been preserved. But as the myth has become more and more threadbare, so a different notion of legitimacy has arisen to take its place: Taiwan's economic robustness in the face of diplomatic adversity. Prosperity has been a sop to the political and social divisiveness of Taiwan society, between those who arrived from the mainland after 1949 (the Kuomintang and its followers), and those who were there from the start (the descendants of those immigrants from Fujian province). Money-making has absorbed energies which might otherwise have been channelled into political opposition. This is why an economically resurgent China presents a greater challenge to Taiwan's Kuomintang rulers than revolutionary Maoism ever did.

Of the two countries the People's Republic has been the more conciliatory. If one imagines them as human beings, Taiwan is stony-faced, China all smiles. Tourists who sneak in from Taiwan are welcomed by the People's Republic with open arms, and given the best hotel rooms for the least money. The tactic is part of what is called *tongzhan*, the Chinese abbreviation for the 'United Front'. This is the old Chinese communist policy of trying to persuade as many classes of people as possible that the communists did not look upon them as enemies, but rather as allies in a national United Front—one so broad that, to quote the words of Mao Zedong, 'it includes the working class, the peasantry, the urban petty bourgeois and the national bourgeoisie'.

Though the Taiwan government forbids direct contacts with the People's Republic, the two conduct a sizeable trade through Hong Kong, to which products are shipped, re-labelled and re-packaged before being forwarded to their final destination. Much smuggling occurs across the Taiwan Strait, and no southern mainland Chinese port is without its digital watches and cassette tape-recorders from Taiwan. There are manufacturers and traders in Taiwan who would like nothing better than to cash in on the consumer boom in China, but they thought twice about it when a number of those who defied government rules by selling their goods directly were arrested.

Defections across the Taiwan Strait occur so frequently that they no longer constitute news. But a defection which few observers could be blasé about was the one which took place in the spring of 1986. A Taiwanese pilot on his way back from Bangkok diverted his CAL (Taiwan's China Airlines) Boeing 747 cargo plane to Canton. A native of Sichuan province, the pilot said that he wanted to be reunited with his father there. But though the defection was unusual—over the decades they have generally been in the other direction—the pilot's nostalgia was nothing out of the ordinary. What made onlookers sit up was Taiwan's response. After some hesitation, its president, Chiang Kai-shek's son, stunned conservatives in his own Party by agreeing to face-to-face negotiations for the return of the plane and its valuable cargo between officials of CAL and CAAC, the national airline of the People's Republic. Taipei has not been on speaking terms with Peking since Mao Zedong drove Chiang Kai-shek off the Chinese mainland, and these talks, conducted in Hong Kong, lifted a thirty-seven-year-old taboo. To a delighted Peking, they signified a first step towards eventual negotiations with Taiwan over its reintegration with the mainland.

The second half of 1987 saw a softening in the Kuomintang's attitude towards the mainland, with a series of liberalisations which included the lifting of the ban on family visits to China. The renewal of contact between the two Chinas was dramatised by the widely publicised visit of a couple of Taiwanese journalists to Peking, Shanghai, Canton, Shenzhen and Xiamen. The two journalists risked punishment in doing so, and they were disappointed by what they saw (the low standard of living, the backwardness), but their curiosity was shared by the countless Taiwanese to whom China is still the ancestral home.

But how to go about reunification? The People's Republic has expressed her willingness to apply to Taiwan the formula she proposed for Hong Kong—that of 'one country, two systems'. Taipei denies the appropriateness of this formula to itself. Yet there is a saying which enjoys much currency in the People's Republic: 'Taiwan watches Hong Kong, Hong Kong watches Shenzhen.' To Peking's thinking the issue is not beyond happy solution, as long as China brings herself up to economic parity by pursuing those very strategies which have gone to make Taiwan what it is today.

The fourteen coastal ports along China's Pacific seaboard, announced open to foreign investment in the spring of 1984, are a territorial extension of these strategies. From north to south they were Qinhuangdao, Dalian, Tianjin, Yantai, Qingdao, Lianyungang, Nantong, Shanghai, Ningbo, Wenzhou, Fuzhou, Canton, Beihai and Zhanjiang. Though not as 'special' as the Special Economic Zones, these cities were given varying degrees of authority to decide on projects financed by foreign capital.

A year later, Shenzhen's difficulties, the size of the trade deficit and the runaway economy had prompted second thoughts about the open door and, in one of those familiar twists of policy, Peking reduced the scope of all but four of the fourteen cities. (The four which escaped the cutback were the largest and the most developed ones: Dalian, Tianjin, Shanghai and Canton.)

It is impossible to say at this stage how the new development plans will work out for the remaining ten. What can be said with certainty is that the attraction of overseas Chinese capital to the cities is regarded as a matter of the first importance, and figures prominently in the planners' calculations. For illustration let us consider the case of Ningbo, of which this is particularly true.

Ningbo, lying to the south of Hangzhou Bay, may be described as a might-have-been. In palmier days it was the main port of entry for China's trade with Japan, a busy entrepôt for the coastal trade, and a trading station where Portuguese merchants found a lively market for European wares. British merchants eyed it greedily, seeking time and again to break into its trade. But Ningbo did not live up to its promise, after the British merchants got what they wanted and opened it up as a treaty port. The stream of foreign trade passed it by, and flowed to Shanghai instead. Ningbo was eclipsed, robbed of its hinterland and its gateway function.

The Ningbonese are old hands at making money, though. Their entrepreneurial gift is not much in evidence in Ningbo today, after those long sapping years of central planning, but there seems to be no shortage of it abroad, and it is on this that Ningbo's planners are pinning their hopes. Ningbo is a small city by Chinese standards, but its planners, who have done their homework, have come up with a sizeable figure for the number of Ningbo émigrés abroad: 73,000 people in fifty-five countries. This, they believe, is a considerable resource—a view evidently shared by China's top leaders, who have called for 'the mobilisation of all the Ningbonese in the world to assist in the reconstruction of Ningbo'.

The most famous of the Ningbo natives made good is Chiang Kai-shek, whose old family home in Xikou has been lavishly restored. The media treatment of this is unlikely to have escaped the notice of Chiang Kai-shek's son, the president of Taiwan, but the move was calculated to serve a political purpose and not an economic one. The native son Ningbo does count upon to rally to its call is someone who has made his name in a classically Ningbonese way. He is Sir Y. K. Pao, the world-class shipping tycoon.

Sir Y. K. Pao had struck Clive James, who named him Powie in a story in the *Observer* about Margaret Thatcher's visit to China in 1982, as someone bearing 'a truly remarkable resemblance to the late Edward G. Robinson', and as having 'an infallible nose for the main action'. Pao has had more commercial shipping afloat than anyone on earth. While the likes of Onassis had had all the publicity, it was he who had the tonnages.

Pao had made his fortune in Hong Kong, and it was not until 1984, after half a lifetime had passed, that he returned to his native home. In Ningbo he was naturally shown the sights, one of them being the famous Tianyige Library, housing local gazetteers and priceless block-printed editions from the Ming dynasty. There, so the story goes, an extraordinary discovery was made. Rummaging among Tianyige's dusty volumes, the historians at the book repository came up with the Pao family tree. Tracing Sir Y. K.'s genealogy back five centuries, they discovered that he was descended from Judge Bao (Pao) Zheng, an upright official who lived in the eleventh century.

No one could have wished for a better pedigree, for Judge Bao, whose name is a synonym for wisdom and fairness, is one of the best loved figures in Chinese history. When the historians completed their research, they set it all down in a three-volume traditional thread-bound edition and sent it to Sir Y. K. in Hong Kong. Sir Y. K. could not have been more pleased. He put down the volumes, picked up his cheque book, and wrote out a cheque for fifty million yuan to build Ningbo a university.

What else would he do for his native town? China's top leaders, from Deng Xiaoping down, invited him to explore Ningbo's business possibilities. Could better use be made of Ningbo's deepwater Beilun harbour, built to accommodate the 100,000-ton carriers bringing Australian ore to the Baoshan iron and steel mill? Sir Y. K.'s suggestion was for a giant twelve-billion-dollar iron and steel plant to be built near the harbour. Bankers and businessmen from Britain and West Germany have been invited to consider the proposition, and a British engineering group, Davy McKee, has undertaken a preliminary feasibility study on the project. Between Ningbo and Sir Y. K. themselves, a joint venture has already been agreed upon, the raising of a multi-purpose block on the Economic and Technological Development Estate.

With such a son as Y. K. Pao, Ningbo might yet know happier times.

In 1982 Pao accompanied Margaret Thatcher to Shanghai where she launched one of his ships from the Jiangnan shipyards. This trip was the same one during which the British prime minister held talks with China's top leadership on the future status of Hong Kong. I happened to be in Hong Kong shortly after the event, and a friend there showed me a video recording of the television coverage of Mrs Thatcher's visit. One part of the film was run in slow motion. It was the scene in which, descending the steps of the Great Hall of the People in Peking, she was seen to trip and fall to her knees. This, my friend told me, was taken by the people of Hong Kong to be a very bad sign indeed, auguring ill for Hong Kong's future.

Certainly Mrs Thatcher had got the discussions off to a faltering start by insisting that the three treaties ceding and leasing the three parts of Hong Kong—Hong Kong island, the Kowloon peninsula, and the New Territories bordering Shenzhen—were valid in international law. Hackles rose at this in China, where every history textbook tells you that Hong Kong was seized by British imperialists on the eve of the Opium War and conceded by the abject officers of the Manchu court under threat of a bombardment of Canton. As far as Peking was concerned, the only sensible way for the British to end this ignominious chapter in their imperial history was to tear up those 'unequal' treaties and return Hong Kong's sovereignty to the People's Republic.

The matter had some urgency for Hong Kong's business community, because although Hong Kong island and Kowloon were ceded to the British 'in perpetuity', the New Territories had come under British administration in what is usually described as a lease; and this, ninety-nine years long, was due to expire at midnight on June 30, 1997.

Upon arriving in Hong Kong from Peking, Mrs Thatcher had said that people who did not stand by one treaty would not stand by another, and that Britain kept her treaties. But she had to eat her words. It turned out that Hong Kong is not quite like the Falklands, and in the negotiations which followed her claims for Britain simply shrivelled away.

In the meantime, the barometer of confidence in Hong Kong, the Stock Exchange's famous Hang Seng Index, registered the general unease by slipping an alarming number of points. The Hong Kong dollar plummeted on foreign exchange markets, the property market all but collapsed, companies went bankrupt, and applicants for immigrant visas besieged the foreign consulates and high commissions. Nobody could talk of anything else and, patently cashing in on this, there was even a restaurant that opened up called '1997'.

Everybody was agreed that Hong Kong would become a very different place after 1997. Then opinions diverged. Though China and Britain had both pledged to maintain its 'prosperity and stability', many were convinced that Peking would ruin Hong Kong. The territory, they argued, was the epitome of those values least cherished in the communist State: commercial freedom and initiative, and the principle that whatever is good for business is good for Hong Kong. Others were more hopeful, pointing to China's plans for modernisation and the crucial role which Hong Kong could play in those.

Among those who saw only doom ahead was Bernard Levin, who wrote in *The Times* in September 1983 that 'We must regard Hong Kong as a ship that is going to sink fourteen years from now, and we must mount a rescue operation to save all its passengers and crew.' Most people in Hong Kong assumed that the privileged among them would leave—the Chinese plutocrats to their properties in California or Vancouver; the British expatriates to their cottages in the Home Counties. The very poorest would have no alternative but to stay. The really big question mark over the five and a half million or so Chinese in Hong Kong was the one faced by the professional and middle classes, the most highly skilled and sophisticated people in all the Chinese world. Many of them have become British naturalised subjects, but although Mrs Thatcher has said that Britain has a 'responsibility' to the people of Hong Kong, the new British Nationality Act will deny them full citizenship of the United Kingdom.

There were fears of a 'sell-out' by the British negotiators. There was the bombshell dropped by Jardine Matheson, the princely hong whose nineteenth-century Scottish founder, William Jardine, was the one who gave Britain the idea of annexing Hong Kong. While affirming its continued confidence in Hong Kong, the company declared that it would move its headquarters from Hong Kong to Bermuda, in an announcement which the *Observer* described as falling well in line with the practice of a firm which 'upheld strong Presbyterian principles while poisoning the Chinese people with opium'.

Moves by Peking itself were anything but reassuring. In the summer of 1983, a new man was sent from Peking to head the shadowy 300-strong New China News Agency. Just as New China is no ordinary 'news agency', so Mr Xu Jiatun, as the newcomer is called, is no ordinary functionary. One look at Mr Xu as he stepped off his train that blistering June day—loose, open-necked white shirt over dark baggy trousers; short, spiky haircut; the sinister tinted glasses beloved of Chinese cadres—and one could tell a world of difference lay between the style of things in Hong Kong and the People's Republic.

Almost the first thing Mr Xu did was conduct a walkabout in the Walled City of Kowloon, a squalid six-and-a-half acre slum which the treaty leasing the New Territories to the British had reserved for Chinese rule. In theory it remains answerable to China. In practice it has been a law unto itself, infested with dope dealers, child prostitutes and the Triads. It is the least savoury neighbourhood in the territory, but the point of it was that its people did without British administration. Mr Xu praised the inhabitants for their handling of their own affairs. Here was a model for the future, he seemed to be saying. At this, a wave of anxiety passed over Hong Kong.

It was with a great sigh of relief, therefore, that everyone greeted the initialling of the Sino-British Joint Declaration on Hong Kong on December 19, 1984. After more than two years of racking uncertainty, something was clinched at last. The agreement, which embodied Deng Xiaoping's formula of 'one country, two systems', was widely praised as a document unprecedented in its inspired compromise.

Its chief points are as follows. The People's Republic is to resume the exercise of sovereignty over Hong Kong (including Hong Kong island, Kowloon and the New Territories) from July 1, 1997. Hong Kong, as a Special Administrative Region of the People's Republic, will enjoy a high degree of autonomy for fifty years after 1997, with an elected legislature, a government of local inhabitants, and perhaps an elected chief executive. During that time its capitalist system, and even its lifestyle (including gambling, as many foreign reporters noted), will remain unchanged; and all the freedoms currently enjoyed by the Hong Kong citizen—such as the rights to free speech, a free press, freedom of movement and religion—will in general be guaranteed. Current trading, monetary and financial arrangements will remain as they are, and the central government in Peking will not levy taxes on the territory. (This last provision, little noted by other writers, should be specially heartening to the Hong Kong citizenry: China has habitually taken from the richer regions to give to the poorer ones.)

The document put a seal on what one British journalist described as the 'Great Chinese Takeaway'. But it did not mark an end, only a beginning. There are practical details to work out; the Special Administrative Region's Basic Law—providing for the continuation of capitalist practices until June 30, 2047—to be drafted. The British administrators cannot just clear their desks, tick off the days, and leave the Chinese to it. A Joint Liaison Group of officials from Peking and London has been set up to oversee arrangements for the transition. Elsewhere in the former British Empire, colonial administrators have prepared their subjects for independence, and in Hong Kong too the British are concerned to reinforce, before they leave, Hong Kong's ability to govern itself when the time comes. Though they may not always recognise it, deep down the British harbour no very high hopes for Hong Kong's continued success under its new masters. They have a sense of history, and neither the history of decolonisation nor the history of China is without its pages of tattered illusions and sectarian violence. But still they want to use the remaining years of British administration to help build up the political structures that will underpin Hong Kong's survival as a free enterprise system under the rule of a socialist government.

But what arrangements should replace the present order? In other colonies, the sequence of transition has been from appointed assemblies to elected assemblies to independence. But there is no agreement on whether or not the best political system for ensuring Hong Kong's economic liberty is a democratically elected government. Hong Kong's intelligentsia and younger generation are convinced that it is, but they are opposed by the local plutocrats, who believe that direct elections will clash with their business interests, because left-wingers might be elected and, before they know it, employers will have social security, unemployment benefits and higher taxes thrust down their throats. The present structure has worked well enough, they argue, and it is certainly no democracy. Theoretically the present system is indeed a dictatorship, out of the classic colonial mould. But it is a benevolent kind of dictatorship, in which the Governor does not exercise to the full the enormous power with which he is endowed by the British sovereign, seeking instead to govern by consent, listening whenever necessary to his two advisory bodies, the Executive and Legislative Councils. Matters are decided in what has been described as a 'clubby' atmosphere, with business interests exerting so much power that Hong Kong is said to be run by an old-boy network of the Hong Kong and Shanghai Bank, the Jockey Club, Jardine Matheson and the Governor.

As the undoubted beneficiaries of such a system, the plutocrats were naturally disturbed by the steps taken towards representative government after the initialling of the joint declaration, with the British administration initiating political reforms and nascent political parties sprouting. In decrying these developments, they have the ear of Mr Xu Jiatun, whose sartorial style and public manner have softened with the passing months, thanks to the influence of Hong Kong's urbane ways, but who remains as staunchly Peking's man as ever. Though they make strange bedfellows, no cynic will wonder at the sympathy between Peking's representative and Hong Kong's plutocrats. By the nature of things they are both averse to democracy, and they both have an interest in keeping Hong Kong's capital safe—the one from fleeing, the other from nationalisation or worse. So these 'red taipans', as the latter have been called, have not hesitated to switch their allegiance from London to Peking, striving for seats on the Basic Law drafting and consultative committees with as much ardour as they once sought knighthoods.

There can be no doubt that Mr Xu cared very little for the British administration's political reforms, which began with elections to a handful of seats on the Legislative Council. He did not name the British, but he gave the press to understand that it was not for such as them to introduce politics into Hong Kong. To be rebuked, however indirectly, by Mr Xu was an experience the British administrators were not anxious to repeat, and they meekly agreed to consult the Chinese before introducing further reforms. In the local Chinese press, this won them the epithet of a 'lame duck' government, and one periodical observed, with a nod to Mao Zedong, that it was a case of 'the east wind prevailing over the west'.

The British government, it was widely assumed, wanted now only to wash its hands of the whole affair, reckoning it had done all it could for Hong Kong. Was Britain to jeopardise her relations with China, which everyone agrees had improved with the signing of the joint declaration, by championing the cause of one group of Hong Kong citizens—and not even the most powerful group at that—against the interests of Peking? Of course not. There were other purposes, such as China trade, to think of. Britain's interests seem obvious to other European nations; as the trade counsellor of one of them put it, 'British technology is so backward that to win Chinese export orders they had to give Hong Kong away.'

To add insult to injury, the citizens of Hong Kong face the possibility of living within radiation distance of a massive nuclear power station the Chinese have planned at Daya Bay, just up the coast from the British territory. What are Hong Kong's people to do if Daya Bay turns out to be another Chernobyl? Such is the geography of the region that their only escape routes on land will lead not away from Daya Bay, but towards it. Little wonder, then, that the nuclear project became a burning issue in Hong Kong in the summer of 1986, with some forty environmental and volunteer organisations coming out in vehement opposition, collecting signatures for a petition to Peking, and launching a campaign for shelving the installation.

Meanwhile, relations between China and Britain grow ever more amicable. This was never more clearly shown than in the visit of Her Majesty the Queen to China in October 1986, the first by a reigning British monarch. Earlier, the Chinese had been presented with a letter by the British trade minister. Written over 350 years ago by Queen Elizabeth I, the letter was lost when the ship carrying it sank, and not recovered until 1978. It was addressed to King Zhu Yujun of the Ming dynasty, and it expressed the first Elizabeth's desire to establish diplomatic and trade relations with China. It was, the two sides now agreed, historical evidence that Sino-British friendship went a long way back.

# PART THREE

*

# DENG'S PEOPLE

The people, and the people alone, are the motive force
in the making of world history.

Mao Zedong, 1945

It is easy to move rivers and mountains, hard to change
a man's nature.

A Chinese saying

# CONSUMERS

No people on earth, save perhaps the French, are as preoccupied with food as the Chinese, for whom it has always been the first pleasure of life. It is a food writer's cliché that when Chinese greet each other, they do not say 'Hello' or 'How are you?', but 'Have you eaten?' One expects to eat well in China, just as one expects bad weather in England and good skiing in Switzerland.

I thought I knew all about Chinese cuisine, its rich variety, its sophistication, until I started to travel in China, and found my gastronomic experiences ranging from the merely passable to the unspeakable.

Along with a tired and disheartened citizenry, the three and a half decades of Maoist rule left China with a blighted table. For the gourmet, there is perhaps no darker blot on the Maoist record than the fact that, for most of the past three decades, average food consumption in China has been below the level achieved in the late 1930s, the period before the outbreak of the Sino-Japanese War. It is true that agriculture quickly recovered from the devastation of war after the communists took over in 1949, and that by 1957–58 average food consumption had regained the pre-war level. But we have it from Nicholas R. Lardy, a professor of economics at Yale University who has tirelessly studied Chinese agriculture and consumption, that in the succeeding two decades the quantity and quality of the average Chinese diet distinctly fell, and did not regain the standard of 1957–58 until the end of the 1970s. By 1979 food consumption had risen markedly, surpassing both the 1950s and pre-war levels for the very first time.

So until quite recently in China, one very soon learnt not to be fussy about food, for there was only one rejoinder to any complaint about not getting the quality of cooking one had been led to expect: 'We are lucky to be eating at all.'

I cannot see how the Chinese could have shopped and cooked through those lean years of near-famine, severe shortages and food ration coupons and not be changed in their appetites, palates and cooking. Beyond a certain degree of hunger, eating becomes the carrying out of a mere physical function, something you do to stay alive. It has often been said that it was the constant threat of scarcity that gave such variety and ingenuity to Chinese cooking, with its ability to turn shark's fin, duck's web and even fish lips into delicacies. But the cleverest housewife 'can't make gruel without rice'. Past a certain point of dearth, even the Chinese ingenuity with make do and mend doesn't help.

Until recently, a Peking family, in spite of spending almost half its monthly income on food, was about as ill-fed as a Soviet town dweller in the 1950s. But still the Pekingnese ate a great deal better than people did in many other parts of the country, for food riches are unevenly divided in China, and down the years, as Nicholas Lardy argues, the unequal distribution of food grains has worsened as a result of government policies. The government could have done more to redistribute food grains among the rural areas, some of which were chronically short of supplies; but it didn't because transport was undeveloped and it was in any case much more anxious to promote regional self-sufficiency.

It seems somehow shocking that, until Deng Xiaoping reversed agricultural policies in 1978, the daily average per capita intake of calories by the Chinese population was if anything below that of 1957, because although there were modest increases in the consumption of vegetables, pork and sugar during that period, these were simply not large enough to offset the decline in the consumption of cereals, vegetable oils and soybean products.

By 1981 though, things had looked up. The improvements in agricultural productivity and marketing had begun to be felt in ampler larders and better stocked food stalls. There were the free markets, offering (for the right purse) quality and variety not dreamed of in those lean years of miserably supplied State stores and surly shop assistants. For the shopper and cook it must have been like coming through a war—rationing and make-do monotony giving way to varied fare. Within five years of the change in policy, consumption of the traditional items of the Chinese diet all grew impressively: grain rose 20 per cent, pork rose 60 per cent, vegetable oil doubled, and so on.

Being better fed is of course the result of the rapid growth in national income and the decision of China's economic planners to award a larger share of it to personal consumption. For the first time in years, people have money for more than the barest necessities. It is scarcely possible to open a Chinese newspaper without being assailed by statistics showing how hugely everyone's income has grown: the urban inhabitant by 61 per cent and the farmer's by more than 100 per cent between 1978 and 1983. Though prices have also risen, there is none the less no question, as even cautious Western scholars have concluded, that the rapidity with which real incomes have grown since 1978 is unprecedented.

Visiting relatives in Nanking some years ago, I was both touched and horrified to find that in order to give me a mandarin carp for dinner, my cousin had to start queuing at the market at four o'clock in the morning. Now, whenever I sit down to dinner with my relatives, my protests at their going to so much trouble are invariably brushed aside with the remark, 'Oh, it's no trouble; we just go to the free market.' Before these free markets, to which peasants from the rural periphery bring their produce for private sale to urban dwellers, started proliferating in the cities, you were lucky if you got fresh fruit and vegetables once a week, instead of the blackened and repulsive things that passed for them in the State stores. By late 1985, they had replaced State vegetable outlets in most cities; and since they have become the chief supplier of fresh vegetables, poultry, eggs and fish to the urban shopper, the government announced that it would open some 30,000 of them by 1990.

The food comes lumbering into the city on mule-carts and lorries in the small hours. In Shanghai I noticed people rolling out bedding in rows on the streets, and was told by my cousin, in case I thought them homeless down-and-outs or a sign of the city's housing shortage, that they were free marketeers from the country, camping out before resuming business in the early morning. In Peking, down at the Shuidui free market, nightfall sees 200-odd traders tuck themselves up under the stalls. The market administration exacts a fee, but it is only a tenth of what you might pay for a bed in the cheapest hotel.

Just as it has become easier to shop in China's cities, it-has become easier to dine out. Asked why China should want to restructure her economy, a Chinese economist pointed to the backwardness of her service industry, illustrating his argument with the observation that although urban population increased by 70 per cent between 1957 and 1978, the number of restaurants and snack bars in towns and cities actually fell between those years, from 470,000 to 110,000. Peking, especially, has seen a rash of new eating places open, some of them as gimmicky as any you would find in Hong Kong. There is the new Confucius Restaurant, for example, offering dishes based on recipes gathered from the kitchen of the Sage's family seat in Shandong province. There is also the Longhua Health Food Restaurant, where it is more than likely that your dishes will be cooked with sea slugs, pilose antler, a specially nutritious southern Chinese ant, and tonics for every ailment from dropsy to male impotence. Then, for a very different kind of gastronomic experience, there is the Yili, Peking's very first fast food cafeteria, serving hamburgers and hot dogs and satisfying the younger generation's fascination for things Western. Or there is Kentucky Fried Chicken, with its picture of the Manhattan skyline and its poster saying, 'America—Catch the Spirit'. Meanwhile, if you want to avoid the long queues in front of the duck restaurants serving Peking's famous speciality, you can call up a duck-to-door service, and have a roast duck delivered to your home with all the trimmings.

Recipe books for regional cuisines, for feeding the old or ailing, and even for European cookery have appeared one by one in the bookshops. A five-volume work on the history of Chinese food, spanning the period from the third century BC to the twentieth AD, is being compiled by the editor of

*Chinese Cookery*, a monthly magazine. All this is reinforced by official action, aimed at giving the profession of cook a new respectability. In the autumn of 1983, there was, for the first time in the history of the People's Republic, a grand conference of cooks in the capital. Dignitaries from the Central Committee and the ministries attended, and a national competition was held to choose the top ten chefs of the country. The judges tasted some 400 dishes, served by the participating chefs over a period of eight days.

The courses served turned out to be a form of showmanship, created more for the eye than for the palate. Like those famous French chefs Carême and Dubois, too many Chinese cooks undertook the most laborious work in the kitchen to produce amazing architectural arrangements of food, transforming honest, everyday materials into elaborate spectacles, with bits of egg, prawn, carrot and cucumber appearing on the table as a rose, a lotus, or a peacock. These dishes looked magnificent, but were disappointing to the taste, not to say inedible. The temptation to produce such flashy food, suggested Wang Shixiang, a distinguished art historian and gourmet invited to be one of the judges, should be resisted. He argued for food of more limited pretensions, and suggested that steps be taken to collect recipes for regional dishes from the humble housewife and the farmhouse kitchen. As is perhaps to be expected in a socialist country, there nowadays appears to be no middle-ground of bourgeois cookery between *haute* and *paysanne* in China. In a private conversation, Wang Shixiang told me that he thought the regrettable fashion in grand dishes to have been fostered by foreign tourism, and the Chinese tendency to equate hospitality with costly prodigality.

It is sadly true that the worthy socialist aim of giving everyone a sufficiency at the expense of luxurious consumption by a minority has made for a general lowering of standards in consumer goods and services, and replaced public taste and discrimination with sheer practical necessity. Underused for so long, the old Chinese skills, in cooking as in craft making, are rusty, if not altogether lost. I was not surprised to learn that when restaurants started re-opening in the top tourist cities, Chinese cooks had to take refresher courses from their fellows in Hong Kong.

It would be wrong to suggest that these are signs of a renewed interest in food, because the Chinese preoccupation with eating has never waned, revolution or no revolution. If anything, the failure of the government to make more food available until recently had intensified that preoccupation, turning it into a daily, hourly obsession. So what has emerged is not a keener hunger but a reassertion of taste. For most people life is too hard to make food anything but a necessity, but it would not be too much to say that what we are witnessing is the rebirth of the art of eating.

The stimulus to all this has come, as it does in most spheres of life in China, from above. The government is anxious to develop the food industry, which has been given priority in the economic development plans of many cities. Progress has been rapid, according to Chinese statistics, with the production of sugar, alcoholic drinks, canned food, soft drinks and other foods doubling in the years between 1980 and 1985. From being fourth among China's industries, food processing has jumped to third, falling behind only machinery and textiles. Much of this had to do with handsome State loans and subsidies for technical renovation and expansion, and with the granting of preferential treatment to food enterprises in the form of reduced taxes and higher retention of profits. But for every factory benefiting from new production lines and imported equipment, many more still await revamping. The government selected a hundred counties as testbeds for developing the food processing industry, but a survey conducted in the autumn of 1985 showed that their progress was chiefly hampered by the shortage of funds and technicians.

Elsewhere, we hear of producers adopting new methods and introducing new varieties. Some of these innovations are nothing short of revolutionary. Peking ducks, conventionally force-fed to give them their ample padding of fat, are being reared in the tens of thousands in Anhui province to a revised method, which has them eating by themselves and growing up leaner. Since 1981, a duck farm in Canton has been producing a million ducks a year of a Peking hybrid variety developed by the British Cherry Valley Farms of Lincolnshire, which expect their breeding stock to be adopted by a further twelve farms in China before long. Even pigs have to be slimmer now, as more and more urban shoppers go for lean meat. Until 1984, nobody had thought of changing the 300-year-old method of making Jinhua ham, a famous speciality of eastern China; now, in a bid to win markets, tradition is giving way to innovation, with the ham coming in different forms for different pockets for the first time in its history.

Now that they can eat plentifully, the Chinese are beginning to be concerned that they also eat healthily. They still get most of their calories and proteins from cereals and tubers, and the study of nutrition, condemned as a science pursued for the benefit of the bourgeoisie, has only just been revived. Revelations have emerged that heart disease (caused by the Chinese eating three times the amount of salt judged ideal by the World Health Organisation) now kills 50 per cent of the population, five times the number recorded at the time of the communist victory.

Folk dietetics and lore go back centuries in China, and because they are hypochondriacs as well as gourmets, generally speaking the Chinese eat and drink with an excessive concern for their food's curative and nutritional properties. Their folk wisdom on the subject is well enough in its way, yet the Chinese understanding of proper nutrition is all too often half-baked. A comparatively new aspect of improper feeding is the vogue in milk, which has never really been a part of Chinese diet, but which is believed to be the one thing Chinese babies must absolutely have, in order to be as healthy as their opposite numbers in the West. When they might have given their toddlers high-protein foods like soybean milk, parents eagerly seek out a dairy milk powder and malt mixture called *naigao*, which is low in protein and high in sugar. The head of the Peking Children's Hospital told the press in 1985 that a third of China's children are suffering from iron deficiency, and that the incidence of rickets is also very high. To large numbers of Chinese the concept of baby food (as distinct from food in general) is still remote, but a joint venture between an enterprise in Guangdong province and the American Heinz to produce it is perhaps a sign that this is changing.

'Yifu Sheng Luolang', read the outsize Chinese characters on a brightly painted billboard in downtown Peking, advertising a twenty-five-year retrospective of the work of Yves Saint-Laurent. It was an arresting notice to come upon in the capital of the People's Republic, but its message was not new. Yves Saint-Laurent was not the first Parisian designer to display his clothes in Peking, which had seen a thing or two since Pierre Cardin paved the way in the spring of 1979.

Mouths did fall open then. As French models swept down the catwalk with loud pop music blaring, the four hundred or so spectators in their blue baggy suits could scarcely believe it was ready-to-wear fashion they were seeing, and not some bizarre fancy dress party. 'Some of the women,' reported a Reuters correspondent, 'covered their faces and tittered. The men looked at the ceiling when they could tear their eyes away from all the flesh.'

After Cardin came Halston, bringing American fashion, twelve top New York models and Bianca Jagger. In Shanghai over a thousand employees from the Chinese textile and garment unions came to watch the show, and though Shanghai is urbane by Chinese standards, the audience's reaction was one of fascinated horror. Alluding to the décolletage, one of them later said to me, 'I confess myself deeply shocked.' Bianca Jagger could be seen during the show 'leaning against a pillar wearing a high-collared Chinese Mao jacket and a blue cap with a red star'.

It took very little time for the Chinese to grow accustomed to the idea of Western fashion. Before long they were staging fashion shows themselves. The first place to form a modelling troupe was the Shanghai Fashion Design Institute, but it was quickly copied, and there is now scarcely a big city without one. Peking alone had seven such troupes by 1985, and now boasts even a modelling school. Two large-scale garment fairs were mounted in Peking in 1983, and at one of them, the Shanghai modelling group put on an all-Chinese fashion show, the first show to be staged in the People's Republic. Against a spot-lit backdrop of a giant fan decorated with what looked to me like flying Buddhist angels, twenty-four models (fourteen of them selected from Shanghai's garment industry workers) tripped and danced across the stage. Their coaching, by the Shanghai Academy of Dramatic Arts, was well reflected in their gait, hand movements and make-up. An attempt at a Chinese flavour had been made too: the models showing men's safari suits, for example, had been taught to assume as far as they could the stylised poses of Peking opera.

The clothes will scarcely impress the Western spectator, except perhaps by the quality of their tailoring and their fine intentions. They cried out for a good designer. Fashion had begun its comeback to the People's Republic, but it was imperfectly understood. This was quickly realised by *Fashion* magazine, which, as well as being the first publication of its kind to appear in China, was the first to sponsor a national design competition. Among the judges were two Japanese designers. The first prize went to a twenty-year-old graduate of Peking's School of Applied Arts called Yao Hong, who designed and made up a long gown based on the *cheongsam*, the high-necked dress with the slit skirt which Chinese women wore up to the first years of the revolution, before socialist unisex took over, and which is popularly linked in the West with the movie *The World of Suzie Wong*.

If they were not inspired by the *cheongsam*, many of the entries were influenced by the decorative folk arts of China's ethnic minorities. They were a far cry from the conventions of Paris and Milan, and it was clear that Chinese designers still had to find their feet. By 1985, though, China had become bolder. She would start participating in the Paris fairs, it was announced. Nor was she above gimmickry: it was further announced that one of the new products she would be taking to Paris were garments with a medicinal effect. These were clothes padded at the shoulder, stomach, waist, chest or knee with Chinese medicinal herbs good for 'pain caused by cold, dampness or stress'.

China's designers had begun the long, difficult haul towards adapting themselves to the norms of the world. In 1985, a Chinese dress won first prize at the 50th Paris International Fashion Fair. This was not just a personal triumph for Tu Tianfang, the young Shanghai woman who designed the dress; it was a milestone for the Chinese garment industry. Tu Tianfang's clothes are manifestly different from the ones displayed at the national fashion contest two years before: they are abreast with international fashion, and look perfectly in tune with the post-punk hairstyles sported by the models who show them. Western styles have rubbed off.

But the clothes China designs for the domestic market are altogether more subdued. The urban girl in China certainly dresses more colourfully now than a few years ago, but China's new designers don't always have her in mind. The raising of fashion consciousness in China was harnessed to another purpose—the expansion of her textiles and garment industry and the pursuit of new export markets. China wants to break into the global fashion market, and it was as a consultant to the Chinese National Import–Export Company for Textile Products that Pierre Cardin was invited to China. Garment factories have been renovated in quick succession, using compensation trade with foreign companies as a means of financing imports of advanced equipment. But for her products to compete on the world market China has to tailor them to Western tastes. And this is where the likes of Cardin and Halston come in: they represented 'Western learning', invited, as the American writer Orville Schell rightly puts it, 'much in the way that experts in hydroelectric projects or oil exploration might be brought in to advise on technical matters.'

This is only too necessary, because in common with other developing countries, China faces intensifying competition and protectionism. China was largely spared the quota restrictions considered by the US Congress in late 1985, including the notorious Jenkins Bill to limit textile and shoe imports, which passed Congress but was vetoed by President Reagan. Nevertheless, China expects protectionism to grow. Consciousness of this has persuaded her to consider building a textile mill in Britain's answer to Shenzhen, the special enterprise zone in Swansea.

If the overseas sales are uncertain, the home market can hardly be livelier. Of all spending, that on clothes has grown the fastest, with people spending as much as a seventh of their monthly wages on changing their wardrobe. Sales of every kind of fabric have soared, and eager customers pack the shops. There is a picture which catches this thirst. It is of a shop in the inland city of Chongqing, selling T-shirts newly arrived from Canton. To the right are the shop assistants, handing goods over the counter. On the left are the customers—rank upon rank of them. Between the two, in front of the counter, a floor-to-ceiling railing has been erected. It is to protect the shop assistants from being engulfed by the swarming crowd.

Now that there is more variety and more money, consumers have become more choosey. 'People don't just want durable and dirt-resistant clothes,' the retailers reported, 'they go for fashion.' The vast readership of popular magazines lapped up stuff like this news item: 'Bat-wing sweaters, loose tops and close-fitting slacks, worsted coats and skirts, are in vogue among women in Peking.' The very latest thing in Peking or Shanghai may have little to do with what is fashionable in Tokyo or London, but trends are detectable all the same. It is true that there is the inevitable cultural lag, and that bell-bottoms and mini-skirts came into vogue in China years after they had gone out of fashion everywhere else, but it is taking the Chinese less and less time to work through the successive modes of yesterday. As may have been observed in other countries, the first thing to happen to clothes in China in the flush of liberalisation was that they became more tight-fitting, but this phase has given ground to other enthusiasms—such as see-through pleated skirts and frilly ankle-socks.

What has also burst explosively into life is the beauty business. Its growth has been phenomonal: in 1984 alone, State-run factories manufactured 560 million yuan worth of cosmetics. There is no lack of customers, though a cosmetics kit like the Shanghai-made Lumei could cost as much as 70 yuan, more than a month's wage to the average worker. But 'the Chinese clamour for glamour', noted the *China Daily* in late 1985, and goes on to quote from a letter received by a Peking cosmetics factory. 'We're in our twenties,' some soldiers in Laoshan, one of the battlefronts along the Sino-Vietnamese border, had written; 'yet the rough life here has covered our faces with wrinkles. Could you send us some Oqi [sic] anti-wrinkle cream?'

To cash in on the boom in beauty products, it seems that some manu-facturers will stop at nothing. Many fakes and even harmful cosmetics were put on the market, and the Ministry of Light Industry had to decree that products be screened by the provincial health bureaus before going on sale. I found on a visit to Shanghai in 1985 that complete novices were engaged in making perfumes. One of them seized upon a bottle of French eau de cologne I had given to a friend there and asked to buy the empty bottle from her so that he could copy its design. 'It doesn't matter about the fragrance;' he blithely explained to me, 'it's the packaging that sells the product.'

In the cosmetics business as in garment manufacturing, Western expertise has been brought in. The first foreign companies to produce skin care products and shampoos in China were the American Avon, the Japanese Shiseido, the West German Wella, and the French L'Oréal. At the same time the Chinese are trying to create products of their own, drawing inspiration from old herbals and traditional lore. Some of their more elaborate formulations contain expensive medicinal ingredients such as ginseng, pilose antlers, and marten grease. But if a manufacturer had to choose a cheap but effective ingredient to put into his skin care formulation, he might do worse than to select a liquid brewed from earthworms. The institutions which jointly succeeded in distilling it in 1985, Shanghai's Fudan University and Light Industry College, recommend it as a skin food as well as a nourishing additive to alcoholic drinks, soft drinks and even cakes.

When I was in Hangzhou, China's pre-eminent resort city, I was asked would I like to buy some Qingchun Bao, an anti-ageing liquid distilled from ginseng and royal jelly. This comes packed in pseudo-medicinal phials, and not only is it very popular with Japanese tourists, it is rumoured to be widely used by China's elderly leadership. The lucky factory which produces this bestseller also boasts sexual potency boosters like donkey skin gelatin and Spring Returns, a product based on powdered deer antlers.

Women have responded with eager appetites to beauty treatments. Pre-eminent among the salons is the Ruby in Shanghai, where women from outlying suburbs start queueing for appointments from as early as two or three o'clock in the morning. Nicky Smith, a British writer on beauty, has described it as 'a glittering red and gold parlour with Soviet-style chandeliers threatening to bring down the ceiling', where 'girls sit like birds in a gilded cage'. It is a thriving concern, attracting so many customers that it was not long before it opened branches in four other cities as well as three more in Shanghai. Everybody knows that it has had a Hong Kong beautician to lecture—all the more reason for going there.

On an earlier visit to China, I had been asked by a Chinese woman how Hong Kong ladies of leisure whiled away their afternoons—if it was by playing mahjong. My answer—that it was more likely to be aerobics or workouts—had completely baffled my inquirer. A year later, I read that the larger Chinese cities were gripped by a keep-fit fever. In imperial days court ladies starved themselves to death to stay slim, but dieting is a sign of plenty, and until recently people cared far too much about eating enough to bother about their figures. But this is changing, to judge by the easy availability of 'slimming teas' and the number of people signing up for weight-reducing classes in the big cities. Passing a fly-blown bookshop in the city of Chengdu one day in early 1986, I was stopped dead in my tracks by what I saw in its window—the Chinese edition of Jane Fonda's *Workout Book*, pirated by the Sichuan Science and Technology Publishing Company.

Pumping iron, the new Chinese fad, swept the country in the mid-1980s, and a magazine devoted to body-building has a circulation of a million. After years of stressing inner beauty, outer beauty could scarcely wait to have its day. This may be deemed to have dawned in 1985, with the nation's first post-revolution beauty contest in Canton; organised by the Nanda Department Store, it crowned a Mr and Miss Nanda on the basis of looks, height, manner and educational attainment.

What also betokens a shift in attitudes to beauty is the official approval of cosmetic surgery. This is apparent in the publicity given to Professor Song Ruyao of the Hospital of Plastic Surgery in Peking. Dr Song is a gifted surgeon, best known for his one-stage ear reconstruction. With degrees from Chinese and American universities, he began his career doing pioneering work in Korea, treating soldiers maimed by napalm bombs. The hospital he now runs in Peking has treated thousands of cases, from correcting congenital deformities to rebuilding noses, buttocks, and even penises. There has also been a small number of sex changes, such as the one which transformed a twenty-two-year-old woman pharmacist suffering from a genital deformity into a man.

The surgeons are concerned to alleviate distress, accepting patients on the basis of greatest need. But the hospital also performs about 1000 cosmetic surgery operations a year, from face-lifts to breast reconstruction after mastectomy. Dr Song has told the press that he expects demand for such operations to rise, with the improvement in the standard of living—they are, after all, 'of enormous psychological, if not physical, benefit to the patient'. 'Eye jobs' are the commonest kind of cosmetic surgery in China; there are now even private doctors to do it, at forty yuan a go. In this Chinese women resemble those of Japan, Thailand, South Korea and Vietnam. The wish to look more Caucasian by having a second epicanthic fold to the eyelid is remarkably persistent—it was widespread among my mother's generation—but it is only of late that it can be openly granted. A very large number of girls who undergo the operation feel that it would make them more attractive to their boyfriends or husbands. This brings to mind the classical Chinese expression *wei jun rong* ('to wear make-up for you'), a common idiom describing a wife's duty.

Though these eye operations smack of 'cultural cringe', the belief that everything Western is automatically better than anything produced at home, they have not been subjected to the same degree of public condemnation as certain styles of foreign clothing. Perhaps this is because they are deemed to belong in the same harmless category as traditional cosmetic devices like ear-piercing. A creased eyelid is not a powerful symbol of any kind of ideology, whereas long hair and blue jeans most assuredly are. It forms no part of the threatening imagery conjured up in Chinese minds by the idea of modern youth culture.

It goes without saying that there are boundaries to the new liberties. For instance, there exists a regulation, prompted ostensibly by health considerations, which sets the maximum heel height of men's shoes at 40 millimetres and that of women's at 60 millimetres. In China everything can be a political matter, and dress is certainly no exception. There is nothing random, for instance, about the adoption of the Western suit and tie by Zhao Ziyang and Hu Yaobang. It is to signify their international outlook, China's pursuit of modernity, and their wish to be in step with the world.

To sum all this up, I can do no better than to quote Hu Yaobang himself, who had this to say to Party cadres about social change, lifestyle, and dress in 1984: 'Ours is a time of great transformation and take-off. In meeting this change, three things deserve our attention: first, the need to revise our ideology; second, the courage to break old rules and regulations; and third, the heed to be paid to lifestyle. Great transformations, whatever may be their nature, are often linked to lifestyles. The overthrow of the Manchu dynasty by Sun Yat-sen was reflected in the lifestyle by the replacement of the long robe and the mandarin jacket by the Sun Yat-sen suit. The Taiping Rebellion had people wearing long hair. The 1911 republican revolution and the May Fourth Movement saw people chopping off their hair ... The current reforms too have a connection to lifestyles. How we live, how we eat, what houses we build, what clothes we wear—in all these the values of the petty peasant economy and the feudal patriarchal society still persist. We want to expunge these things.

'We mustn't equate modernity with capitalist lifestyles. Why do I wear a Western suit and tie; why does comrade Zhao Ziyang? It wasn't unpremeditated. It aroused opposition of course: a Democratic Party dignitary said in a letter to me, "I admire everything about you, but this adoption of Western garb is not right." Yet I say that unless we adopt such changes, the backward elements in our lifestyle will continue to restrain our thinking.'

Rose Zhang is seventeen and sports an Afro hairstyle. She wears the most outré of dresses, clinging costumes with a fox fur slung racily around her neck. She is that new phenomenon in the People's Republic, a teenage pop idol.

She comes complete with a doting mother, who is something of a celebrity herself, if a rather minor one: she had had a small hit in the 1960s with a song called 'Thinking of Chairman Mao'. Rose's songs though, swing to a rock beat borrowed from Western pop tunes, and their theme is young love. The first of her many cassette-tape recordings sold over a million copies, and Rose has no doubt at all that she is China's most popular pop megastar. Her fan mail tells her as much.

She is very far from the world of razzle-dazzle inhabited by Western pop stars; mother and daughter live in a shabby one-room dormitory in Peking. Yet the room houses a refrigerator and a piano, presents (or incentives) from her State-run recording company. These make up for the fact that though her recordings are among the hottest selling things in the country, she is paid only $500 per tape, a pittance by Western standards, though good money in China.

Mother will probably see to it that Rose stays clear of the hazards of her trade. Everybody knows the fate which befell Zhang Hang (or Zhang Xing, as some Western reporters have it), the Shanghai rock singer who soared to stardom with hits like 'There's More than One Way to Make It' and 'Too Late', only to be whisked out of the public eye by the police on a charge of hooliganism. Zhang Hang had played around, it seemed, his sexual horizons widening with rising fame. When it was found that two of his girlfriends had had nine abortions between them, the Public Security men decided it was time to step in.

But pop music has become an ineradicable part of urban Chinese youth culture, something which arresting a rock star will not stamp out. The cult which surrounded Teresa Deng Lijun, the popular Taiwanese singer, was only the first of a series. Though she was banned at first, authority was openly flouted; it was difficult to go anywhere without hearing her, and there was truth in the popular saying that 'Two Dengs rule China: Deng Xiaoping by day and Deng Lijun by night.' The irresistible allure of Western popular culture is very well reflected in a description of a variety show in Canton by a Swedish visitor. The evening begins with musicians playing traditional Chinese musical instruments. The audience, aged between fifteen and thirty, murmurs and fidgets. Then, as the performance draws to a close, what everyone has been waiting for happens. A young couple steps on to the stage, dressed as Western teenagers might have done in the 1940s and 1950s; they sing a song about love, and the audience is rapturous. The couple are seen, as they sing their encore, to make some dance movements to the music. The body movements are unnatural, and made in the wrong order. But they trigger off 'a riot of acclamation'. When the Swedish spectator recovers from her surprise, she turns to look at the audience. It is utterly captivated. 'A happy teenage girl has tears in her eyes.'

But this was 1982. Just a couple of years later, the audience would not have been so impressed. By 1985, the British pop duo Wham! had been permitted to perform in China. On April 7, they gave a concert to 12,000 Chinese in the People's Gymnasium in Peking. A friend who attended it told me how it went: 'Towards the end of the concert the foreign students in the audience got up to dance. A group of young Chinese started to follow, but then the Public Security men moved in and put a stop to it.' By 1986, it was not just pop music that brought audiences out in huge numbers. In Shanghai, there appeared such a hunger for high-brow music that a concert hall had only to announce a Beethoven symphony to find its box office besieged.

Saturday night fever has caught on. *Disike*, Chinese for disco, has entered everyday vocabulary, and there can be few cities where the young do not pulsate to the sound of a Japanese stereo on a Saturday evening. In November 1984, the authorities closed eighty-four of the 136 dance halls in Shanghai because, reported the city's daily *Wenhui bao*, they were badly managed and their singers gave unseemly performances. But their patrons did not think they would be closed for long; the authorities can no longer so easily stop people from having fun.

Towards the end of 1983, there was the infamous campaign against 'spiritual pollution', which combined media browbeating with practical restrictions, and affected every domain from mode of dress to literary techniques. But what was 'spiritual pollution'? Deng Liqun, the Party's propaganda chief and instigator of the campaign, defined it as encompassing the following: 'obscene, barbarous, treacherous or reactionary things; vulgar taste in artistic performances; efforts to seek personal gain and indulgence in individualism, anarchism and liberalism; writing articles or delivering speeches that run counter to the country's social system'.

As the campaign mounted to a climax, men were ordered to shave their moustaches and cut their hair, girls were forbidden to wear earrings and 'way-out' clothes. Avant-garde artists and writers were hauled over the coals. There was to be no more foreign rubbish, or contamination by what the Minister of Culture called 'stinking bourgeois lifestyles dedicated to nothing more than having a good time, drinking, idling and hedonism'.

In the succeeding weeks admonitions resounded across the country, with those who had an axe to grind or an appetite for extremism seizing the chance to chime in. That is exactly the way these campaigns work: it is not always the authorities who single out and persecute the victim. Colleagues, neighbours and 'friends' are often happy enough to do the dirty work for them, out of frustration or jealousy, or a wish to settle old scores. There is ample evidence of this in the artistic community, where, once a political campaign starts, the leadership can more or less withdraw from the scene and let the opposing factions fight it out among themselves.

It was soon evident, though, that the campaign was going to cost far more than it was worth. It interfered with the means by which Deng Xiaoping hoped to turn China into a modern nation—the release of individual initiative and energy, and the flow of foreign money and expertise through the open door. Matters used to lie at the mercy of politics. Such is no longer the case. There are now foreign investors to think of, Japanese businessmen murmuring their anxieties. So the campaign was allowed to fizzle out, with editorials such as this appearing in the Party press: 'The young ought not to be taken to task for appreciating stylish clothes and good food, and for having fun. No significance need be attached to the shape of trousers, the height of heels, or the style of hairdo. Rather, the legitimate desires of the young to embellish their lives should be supported.'

Its failure was the most heartening thing about the campaign. This, above all, marked it as an event of the eighties, a hard time for the Party, which no longer commands events so absolutely. This is not to say that there are no blitzes on what are called 'unhealthy tendencies' at regular intervals. The People's Daily complained in September 1985 that people turned a deaf ear to the government injunctions against the showing of pornographic videotapes imported from Hong Kong. But the local Party heads took a risk and ignored the complaint, because screening such shows is a profitable means of making money for their work units.

Similarly ironic is the trend in the book trade. Officially encouraged to think in terms of profits, publishers now vie to give the public what it wants, rather than what is considered to be good for it. It has distressed the Party's propaganda department to discover that, of the six billion and more books printed annually in recent years, an inordinately large number have had only entertainment value. The implications are varied and, for the propaganda department, disconcerting. The reason why there has been such a paper shortage of late, despite increased imports and production, is that much of it has been used to produce books and newspapers not included in the State plan. Textbooks cannot be printed in time, newspapers and magazines have missed publication deadlines—and all because tons of paper have been used to produce kung-fu novels and tabloids. The boom in such reading matter, catering to the age-old Chinese taste for adventure-packed stories of martial arts masters and their chivalrous exploits in ancient times, is only a reflection of one of the most dramatic developments in recent years, the enormous consumer market for potboilers, pulp magazines, and foreign literature. A common sight these days is the row upon row of unsold serious novels on bookshop shelves; this is in striking contrast to the brisk sales of works by Western authors, large numbers of whom have been translated, from Agatha Christie and Ken Follett to John Updike and John Fowles.

In the cinema too, popular tastes run to Chinese kung-fu and foreign films—the more action-packed the better. In Shanghai, a video-tape screening of a kung-fu classic drew such huge audiences that it had to be shown round the clock. When *Superman* was shown, scalpers were able to sell tickets for ten times their original price. As for *First Blood*, the violent Hollywood film with Sylvester Stallone playing a Vietnam war veteran called Johnny Rambo, it created a veritable cult among the urban young. A young Chinese I met once showed me an edition of a popular Chinese magazine, *World Affairs Pictorial*, in which Rambo was the cover feature; the boy's eyes positively shone when he turned to the photographs of the hero's custom-made machine-gun, and a knife with the words 'First Blood' inscribed on the blade.

What is so odd about this craze is that it has taken place in a country where the authorities have full control over what foreign films to let in. The foreign residents were puzzled that a film which so glorified violence should have been judged appropriate for Chinese consumption. 'Rambo is no hero,' one of them said in a letter to the *China Daily*; 'he was a madman.' And *First Blood* was a movie she would boycott even in her native America. Yet the savageries simply delighted the Chinese spectators, whose tastes are frankly rudimentary. One Chinese review went so far as to applaud the film as a 'serious work, with a healthy content, a profound social significance, and much artistry'. As for Rambo himself, he was proclaimed 'a symbol of the American spirit' and a latterday Lin Chong, a legendary folk hero of the Song dynasty, known to almost every Chinese through the popular classic *The Water Margin*.

As the standard of living grows, so there are more of all kinds of consumption. I was impressed to learn in Shaoxing, a minor town in eastern China, that in two years the villages around had built no fewer than sixty cinemas, a remarkable rate by any standard. Shanghai has seen a proliferation of video-tape screening venues in the last couple of years, and there has even opened an all-night cinema devoted to showing foreign films, where a doctor stands guard should any cases of over-exhaustion arise.

The cinema industry itself has undergone some dramatic changes, good ones as well as bad. Movies have always been vehicles for propagating the regime's ideas, but of late they have reflected official values in a different way. Told to be responsible for their own profits and losses, studios have rushed to produce money-spinning ventures catering to the most vulgar tastes. People with more upmarket tastes have sneered at this; but who would begrudge the Chinese, who for so long have seen nothing but preachy and maudlin revolutionary movies, their first taste of pure entertainment? Such has been the monotony of their cultural diet that when controls were first loosened in the late 1970s, even the screening of thirty-year-old movies unearthed from the archives caused a stir.

But the most striking change to have occurred in Chinese cinema is not the record crop of commercial feature films, but the appearance, for the first time since the founding of the People's Republic, of true originality. In 1984 there came a film which would win more international film awards than any Chinese film in history, Chen Kaige's debut feature *Yellow Earth*. The film tells the story of a communist soldier who arrives in a village in northern Shaanxi to collect folk songs for propagation by the Red Army as campaign songs and as examples of authentic peasant culture. It is 1939, four years after the communists established their headquarters in Yanan, and the soldier's mission is underpinned by the communist resolve to penetrate the surrounding countryside and transform it. The soldier is billeted with a poor peasant family—a widower, his son and his twelve-year-old daughter. Their life is harsh, but harsher still is the fate which awaits the daughter: she is to be married off as a child-bride to a much older person she has never seen. Hearing how life is changing in the revolutionary base, she asks the soldier if she might follow him there. He promises to come for her, but the days pass, and she is married. In a final bid to escape to Yanan, she drowns in the Yellow River, the waterer of this most arid of regions in China. When we next see her father and brother, they look wild and half-crazed, supplicating with hundreds of other villagers to the gods for rain. The figure of the returning communist soldier is glimpsed mirage-like on a far horizon. It strikes with a quality of terrible remoteness, and the last scenes freeze on the brother running to reach him, against a stampede of villagers in the opposite direction.

*Yellow Earth* is a deeply political film, asking the question of how successful socialism has been in prising free the Chinese race from the tyranny of their civilisation, which is symbolised in the film by the Yellow River, the seedbed of Chinese culture, and whose ugliest aspects (such as the custom of child-brides) survives? The film ends ambiguously, but still the answer to which I was led could only be that it has not been successful. This is not a point which many British viewers, who saw the film at festivals in London and Edinburgh, will have caught, because to do so one would have to share the sadness felt by Chen Kaige's kind and generation at the failure of three decades of socialist transformation to come to grips with the grimmer facets of the Chinese heritage.

*Yellow Earth* is an extraordinary film to have come out of China, the first to be able to hold its own in the context of world cinema. It received an award from the British Film Institute, which judged it to be the most imaginative and original film to be shown at the London Film Festival in 1985. 'It isn't interesting just because it comes from China,' wrote the British film critic Derek Malcolm, 'but because it would look good in any company.' Chen Kaige, he went on to say, had the makings of a world-class director. *Yellow Earth* is a truly ground-breaking work, beautiful in its images; innovative in its use of song and sparseness of dialogue; very un-Chinese in its restraint, in its ability to leave well alone, and in its eschewal of those stylised operatic posturings which somehow manage to get into everything. Summarising all this, Tony Rayns, the pre-eminent British writer on the Chinese cinema, observes: 'The film speaks a cinematic language that is new to China, a language rooted in the pace of peasant life and the imagery of peasant art, complete with areas of necessary ambiguity. The summit of its achievement is that it makes its new language sing.'

Chen Kaige's success was achieved against a background of conflict within the industry, between, on the one hand, the film-maker and the cultural officialdom, and on the other, the older director and the younger. Chen belongs to the so-called 'fifth generation' of directors, people in their thirties who graduated mostly from the Peking Film Academy in recent years, and who want to create an altogether new kind of cinema in China. But two things worked, and still work, against them. There is first of all the fact that, in China as in other socialist societies, the cinema has a definite didactic function. Though this applies to all art, the film industry is where the orthodoxy of the Maoist past, socialist realism, has been particularly difficult to shake off. Lenin had after all said that: 'Of all arts, for us the cinema is the most important.'

The second obstacle is the prerogative of age. The younger men have little chance to make their mark as long as the studios are dominated by old-timers. And it is not as though they can work outside the system. By and large there is no such thing as independent feature film-making in China. All that a young film school graduate could look forward to was assignment to an assistantship in one of the five established film studios in China (Shanghai, Peking, Changchun, Canton, and the Army studio in Peking), each with its stable of directors, technicians and actors; and its yearly quota for production. But in the early 1980s, an opportunity arose for these young directors. This came of the policy of regional devolution, which spawned a string of small, new studios in the provinces. These were in comparatively backward spots like Xian and Guangxi, hardly places where the established directors would want to work. But they were a godsend to the young directors, who transferred there one by one, and got to do more or less what they wanted.

Making a film of one's own choice is one thing. Getting it past the censors is another. Chen Kaige was lucky that his film was not relegated to an old vault to gather dust, but still it came under fire when, in the first months of 1986, cultural orthodoxy had its moment. It is true that it was not withdrawn from overseas circulation—to do so would risk an international scandal—but the Party general secretary made no bones about his displeasure. It showed how unsuitable was the film, Hu Yaobang observed, how far it was from socialist values, that it fared so well at foreign film festivals, where after all the norms applied were those of bourgeois ideology.

Curiously enough, a paradoxical situation had meanwhile come to a head in the movie industry: for all its commercialisation, the cinema was attracting fewer and fewer movie-goers. The drastic fall in box office receipts was attributed to the rivalry offered by the new variety in leisure pursuits, chief among them television. How was the film industry to compete? By making better, more edifying films, said the top ideologues, who were fuming at the commercial and 'arty' trends in the cinema industry. By co-operating with television for mutual good, suggested others. The chosen solution was disclosed in January 1986, when it was announced that the Film Bureau, hitherto an organ of the Ministry of Culture, would be placed under the aegis of the Ministry of Broadcasting and Television. This is a blow to the film industry, artistically and economically: to move closer to television is to come more directly under the eye of the Party's propaganda machine, and perhaps also to suffer a drain on its financial and technical resources.

Film-makers had felt the pressure months before. They knew that what was expected of them were rationales of the economic reforms. They produced them accordingly, but the films were not all a reversion to mediocrity. From the Xian Film Studio, one of those niches for 'fifth generation' directors, came a couple of more than creditable movies. On the surface one of them, *Wild Mountain*, could not be a better apologia for rural reforms, but it is actually a gem of a film, daring, likeable, convincing in its handling of character and relationship. It tells the story of Hehe, a demobbed soldier who, having seen something of the world, is no longer willing to put up with poverty and backwardness. He starts new enterprises in the village, such as pig-raising and brick-making. The villagers' bafflement at his persistence in the face of repeated failures pointedly reflects the resignation and conservatism of their kind. His wife sadly concludes that he is nothing but a squanderer and divorces him. The only person who sympathises with Hehe is Guilan, the neighbour's wife. She, too, looks beyond the land and the village, but her amiable husband is rather stick-in-the-mud; and when Guilan's enthusiasm for Hehe's initiative gives rise to gossip, he decides to leave her. The film ends on a happy note, with Hehe marrying Guilan and the neighbour marrying his wife. One would not expect wife-swopping in a Chinese film, but *Wild Mountain* gets away with it because in this case a change of partner can only contribute to the success of the rural reforms.

To help kindle enthusiasm for the country's modernisation is a task for television no less than it is for the cinema, though it is admitted that giving audiences something enjoyable to watch when they come home from work is also a way of 'serving socialism and the people'. The rule to remember, TV producers have been told, is Deng Xiaoping's pronouncement on matters of culture: that the sole criterion for evaluating them is their 'social effect'. It is thought very healthy that sports programmes are so popular. Here the mass audience and cultural officialdom are at one. So enthusiastic are Chinese of all classes about sport that on the days they show the World Cup volleyball match or the soccer championships, you can be certain of empty cinemas.

Soap operas come a close second. The first serials were the ones imported from Hong Kong, with the Cantonese dialogues dubbed into Mandarin, the national language that is called *putonghua* in China. One of the most popular of the imported programmes was *The Shanghai Bund*, which was based on the life and times of a real life gangster in pre-revolution Shanghai, and by which everybody I spoke to in China was riveted. Another was *The Adventures of Sherlock Holmes*, sold to the Chinese by Britain's Granada TV which, at the time of writing, is also negotiating the sale of the rights to *The Jewel in the Crown*. Not to be outdone, Chinese networks have started producing drama themselves. Between 1983 and 1985, the number of TV plays produced more than tripled, from 400 to 1300. These include much routine stuff, but a serial adaptation of a novel by Lao She, a famous writer whom the Red Guards hounded to death during the Cultural Revolution, was favourably received as a 'quality' production. Entertaining too, will be the fourteen-part adaptation of *Begonia*, which is a tear-jerker published in Shanghai in the 1930s, and popular fiction at its most romantic and beguiling. The novel is based on a real story whose dramatic possibilities can scarcely be bettered. An educated young woman is forced to become the concubine of a warlord, but finds happiness only when she meets the opera singer Begonia, who becomes her secret lover. But they are discovered, and the warlord in his fury kills them both and smashes Begonia's handsome face to a pulp.

The most talked-about serial in 1986 was *The New Star*; the studio was deluged with letters requesting repeats. Described as the most daring TV film ever to have been made on contemporary themes in China, it is an indictment of the bureaucratic system. It is about a new broom who comes to a small, remote county as the Party secretary. He is determined to right wrongs, solve problems, and end corruption; but he runs slap into the vested interests of entrenched cadres, who do all they can to thwart him. It is all so believable, so true a mirror of real life, that TV sets throughout China were compulsively switched to it. Almost every corner of China could do with a 'new star', and one viewer even went so far as to say that it would help the reforms if cadres across the country could be organised to see it—and to recognise themselves in the conniving, power-hungry, arrogant and mediocre officials in the film.

For me the most dramatic change to appear on Chinese television screens remain the foreign commercials. It would have been hard a few years ago to imagine airings of commercials for Tide detergent, Nescafé and Colgate toothpaste on Chinese TV, but these are exactly what viewers were introduced to in February 1986. The advertisements precede a programme they sponsor, the first foreign series to be made for a Chinese audience. Produced by a Chinese émigré from America, *One World* (as the series is called) offers such assorted topics as Egyptian pyramids, Iowa farmers and microwave cooking. The producer disposed of the suggestion of Chinese censorship by telling the foreign press that she had been given a free hand, though she no doubt uses her discretion: an episode on New York shows footage of people scavenging for food in garbage cans, proof that life is not all roses in the ultimate capitalist metropolis.

Yet despite the surge in the ownership of TV sets in recent years, they are still thin on the ground. One count puts the total for 1985 at 50 million. There are few places, for example, with as many owners as Canton, where a survey found that out of 1000 people polled, more than 900 had TV sets at home. Canton is also exceptional in that its citizens could pick up Hong Kong television with special 'fishbone' aerials, a proscribed practice which the authorities have countered by jamming the Hong Kong channels.

For many parts of interior China, and especially for the elderly, the chief form of dramatic entertainment is still the local opera, whose traditional repertoires have returned to grace with the fall of Madam Mao (who had made opera her fief). It says something for the resilience of this traditional diversion that regional troupes abound; yet although opera is popular enough in many parts of China, its steady waning as a whole looks to be inevitable. How to save Peking opera, the style of Chinese opera with the greatest international renown, is a matter of grave concern to cultural circles in the big cities, and performers have gone as far as to suggest altering performing styles to suit younger tastes. Purists were horrified to see this put into practice, with devices verging on gimmickry, at a recent festival:

during a performance by the Peking Opera Company, dry ice emitted cloud, lasers beamed colours, and electric musical instruments twanged.

But then eclecticism is a strong Chinese trait. Chinese opera has even been combined with Shakespeare, to produce entirely novel versions of *Othello, Twelfth Night* and *Macbeth*. This took place in the spring of 1986 at the Shakespeare Festival of China, which marked the rehabilitation of the Bard after his fall from official Chinese esteem during the Cultural Revolution. Of what the Bard and Chinese opera have in common, the president of the Shakespeare Research Centre said: 'He is very free with the unities of time and place, much like Chinese opera.' The festival's organisers were much gratified that Britain's prime minister agreed with them; the congratulatory letter they received from Margaret Thatcher had read, 'Were Shakespeare still alive, he would be very appreciative of those who adapted his plays to Chinese traditional operas.'

It was also the opinion of the Shakespeare Research Society that the Chinese had had enough of naturalism and socialist realism. Nobody could agree more than the new playwrights who have recently emerged to break down the barriers of conventional drama. China's modern theatre has scarcely made any artistic headway since the early decades of this century, when Western dramatists like Ibsen and O'Neill brought a new mould and method to the Chinese stage. Having been closely shackled by the demands of propaganda in the last several decades, it has not had much chance to outgrow its origins in performing styles and techniques. But in the early 1980s, a playwright emerged to change all this. He is Gao Xingjian, a writer we shall have occasion to meet again. Gao brought to the Chinese theatre his wide familiarity with Chinese and French literature, and what he did was to make modern Chinese drama take an avant-garde turn: he offered the Chinese public their first glimpse of the Theatre of the Absurd.

The play with which he most effectively did this was *Bus Stop*, staged theatre-in-the-round fashion at the Capital Theatre in Peking. We see a group of people gathered to await a bus into town; buses (represented by stage effects) pass, but do not stop; bewilderment sets in, then panic; nobody can decide whether or not to walk into town. Music sounds, lights flash; years are found to have gone by, but still nobody has moved. One is right to assume *Waiting for Godot* to be the inspiration behind this play, and Gao Xingjian himself readily acknowledges his debt to Samuel Beckett. But he means the play to say something about the Chinese condition, and he inserts a prelude to express this. The prelude is borrowed from a short scene, revolving round a lone traveller, which the great modern writer Lu Xun wrote in 1925, and which Gao has read as an allegory of the journey of the Chinese people towards a brighter if far from certain future.

Unconventional too, is the play which opened at the Cultural Palace of Nationalities in the autumn of 1985, and which eschewed the means to a suspension of belief in favour of Brechtian methods for distancing the audience from the played action. Its title, *WM*, stands for *women*, the transliteration of the Chinese word for 'we', and the plot—such as it is—revolves round seven young people who were sent off to be rusticated in the great northeast wastelands during the Cultural Revolution, and who are now returned to the city. In these seven characters many members of the younger generation will recognise themselves. The group is neither one thing nor another, neither wholly good nor wholly bad: its members are perhaps just people trying to survive, responding to the uglier aspects of their society with sneers, despair and self-questionings. *WM* played to full houses in Peking and Shanghai, but it was judged anti-Party, and closed down by the authorities. It remained the most talked-about play between late 1985 and early 1986, and a group of students, Chinese as well as French, staged its first act in Paris not long after it was banned, as a gesture of their solidarity with it.

An evening at the theatre, though, is not everybody's idea of distraction, and the Chinese have always been good at devising pleasurable pursuits for themselves. Their age-old passion for gambling, for example, has never ceased, and no sooner was official control relaxed than it was pursued throughout the country. Just one figure will suffice to illustrate its tenacity: in Wuxi, not a particularly large city, 2500 gambling dens were raided between January and October of 1985. Probably no other pastime is quite so compulsive, and it has been reported that in one village, even the local police indulged in the habit.

Another escape from daily monotony is tourism. This is something of a novelty in the People's Republic, but since it started a few years ago it has amounted to a craze. The Chinese do not exactly have holidays, but their work units miss no opportunity for organising sightseeing trips on government money. The Party's call for unclogging marketing channels has led to many inter-regional meetings, and these provide a good enough excuse to travel away from home and to take in another part of the country.

The Chinese are by and large conventional sightseers: they are not ones to get off the beaten track, or to enjoy losing themselves in lonely spots in unpeopled country. In fact, they are not looking to be by themselves when they travel; a historical site swarming with tourists would not put them off as it would a European visitor. Nor are they disappointed when, arriving at a renowned tourist site, they find nothing but a stele marking the spot. If they know their Chinese history or legend, the place, while offering nothing to look at, will assume a significance in proportion to the associations it will evoke in their minds.

In the propaganda posters of yesterday, one saw face after Chinese face split irrepressibly in a smile. We know that life was anything but fun for them, and yet the smiles were not entirely a pretence; the Chinese have always known how to make the best of things, and to enjoy themselves whenever they can. It seems inevitable, and no bad thing, that the Chinese should now want to consume more, to be more comfortable, and to be better entertained. But though there is no doubt that China has recently undergone an unprecedented boom in leisure spending, the hedonism and bourgeois lifestyles that the anti-spiritual pollution ideologues have ranted at are still a long way off.

# 8

# COUPLES

Until as recently as 1978, you knew what true love was. True love was what two politically united people felt for each other when they became man and wife. The romantic ideal was altogether suppressed during the Cultural Revolution, and your heart glowed red only for love of Chairman Mao. It was not an acceptable theme for film or literature, and to suggest it you had to present it in politically uncontroversial ways, such as when a couple married out of a common intense hatred of the class enemy.

All this changed from about 1979, when love was suddenly everything, and all over China people wrote and devoured love stories. Even so, the initial steps towards a definition of true love were tentative: as *The Place of Love*, the first romantic story to appear in ten years, had it, love was something 'built on a shared revolutionary goal and purpose' which, as it grew over time, 'enriched and enhanced itself'. In the West this would be judged naïve, propagandist and hypocritical. But to the Chinese, who had had to pretend for a whole decade that romantic love did not matter, the mere possibility of discussing the subject openly was enough to make one sit up. They besieged the author with letters, some hoping for advice, others offering to share romantic feelings of their own.

If love was the secret preoccupation of people's daydreams during the Cultural Revolution, it was not a condition of marriage. In fact this was nothing new in Chinese society, where love did not generally precede marriage (it could hardly do so if the couple had barely met). But a new sort of alliance came into being under communism, one based on class sympathy rather than personal feeling. This has left China with millions of loveless marriages, but it is only in the late 1970s that the fact was openly acknowledged. When Chinese fiction started dealing with this theme, countless readers recognised themselves in its pages. The best known case of this was the furore over *Love Must Not be Forgotten*, a short story which the woman novelist Zhang Jie published in 1980. By Chinese standards it is a daring story, because it makes bold to suggest that unless Mr Right were to come along, a woman shouldn't marry. The narrator of the story is in the unenviable position of being still unmarried at thirty. When she receives a proposal of marriage, she should accept with alacrity. Instead, she decides that 'remaining single is not such a terrible thing. Perhaps it's just a sign of social progress. ...'

She is reinforced in her view by the example of her mother, the great love of whose life is not our heroine's father, but a certain married man. The love is returned, but never physically expressed, so the mother dies an unhappy and unfulfilled woman. Zhang Jie's story provoked much hostile public reaction; her sympathetic treatment of extra-marital love, even if unconsummated, was too much for some people. Nor was it only the Party ideologues who were outraged; the author received anonymous letters from the general public, charging her with immorality and with having undermined the conventions which give marriage and family their stability.

Here and there you might find Chinese professing a belief in the idea of the *grand amour*, but you have to try hard. Youthful yearnings there may be, but by and large the Chinese do not view marriage romantically. This has long been so. Fei Xiaotong, an anthropologist we shall meet again, was struck by the emotional shallowness between married couples in Chinese rural society when he did fieldwork in the country in the 1930s. It seemed to him that, with their constant stress on filial piety, the Chinese had become incapable of experiencing or understanding romantic love. 'Except for tears,' he said, 'which we never lack,' the Chinese were reserved about their emotions to the point of being 'emotionally numb'.

Yet if love is not a must, marriage certainly is. The Chinese abhor the single status, and I know of no society where spinsterhood is more of a misery. In China it is taken for granted that everyone must marry, and a person who doesn't is the object of cruel scorn or pity. It is assumed that no one remains single from choice, and not marrying is invariably put down to some physical defect or social inferiority. Marriage is regarded as an inevitable passage in life, second to none in its importance in individual experience; without it, no person is thought to be complete.

These attitudes represent traditional values at their most oppressive. It is the Confucian emphasis on family that keeps the Chinese so opposed to celibacy. It is not at all uncommon to hear of young Chinese women killing themselves because they have failed to find a husband, so inescapable is the stigma of the unfamilied status. In China if you are over thirty and unmarried, you are defined as a social problem, a matter of concern to the State. There is of course a traditional core to the government's attitude. It is not merely that the tentacular control of the imperial mandarinate lives on in the communist bureaucracy; it is that we can recognise in today's pressures towards conformity just the same mixture of convention and compliance that the Confucian State imposed on public and private lives in its time. Generally speaking the Chinese prefer to live in a world where there are few distinctions and where people do not exceed what is proper. An unmarried person jars upon the State, which is concerned to maintain social harmony. 'Now over the kingdom,' goes a Confucian passage expressing the ideal of conformity, 'carriages have all wheels of the same size; all writing is with the same characters; and for conduct there are the same rules.' One can't help hearing echoes of this ideal in present-day Chinese attitudes to matrimony.

Of the women who feel the predicament of being unmarried at thirty, a large number are returnees from the countryside, where they had been 'sent down' for rustication in the Cultural Revolution. In the rural areas in which they found themselves, the chances of finding suitable husbands were slim. It was only when they returned to their homes in the city in the late 1970s that they started to think about marriage, but by then they had missed the boat.

Others have remained single because they devoted themselves to work or study in their 'twenties, and are now too scholastically accomplished, or too advanced in their careers to be attractive to the mass of Chinese men, who are in no mood to be overshadowed by their women. It rankles with some women that they should have to play at being inferior, but many more connive at it. In a letter to the editor, a reader of *China Daily* pointed out that this was male chauvinism. 'It made me sick,' the letter-writer said, to hear courting couples talk in parks and buses—the way a boy would show off by inserting a couple of words of English into his conversation and the girl would drink it all in, allowing her boyfriend to correct her pronunciation as though she knew nothing.

Though most Chinese spinsters would marry if they could, there are some who hold themselves aloof deliberately. In an article on the increase in the number of unmarried people in the big cities, the Shanghai-based *Liberation Daily* described single women as being of six kinds: those who are simply not alluring enough, those who harbour unrealistically high expectations and fail to find anyone to meet their requirements, 'emotional types' who cannot bear the thought of setting up home with anyone 'who has not fully captured their heart', those who reject the opposite sex because they have been deeply wounded in love, divorcees who have given up hope of making a happy marriage, and those whose minds have been warped by books.

What qualities do Chinese men and women seek in their mates? In the 1950s, the most eligible people in Shanghai were teachers, cadres and technically qualified professionals. Political criteria became more pronounced in the 1960s, when Party members were much sought after. The ideological climate of the 1970s gave people cause to attach absolute and primary importance to the factor of class origin in their choice of marriage partners, and scarcely any working-class man would consider taking a former capitalist's daughter to wife, any more than a peasant's daughter would marry the son of a landlord. Now political considerations have given way to economic ones, as befits an age of material progress and opportunity, and it is widely accepted that income levels have to be satisfactory. As a rule women are not attracted to porters, cooks, cleaners or construction workers, because these jobs are lowly and badly paid. By contrast, miners are thought very eligible. The Youth League officers in the Datong Coalfields, for example, receive letters from girls all over the country asking them to help match-make. The reason is not hard to find: miners there earn double the normal salary, and their homes are equipped with 'modern' furniture, colour television sets, washing machines, tape-recorders and sewing machines.

Ask any Chinese girl for her requirements and she will specify a minimum height of 1·70 metres. As for other priorities, one can often read them between the lines of the 'Spouse Wanted' ads in local Chinese newspapers. Here is one from the *Chengdu Evening News*, dated April 17, 1986: 'Li, unmarried, 30, 1·6 metres, college graduate, employed by an enterprise in this city, temperamentally introverted, looks and conduct well thought of, healthy, kind, strong survival instincts. Seeks unmarried male, 35 or younger, over 1·65 metres tall, honest and upright, healthy, educationally equal, employed in this city. Please send recent photo (returnable) to *Chengdu Evening News*.' Here, from the *Chengdu Daily* (April 22, 1986), is another: 'Jiang Nan, male, 31, divorced, 1·74 metres, healthy, TV University graduate, broad interests. Middle-level cadre in a State enterprise in Yanan, monthly salary 100 + . Wishes to meet woman under 30, over 1·6 metres tall, healthy, reasonably good-looking, employed in a State organisation. Please send recent photo to Yanan P.O. Box 1.'

The picture is different in the countryside around. When rural inhabitants there were asked how they chose their mates, they said that finding one another congenial was the first necessity. Town folk are not only fussier, they have matters like availability of housing to consider. So terrible is the congestion in Shanghai, for example, that any suitor who has a spare room to offer is instantly eligible. You also have a lot going for you if you have relatives living abroad, 'overseas connections' to the dazzling world of Hong Kong or the wider capitalist West. In China, as elsewhere, marriage is the great means to self-betterment, and when you hear of a Chinese marrying a foreigner, you can never know for sure how much the alliance is genuine, how much a ploy for the Chinese partner to get out of China. Genuine relationships there doubtless are, but all too often, one hears of wide-eyed European students of Sinology marrying Chinese girls who turn out only to have had exit visas in mind.

Standards have changed in recent years, and the intellectual, for so long the pariah of society, is very respectable again. Educated girls set much store by academic distinction, and some even make it their first criterion in choosing a husband. In late 1985 the papers reported the case of an attractive and well-educated girl in Shandong province selecting her husband by open competitive examinations; the winner was a soldier who averaged ninety-four marks on every one of the subjects she had set. This was a return to form, for in Chinese stories the happy ending only comes with the groom passing the imperial examinations.

But high educational qualifications came second in a public survey conducted in 1984 in Peking, in which 525 young people were asked what they looked for in their ideal spouse. A third of those questioned laid greatest stress on character, and 8 per cent thought looks and manners were the most important. However, in an enquiry among 894 Shanghai undergraduates in 1985, nearly half expressed a preference for university graduates—in other words people as well qualified as themselves. As for other attributes, half said they would be satisfied with an average income, over 38 per cent wanted their future spouses to be Party members, and 33 per cent required good looks. The meaning of this last figure will not escape anyone who remembers how vehemently people used to protest that looks did not matter, only revolutionary zeal did.

Though the poll was conducted among university students, in theory romance is forbidden on the campus. In practice, of course, it thrives: university is where boys and girls find their future mates. As a popular song has it, it is where boys

> Cast their nets wide,
> Then cultivate 'key points';
> Set long-term tests
> And select the best.

And where girls are

> Haughty in the first year,
> Choosy in the second,
> Panicky in the third,
> And shrieking in the fourth.

Nor is it only at university that the pairing off begins. 'We have detected an alarming trend,' said a Youth League leader I interviewed in 1986. 'Boys and girls are reaching puberty and awakening to their sexuality earlier than their parents.' The authorities think that adolescents are much too young to be thinking about love, but teachers and social workers report that more and more secondary school children are taking an interest in the opposite sex. 'Many are satisfied just to play together,' declared the *Liberation Daily*, 'but there are also some youths who, imitating adults, hold hands, embrace, kiss, and a very few even have sexual relations.' The paper went on to give reasons; the increased exposure to sex through magazines, movies and television; the attitude of defiance created in children by their parents' traditional attitudes to sex, the lack of proper guidance and sex education.

In the autumn of 1985, forty schools in Shanghai added sex classes to the curriculum, lifting an age-old taboo. What persuaded the authorities to start sex education was the discovery that most of the female delinquents in the reform schools they investigated were sexually promiscuous; it was because young people did not know any better, the authorities concluded, that such 'abnormal phenomena' as sexual precocity arose. Sex education, they believed, would not only demystify the physiological and psychological changes that accompany sexual development, it would also help adolescents to evolve 'a correct attitude to sex'.

With the lifting of the taboo on sex discussion, nothing was ever quite the same again. The seed of sexual frankness had been planted, and quickly during the following months it would swell and split. The Shanghai Family Planning Advisory Services and the journal *Modern Family* opened the Xinhun (Newlywed) School to offer seminars on sex to married couples, and suddenly Chinese couples found that they still had everything to learn about how their sex lives might be improved. Six months later, China's very first sex clinic for women opened in the northeastern city of Dalian, to deal with problems of 'frigidity, nymphomania, perversions and infertility'. Not long before, a school in Canton opened to teach seventeen- to thirty-year-old unmarried women about love, offering a choice of seven courses, including 'How to be a New Woman of the Eighties', 'The Dangers of Pre-marital Sex', and 'How to Choose a Lover'.

Women are seen to need more help than men to overcome their sexual inhibitions. The female right to sexual pleasure is recognised, and there is even a film to plead for it. In *Virtuous Woman*, a feature film made in 1985, an eighteen-year-old girl is given in marriage to a six-year-old boy. The time is 1948, and in the remote village where the action takes place, child-brides and child-bridegrooms are nothing out of the ordinary. During the day, with all the work there is to do on the farm, it is not difficult for the heroine to forget her misfortune, but at night she cannot help feeling frustrated and lonely. Lying in bed beside her under-aged husband, she hears cats in heat howling in the distance. Later she falls in love with a young farmer and, defying the disapproval of the villagers, divorces her little husband. That, suggests the film audaciously, is as it should be.

The Chinese are not frank in their sexuality, and are not generally thought of as profligates. A Chinese gynaecologist I once met told me that, in his experience, the vast majority of young people in China have only a dim notion of sex. Much may go on in the hayloft in the country, but wide-eyed innocence characterises the general approach to love-making. Sun Longji, a Chinese scholar in America and the author of a book called *The Deep Structure of Chinese Culture*, goes so far as to suggest that the Chinese are arrested in their sexual development. His views, which I simplify, are based on Freud's theory of infantile sexuality, according to which maturation consists in passing through a number of erotic phases or stages, these being named after the predominant sources of erotic pleasure, namely oral, anal and phallic. Sun Longji says that the Chinese are subject above all to their oral tendencies; it is as if the phallic phase has been interfered with, and fixation has occurred at an oral level. It is no coincidence, he says, that the Chinese are so obsessed with food; it is in gastronomy that they find their fulfilment, not in love-making.

For all the burgeoning of sex classes and counselling, Chinese society is at a very early stage of sexual emancipation, and most girls remain virgins until they marry. Indeed, pre-marital sex is not allowed, and when it happens, is vehemently denounced as immorality. Nevertheless, cases of pregnancy before marriage are on the rise in some cities, and so are sexual offences among the young. Despite appearances, Chinese society is not as chaste as one might suppose, and to judge from the press reporting of crime in high places, a favourite pastime of the sons of Party bigwigs seems to be committing 'rape' (a term the Chinese use loosely, to mean anything from taking a woman by force to tempting her to sexual intercourse). The Minister of Public Security has openly acknowledged the existence of prostitution in the cities most subject to outside influence, though almost all the customers appear to be foreign visitors.

For all these hints of debauchery though, the Chinese remain a straitlaced people. An open-air dance hall I looked in on in Chengdu had a notice at the entrance forbidding couples to dance cheek-to-cheek; the rule was followed, I noticed, and most couples dancing to slow numbers held each other at arm's length. Large numbers were dancing with members of their own sex. This is a hangover from the traditional segregation of the sexes— young men strolling down the street hand in hand is a common sight in many Asian countries—and need not be seen to connote latent homosexuality. Nevertheless, homosexuals are able to hide behind it.

Homosexuality is looked upon as a mental disease in China and rigorously suppressed, but Chinese history and literature abound in references to love affairs between men. Such tastes particularly prevailed among male actors, many of whom habitually impersonated women on stage, it being rare to include both men and women in any one theatrical company. Yet ask any Chinese official about homosexuality today, and he will swear it doesn't exist.

It would be an exaggeration to say that a gay scene is evolving in China, but the near absence of AIDS has made at least two of her open cities, Canton and Shanghai, attractive to homosexuals from Hong Kong and Macao. An investigation carried out in the spring of 1986 by the Hong Kong daily, the *South China Morning Post*, reveals that these two cities have become something of a gay haven, to which more and more overseas Chinese and European homosexuals gravitate in search of partners.

*        *        *

The day after the marriage bureau of the Elderly People's Association opened for business in Chengdu's Wash-and-Starch Street, a man of middle age and middle height could be seen to step into its office. He wore spectacles, and had a shock of stiff greying hair. Inside, two matronly women both easily to be imagined in a farmhouse kitchen greeted him with a smile. After some preamble, the man got down to explaining his domestic situation. He had been divorced six years, and now he wished to be married again. He had three children; the boy lived with him, the two girls with their mother. On the subject of the mother, he was loud and vocal; she sounded a perfect shrew, ill-tempered and always scolding. His new wife, he said more than once, would have to be the opposite of that.

I had been hovering at the door, and when the man took his leave, the two ladies indicated that my turn was next. I had not come to the marriage bureau to sign up, but as it was inquisitiveness which had brought me, I decided to play along to see what I could learn. As soon as I sat down the ladies pushed a form at me. One of them asked if I had ever been married before, and when I said no, it was instantly assumed that there was something the matter with me—and I was asked what. I could have named at least a dozen things, but I mentioned the one that bothers me the most.

'I am half-deaf,' I said, 'like Deng Xiaoping.'

They did not smile at this, but declared with an air of calm kindness that it was not such a grave handicap, as handicaps went. One of them observed that a match-making agency for the physically disabled had just been set up in Peking, but that such facilities did not yet exist in Chengdu.

They then inquired about my wishes, and when I asked them if they had any university graduates on their books, they beamed and exclaimed, 'Oh, plenty!' The man that was here just now, one of them continued, 'now he's a university graduate.' I found this hard to believe, but was assured that he was an engineer.

The registration procedure was simple: one had only to produce proof of identity—whether this was one's residence booklet, an employment card, or a retirement certificate—two one-and-a-half-inch photographs, and a fee of 5 yuan. 'If the couple so wishes,' the ladies said, 'we can help organise the wedding ceremony itself—the hire of the hall, the wedding photographs, and so forth. Of course we'll do our best to make it a properly grand and lively affair, but we're against lavishness and extravagance.' The match made, the Elderly People's Association expects a fee—'You can give what you like, so long as it's not less than 20 yuan.' If, after three encounters, marriage does not occur, the applicant must re-register and pay another 5 yuan in signing-up fee.

Their role, the ladies explained, was to create opportunities for people to meet and to get to know each other; to this end they organised tea parties, outings, lectures, and all sorts of interesting, 'healthy and beneficial' activities. 'Downstairs we have facilities for billiards, bridge and mahjong.' In addition, they play the part of mediator whenever there is opposition at home, conciliating young people who set themselves against their widowed or divorced parents remarrying because they want them to babysit or do the housework, or because they think that remarriage is unseemly. Elderly people have a right to happiness too, the Association believes, and one of its aims is to find partners for all the lonely old hearts in the city.

Besides widowed old folks, the marriage bureau caters to divorced individuals and a category named *danan danu*, 'older boys and girls'—that is, men over thirty and women over twenty-six. In China the road to marriage is the same for all: a man ought to be married by twenty-five and a woman by twenty-three, and a marriage contracted after these ages is considered a late marriage. Those who are not married by twenty-five—a 1984 survey shows that there were 150,000 such worrying people in Peking and 160,000 in Shanghai—are thought to need a little help from society, which is where match-making services of the kind I have described come in.

They sprang up in a rash in the early 1980s, and now there are at least fifty in the country, including a few which specialise in military personnel and the disabled. They are run as non-profit organisations by local governments and by national mass groupings like the Communist Youth League and the Women's Federation. They nearly all say they could do with more government funding. Unfortunately this is difficult to justify, because none of them seems to be very successful, the rate of matches resulting in marriage hovering around a low 10 per cent in bureau after bureau. Romance seldom blossoms between couples the bureaus bring together. 'It was much too contrived for me,' complained a thirty-year-old woman signed up at the Chaoyang district bureau in Peking. 'They try to talk you into settling for less than what you want because they simply don't have all that many eligible bachelors on their files.' The inequality of the valued assets between male and female does seem to be a problem, as the files of the Shenyang Match-making Centre illustrate: in 1984, while only thirty-one of the 302 men listed had had higher education, and eighteen had professional or white-collar jobs, the corresponding figures for the women were seventy-nine and 138 out of a total of 418.

Though marriage bureaus are a new phenomenon in China, it is easy enough to see the retired cadres and social workers who staff them as the traditional go-between in modern guise. Now it is the State, rather than the parents, which matches boy with girl and arranges their marriage. Though couples have somewhat more chance than in the past to get to know each other before the wedding day, about 70 per cent of Chinese marriages today are still to some degree arranged, if not by the parents then by relatives, friends, and public match-making services.·

Two factors contribute to the continuation of the system of arranged marriage. First, young people have little chance to meet suitable partners on their own, much less to date or go steady. In the countryside particularly, for a couple to meet regularly is tantamount to a declaration of intention to marry, and it is very difficult for a girl whose name has previously been linked with another boy to find a husband. In any case, boys and girls customarily meet in a group, not singly. The second factor is the State's nanny-knows-best attitude to the day-to-day affairs and destinies of its citizens. Well-intentioned as they are, the State's match-making efforts are governed by the knowledge that throughout history, it has ever been hearth and home which gave society its stability. They are anxious for everyone to be familied, even old people who, as the custom of several generations living under one roof wanes and the number of nuclear families increases with growing urbanisation, find themselves bereft of company.

Though increasingly rare, marriages negotiated by parents with the help of go-betweens have not died out completely in China. A survey of nearly 5,000 couples in five major cities shows that they account for less than 1 per cent of the marriages contracted in the early 1980s, whereas they were almost 21 per cent of the total in the 1950s. The figure is doubtless much higher in the rural areas, where thirty years of communist rule have not much weakened old customs. There one often hears of girls being forced to marry someone their parents have chosen. Witness the case of Zuo Xiaoqun, a peasant girl whose letter was published in the *Sichuan Daily News* on April 22, 1986. 'Last December,' she wrote, 'my parents took out a marriage certificate for me with the collaboration of the family of the husband-to-be. I was determined to oppose this marriage, and wrote to a number of newspapers for advice. Before long, the *Sichuan Daily News* replied, not only to say that they had forwarded my letter to the relevant authorities, but to supply me with detailed information on how I might get the marriage annulled. Replies were also received from the other papers, which told me that my case had been referred to the government of the township where the other party's residence is registered, and that my plight was taken very seriously. The two local governments then liaised, mine and the other party's, and after investigations were carried out, they declared my marriage certificate to be invalid. The gifts exchanged between the two families were returned immediately. Not only that, but the registrar was severely reprimanded for breaking the law [which gives everyone the right to choose his or her own spouse], and my parents were subjected to educative censure. I am deeply grateful to the Party papers for their concern and support; their correct handling of the matter has given back to a young country girl her freedom of choice in marriage.'

In China a couple is deemed to be married as soon as a marriage certificate is granted, and it is the registration that is legally binding, not the wedding

ceremony. Getting a certificate can be a protracted business, as the applications have to be stamped by so many offices, from medical authorities to
the couple's respective employers. One couple I know counted the number
of chops on their applications and found that between them they had no
fewer than forty.

Registration is usually followed by a wedding ceremony. Seven or eight
years ago, when proletarian austerity prevailed, no one would dream of
making a splash, and a wedding was a simple affair where guests were
merely treated to tea and sweets (usually paper-wrapped toffee). More
recently there has been a return to form, and weddings have become—
for those who can afford it, and even for those who can't—an occasion for
conspicuous consumption. They are times of preparation, saving, shopping,
booking, and endless expense. In the country, the whole village may be
involved, and no occasion, unless it be the Chinese New Year, brings as
much pleasure and interest to the whole community. The Party press
periodically lashes out against such bad old conventions as family negotiations over the size of the bride price, but rural people take it as an axiom
that a fair bargain is a matter of crucial importance. The prosperity brought
by the economic reforms have, if anything, strengthened the custom, and
one hears of direct cash exchanges and payment by instalments. Rural
incomes may have risen 100 per cent in some communities, but bride prices
have soared ten-fold on average.

To appreciate the role of money in Chinese marriages, one has only to
cite a few popular phrases. All over China, you hear that it is not a proper
wedding without the following things: *san zhuan yi ti*, 'the three things that
go round and the one that you carry', namely a bicycle, a sewing machine,
a tape recorder, and a television; *sishiba jiao*, 'the forty-eight legs', a houseful
of furniture the legs of which total forty-eight; *quanji quanya*, 'whole chickens
and whole ducks', or if a play is made on the words, 'the whole range of
available machines (tape recorder, television, refrigerator, and washing
machine), and all articles made of duck down'.

The costs are usually met by the bridegroom and his family. A survey
conducted in the autumn of 1985 on newlyweds in small county towns in
the provinces of Jiangxi and Fujian revealed that the average cost of a
wedding was 3000 yuan but that the figure could be as high as 5700. A
fifth of this goes on the wedding banquet, while the rest is spent on filling
the new home with the latest status symbols, such as name brands of electric
fans and imported cassette tape-recorders. At the actual ceremony, the bride
is usually dressed in red, the traditional colour of joy, but she may have
her picture taken, if she is from a cosmopolitan city like Shanghai, dressed
in the virginal white of a European-style bridal gown, routinely loaned by
the photographic studio. A popular wedding accessory nowadays is a hired
limousine to fetch the bride from her home; and one couple I know,

neighbours in the same block of flats, had a car drive them round the building just for a sense of having had the whole works on their wedding day.

Yet another luxury is the honeymoon, and nowadays one comes upon honeymooning couples in all the most popular tourist resorts, strolling by lake shores under hanging willows, or crowding their way into sightseeing buses. The Mecca of newly married couples is the picturesque town of Hangzhou, where, on boating lake or beside ornamental pavilion, young wives can be seen posing endlessly for their husband's cameras.

In China marriages are unto death, and the old saying 'Better to demolish a thousand temples than break up a single marriage' still holds. When the communists promulgated the Marriage Law shortly after they took power, over a million divorces were granted to women who had suffered oppression and brutality under the old system of arranged marriages, concubinage and male domination. But subsequently the divorce rate tailed off, and it was not until the enactment of the new Marriage Law in 1981—which grants divorce on the grounds of 'complete alienation of mutual affection'—that it began to rise again. However, such is the official disapproval of divorce that only half of the couples who seek a legal end to their marriage are granted it. The rest are reconciled—or pressurised by semi-official local groups such as neighbourhood committees and women's associations— into accepting a settlement. These mediators do their best to make estranged couples try for reconciliation as the lesser of two evils.

What leads Chinese married couples to separate? Just as in the West, it is pointless to generalise. One can only give specific examples. At one extreme is the case of Yu Luojin, who is perhaps more famous as a woman three times married than as a writer. Her autobiographical stories, with their uninhibited descriptions of her matrimonial failures, caused a sensation when they came out, winning her both admiration and scorn. There was more than an element of spite in the sobriquet which some critics gave her: Fallen Woman. But if they had hoped to discredit her, all they succeeded in doing was to make her even more famous.

Her story is this. Because her brother was shot as a counter-revolutionary, the entire family was disgraced. Jobless and penniless, Yu Luojin opted for 'marriage' with a young man working in a commune in northeast China. This was only a means to a meal ticket and a roof over her head, and as far as she understood the arrangement he was not to have any sexual claims upon her. Here are the elements of a tragedy. Though he managed to keep his word for a few days, one night he forced himself on her. She submitted long enough to his embraces for a child to be born. But then she divorced him, accusing him of rape.

She then married a factory worker. But he turned out not to be what she wanted either, and she began to fantasise about a dream lover. Presently her brother's case was reviewed and his name posthumously cleared. For this the literary editor of a prestigious paper was partly responsible. She began to pin her hopes on him, and a lengthy correspondence ensued. However he was to prove yet another disappointment. Though she started out admiring him, she ended up despising him. It turned out that he had no intention of divorcing his wife to marry Yu Luojin. The public got to hear of all this because she published the entire correspondence, and also recounted the affair in a novel. A kind of glamour arose around her, and of her more enthusiastic readers, one, an engineer, became her third husband. In the spring of 1986, she asked for political asylum in West Germany, and because she had left her husband behind in China, it was widely assumed that another divorce was in the offing.

Though hers is far from a typical story, Yu Luojin's matrimonial troubles ring a bell with many Chinese women, all too many of whom have had to marry for the wrong reasons. A case of divorce hotly debated in the press in late 1985 was that of a couple who married during the Cultural Revolution for no more compelling reason than that they were well matched politically. The relationship quickly deteriorated after the wedding, hastened down its plunging course by the fact that the wife developed a gynaecological disease which put paid to their sex life and shattered their hopes of having a child. The adoption of a daughter in 1980 failed to heal the rift, and three years later the husband suggested a split. The wife wouldn't hear of it at first, and when mediation by the court failed to bring about a reconciliation and a divorce was granted, she developed 'hysterical paralysis and threatened to kill herself'. Later she consented, but only on condition that he paid her the equivalent of $9000. This he was neither willing nor able to do, and he too threatened suicide unless the matter was resolved to his satisfaction.

More than 1000 letters were received from readers when the case was published in a legal magazine, some expressing sympathy for the wife ('a sick woman who has no relatives to turn to'), some decrying her dependency ('she should stand on her own two feet'). The majority, though, were of the opinion that a loveless marriage should be dissolved. This surprised the editor of the journal, for his experience, like that of many others, is that on the whole the Chinese still believe that any kind of marriage is better than being divorced.

Some marriages break up because they were precipitately entered into. Examples of a particularly disturbing kind come from the Xuhui district in Shanghai, where a third of the divorce cases handled by the Bureau of Civil Cases between 1980 and 1984 involved couples who filed for divorce before they had even lived together as man and wife. Because it helps to be married in the allocation of housing in Shanghai (as elsewhere in China), people rush into matrimony whenever they hear new accommodation is in the offing, or when they learn of a government scheme to put up residential buildings in the vicinity. All too often, conflict arises after the marriage is registered and the couple realise their mistake before they have even set up home.

The kinds of strain to which marital relations are subject in China are somewhat different from those suffered by relationships focused on emotional satisfaction and personal fulfilment. In China many women are content if their husbands are generous with their money, do not abuse them physically, shoulder some of the domestic workload, treat the children well and do not jeopardise family income by gambling or drinking. Recent surveys in Peking show that often it is when the husbands fail to meet these expectations that married couples quarrel. In the big cities the commonest sources of marital discord are disagreements over domestic chores, money and child rearing. For the great majority of those who decide to terminate their marriage, divorce is the end point of a series of personal conflicts exacerbated by the toll which unending housework takes on their physical and mental well-being. It has been estimated that urban households spend four to six hours a day on housework, and when it is remembered that most Chinese women work an eight-hour day, it is not difficult to see how hard a grind daily life can be for the urban housewife. Women work like slaves to make ends meet, to take care of their husbands and children, and also, in many cases, their aged parents. The domestic helpfulness of husbands varies from family to family, but it is rare to find a man who does not see housework as his wife's duty.

Only a small proportion of marriages is threatened by sexual discord, but this may simply mean that few Chinese couples believe sexual satisfaction to be essential to a happy marriage. To couples who do want to improve their sex lives, however, psychological counselling is now available. This has not been offered for thirty years in China, largely because psychology was dismissed as a pseudo-science created for bourgeois needs.

The number of divorce cases provoked by adultery—what the Chinese coyly call 'an intrusion by a third party'—has risen sharply in recent years, and what to make of it is increasingly debated by the media. Here is Xiaolin, reported one paper in early 1986, thirty-three years old and the mother of a three-year-old daughter; and here is her husband, having an affair with a woman seven years younger, and prettier than she. Though Xiaolin's dark skin was not to his liking, the husband had married her at the urging of friends and relatives, who assured him that she was kind and hardworking. Now he frequently beats her, and to force her to consent to the divorce, even drove her out of their house. The court is unsympathetic, and the neighbourhood committee tries to bring the couple together. But not everyone supports the wronged wife unreservedly. It has been shown by a Peking survey of extra-marital affairs that all the 'third parties' were women who were better educated than their lovers' wives and who wanted more out of life; so the wives are partly to blame, the papers say, if their husbands lose interest in them.

Compared to Western countries the number of divorces in China is tiny, and the reason the matter is debated at all is its comparative novelty. There is no doubt that marital relations are being affected by the economic changes. Take the leap in marital breakdowns among private businessmen, China's new socio-economic grouping. The numbers involved are small, but among private entrepreneurs in a district of Wuhan, for example, each year since 1983 has seen a doubling. One reason is said to be more quarrelling between husband and wife over money, paralleling the rise in incomes; another is said to be the widened social contacts which private business offers, and the expanded opportunities for involvement with 'third parties'.

Take also the effects which the responsibility system is having on the status of rural women. At first glance, the economic reforms, which offer a greater cash return for sideline cultivation and handicrafts, traditionally women's work, appear to be detrimental to their emancipation from home, family labour and male domination. Upon closer investigation, though, the situation is disclosed to be not so simple. A telling investigation in Qingpu, a county in Shanghai's rural outskirts, shows that there were two peaks in the divorce rate among the inhabitants, one coming after the promulgation of the Marriage Law in the early 1950s, the other following the introduction of the system of production responsibility. In most of the recent divorces, it is the wife who seeks to terminate the marriage, either because her husband beats her or because she can no longer put up with his gambling and his neglect of the family. Now that she can earn money for herself from various sideline occupations, many a country woman finds that she no longer derives her sense of security from her husband. Reports from other provinces similarly suggest that while the social changes have by no means benefited all women equally—quite the reverse, in fact, in many cases—they do offer some women more economic independence and opportunity.

Public attitudes to all this remain deeply ambivalent. While divorce is still deeply forwned upon, and those who become involved in extra-marital affairs are seen to be acting immorally, one sometimes hears couples invoking Lenin, who is supposed to have said that a marriage without love is immoral. The debate continues, and it is is a sign of changing times that one of the most authoritative voices to have made itself heard is the one which contends that people are getting divorced not because moral standards are slipping, but rather because their expectations are so much higher that they will not settle for unsatisfactory approximations.

# 9

# CHILDREN, STUDENTS AND SAVANTS

Forty-six-year-old Mother Zheng is the wife of a bamboo craftsman in a hilly part of eastern Sichuan province. She keeps 150 chickens and four pigs, and has given birth to nine children. Childbirth is nothing to her, and some of her children were born in the fields, some in the kitchen. 'Nothing to it,' she says, 'you boil a basin of water and look for a pair of scissors.'

Two of her nine children died—the firstborn, a son, and the sixth daughter. Six of her surviving children are girls, but her youngest child, which she had at about the same time as her eldest daughter had hers, is a boy. His arrival changed everything: no more weeping behind closed doors, no more self-recrimination. Girls are just not the same, thinks Mother Zheng; they get married and go away, and you end up with having no one to leave your house to, the house you have worked and skimped for all these years.

Though childbearing is not a bother, it has not been easy for Mother Zheng to have her last baby. The rule hereabouts is to fine people for having more than the permitted number—400 yuan for a third child, 600 for a fourth, 750 for a fifth, 900 for a sixth, and 1,300 for a seventh. Two of her children having died, Mother Zheng had to pay a 1,300-yuan fine on her baby; she had to go heavily into debt for it, and it was two years before she repaid it.

But she was absolutely set on having the baby. Of course the local government got to hear of it, and sent cadres round to 'work' on her. There came a stream of such officials to her door, and they talked and talked until they dropped. Anyone less determined would have succumbed to the pressure. But not Mother Zheng; she would just listen, and not utter a word. After a while she took to hiding from the officials; she went to her mother's over on the other side of the hill, and would only sneak back now and then to look in on the girls, the chicken and the pigs. She felt some sympathy for the cadres, because she heard that the local Party secretary and the Family Planning Committee representative could be fined personally if their district exceeded the birth quota; but then she felt for herself more. She simply could not contain her yearning for a little boy; she could not bear the other women's scorn.

In this she differs from few Chinese women, whose desire for sons goes back to the earliest times of Chinese history. Traditionally, the worst thing that could happen to a Chinese was to have no male descendants to carry on the family line and offer sacrifices to the ancestors. There are countless stories of the lengths to which Chinese couples go to have a male child. One of the most bizarre, and to my mind the saddest, is the case of a fifteen-month-old baby girl abandoned in the Guangdong People's Hospital because her parents insisted that they had given birth to a boy. The luckless girl was born in the street on a January night in 1985, before the ambulance arrived. Because of the circumstances of the delivery, the doctor didn't examine the baby properly before pronouncing it to be a boy; but the seven doctors who were on duty at the hospital when the ambulance arrived were quite sure the sex of the child was female. Nevertheless, the parents maintained that the hospital had swapped their baby son for a girl, and refused to take the baby home or even to visit her. The Intermediate People's Court instituted investigations and, based on its findings (supplemented by tests which showed the baby's blood group to match her parents'), ruled that the latter had abandoned their daughter and that they must take her home and look after her.

Everyone knew the explanation for the parents' behaviour: it was of course the Chinese government's policy of restricting family size as far as possible to one child per couple. China is one of those countries to which one can truthfully apply the term 'population explosion'. Numbers were doubled within a generation: between 1949 and 1982, Chinese population grew from 540 million to over a billion, more than a fifth of the world's total. This is a monstrous population for any country to be burdened with, and China's planners are only too aware that unless they slow its growth, whatever extra wealth they create will be gobbled up by it. Yet until about 1970 China's leaders did not make it their business to popularise family planning. As usual, Mao Zedong had the last word on the subject—'Every stomach comes with two hands attached,' he said; 'China's populousness is a good thing ... on no account must we think we have too many people.'

Now the family planner can scarcely be escaped. Somewhere behind him loom these alarming statistics: a calculation based on food and diet suggests that China can support 680 million people, while a consideration of ecological balance and the per capita distribution of fresh water yields a figure of 630 to 650 million. Yet even if Chinese women were to bear an average of no more than 2·5 children for the rest of the decade, there will still be a population of 1300 million by the end of the century. This is a frightening prospect for those who think in terms of the ratio of land and resources to inhabitants, and China is determined to avert it. She has set the goal of keeping her population at the 1200 million mark by the year 2000; and because so many young people are now reaching childbearing age, she can see no way of attaining that goal other than by a drastic reduction of family size.

Chinese demographers are amply aware that if the policy of the one-child family were to be maintained for the next two decades, the age structure of the population would become grossly unbalanced, to the point where each economically active person would be supporting two parents and four old and economically dependent grandparents. But China, with no fewer than 240 million women of childbearing age in her population, is not in a position to take account of niceties. And if her project to achieve zero population growth by 2000 by enforcing a one-child policy is something no other country has ever attempted, the sheer size of her population puts China in a class of her own.

The government and the local authorities administer an intricate system of rewards and penalties to persuade families to opt for the one-child ideal. In the city, for example, couples who have pledged to have only one child receive a bonus and a monthly 5-yuan subsidy payable until the child reaches fourteen. Not only will they take precedence over couples with two children in the queue for new housing, their child will go to the top of the list for a place in the kindergarten and local primary school, and have its nursery school fees paid for by the State. But if they change their minds and have a second child, they will forfeit all these benefits.

Every woman of childbearing age is monitored by family planning representatives in her place of work and her neighbourhood committee, to whom she has to report if she plans to have a baby. They will have a dossier on her reproductive history, and will know what contraceptive method she is using. If a woman has already had a child, it will not take many missed periods to set off an official reaction. Every kind of pressure, from interminable nagging to downright arm-twisting, will be exerted to make her have an abortion. And as we saw in the case of Mother Zheng, the punishment for defiance can be dauntingly severe.

It is the workplace and the neighbourhood family planning committee which supply a couple with their free contraceptives. The single most popular method is the intra-uterine device, though nineteen varieties of contraceptives have been produced in China since the late 1960s. These include vas blocking agents which, together with vasectomies, constitute the commonest methods of male birth control. The former Party general secretary Hu Yaobang has declared on more than one occasion that the very best materials should be used in making contraceptives, and that if such materials cannot be had in China, they should be imported from abroad. Firms from Britain, West Germany, Finland, France, Japan, the Netherlands and the United States have all exhibited oral, injectable and external-use contraceptives in Peking, as well as equipment for manufacturing them.

If there are products in China of which there is a more abundant supply than contraceptives, it is difficult to think of them. Yet such are the vagaries of the State distribution system that acute shortages can occur. The country had 600 million condoms in stock at the beginning of 1986, but the products simply were not reaching the customer. In early 1986 a condom manufacturer in the northeastern city of Dalian faced bankruptcy as its supplies piled up in the warehouse.

The government is ready, nevertheless, to help childless couples to procreate. The longing for progeny is a corollary of the restrictions on family size, as it is an immemorial urge and duty, rooted in Mencius' pronouncement that, 'Of the three unfilial acts, the greatest is the leaving of no descendants.' Infertility hits hard in China. Weiwei, a friend of mine in Shanghai who has been trying to conceive for five years, is a typical case. When Western medicine failed to produce results, she turned to Chinese folk remedies, spending enormous sums on rare herbs and healthful brews, and brooding so much that she has become slightly unhinged. The doctor who examined the couple told Weiwei's husband that he had too low a sperm count, but that was probably a well-intentioned untruth; I am told by a relative that it is a matter of policy to tell an infertile couple that there is something the matter with both of them, so as not to create any cause for recrimination. (Sperm banks do exist in China, and artificial insemination is available in six Chinese cities. Donors have to be married, and women who wish to be inseminated may choose the father of her child on the basis of age, ethnic group, blood type, educational level, weight— and that all-important attribute, height.)

What of the millions who are only too fertile? There is no doubt that abortions are sometimes forced upon pregnant women, though how widespread the practice is can only be a matter of conjecture, particularly as degrees of coercion may vary widely. The issue came to a head when the United States International Development Agency accused China of practising forced abortions and withheld a part of its pledged contribution to the United Nations Fund for Population Activities in protest. The Chinese government was understandably indignant. China's internal affairs, its spokesmen said, were no concern of the USA's. It also refuted the American suggestion that the one-child campaign encouraged female infanticide, but here it is more obviously on the defensive. The killing of baby girls by parents who want to try again for a boy has been widely documented, not least by China's own media. The horror of what some people are driven to do under the impact of the campaign is more easily grasped when we consider specific cases. In Peking, a woman worker was sentenced to nineteen years' imprisonment in early 1986 for mutilating the face and body of a nephew with nitric acid; she was under the impression that her husband preferred the boy to his own baby daughter, and thought his family treated her badly because she had given birth to a girl instead of the boy they all wanted. In Hebei province, a country woman was so crazed by the thought of not having a son that she took a cleaver to her two daughters before drowning herself in a well.

The cost of the campaign in physical and mental anguish has been enormous, and in recent years the rules have been eased in a few places: in parts of Shandong, Zhejiang, Guangdong and Guangxi, a couple may now have a second child if the firstborn is a girl, but only if four years have elapsed since her birth. Elsewhere family planning regulations have been modified to suit local economic and cultural conditions; they have always been slackly applied, for instance, and often not at all, in sparsely populated areas inhabited by China's ethnic minorities. And in Tangshan, a northeastern region which suffered the country's worst natural disaster for decades, an earthquake which killed 200,000 people, family planning rules are altogether waived.

Even in crowded cities, the policy has of late not been applied across the board. Allocated a quota of so many second births, a community gives special consideration to couples who are themselves single children, parents with a disabled firstborn, couples who have adopted a child and would like to try for one of their own, parents who remarry and have only one child from their previous marriages, and husbands or wives who have worked for more than five consecutive years in an underground mine or under submarine conditions.

How much of a difference has the campaign made to the birth rate? Since 1980, the annual rate of population growth has been 1·17 per cent, a figure which suggests to Chinese demographers that the country has managed to move out of its first post-1949 baby boom without creating another one for the future. Behind the figures, though, lie great regional disparities. In China, as in other Third World countries, it is tempting to see a link between the education of individuals (particularly women) and a willingness to limit their families. Certainly, of all China's province-level regions, Shanghai's birth rate is the lowest, whereas the highest are to be found in Tibet, Ningxia, Xinjiang (Chinese Turkestan) and Guizhou, all comparatively underdeveloped areas.

It is axiomatic that modern industrialised countries have lower fertility rates than developing ones—the theory, propounded by United Nations demographers, is that 'once a certain economic and social level is reached, fertility is likely to enter a marked decline and to continue downward until it is again stabilised on a much lower plane'. Though no area in China, not even the most developed, approaches the threshold indicated by this theory, nevertheless eight province-level regions display demographic features comparable to the world's most advanced nations. Three of these regions are the metropolises of Peking, Shanghai and Tianjin; while the others are found either along the northeastern seaboard or in the northeast (an area developed by the Japanese in the 1930s). At 2·1 or less, the fertility rates in these areas are similar to those of Western Europe, the United States and Japan; so demographically China is patchy, a mixture of the characteristics of both backward and modern countries.

Part of the formula for population control is the promotion of delayed marriages, and in that practice too, the eastern coastal regions differ sharply from the hinterland. The legal marriageable age is twenty for women and twenty-two for men. Shanghai had been held up as the one place in China where an average marriage age of twenty-six—unarguably late by Chinese reckoning—has been achieved. Yet though the proportion of late marriages has on the whole risen substantially over the years, from about 16 per cent in the early 1970s to 59 per cent in 1984, the old practice of marrying at fifteen or sixteen is by no means ended. Teenage brides are still to be encountered in many a village, where the legal marriageable age means little or nothing to the peasant, and where it is common for girls to become mothers who are still wet behind the ears.

For China's policy-makers these are disturbing practices, all the more worrying for having been stimulated by the unshackling of the peasant from the economic and social constraints which previously bound him. What is more, family planning sometimes finds itself at cross-purposes with the rural economic reforms; for it is the larger household, with many hands, which has the advantage in the handicraft and service trades. The new rural prosperity works against the success of the birth control campaign, because the fines on over-procreation do not deter the affluent peasant, flush with the proceeds of his entrepreneurial activities.

Perhaps the most revolutionary of the differences which the campaign will make to China is its destruction, at a stroke, of the ramifications of the Chinese kinship system. Just as the Eskimo has many words for 'snow', so the Chinese have no single collective word for sisters, brothers, uncles, aunts or cousins, but instead separate terms which make clear the exact relationship of these kinsmen—whether older or younger, maternally connected or paternally—to oneself or one's parents. That kinship terms, such as Second Elder Brother or Third Elder Sister, are used rather than personal names as forms of address within the family is another symbol of the importance of the family. But today, 32 million single children are growing up in China bereft or siblings.

Already, they have been termed the 'troublesome generation', a new breed of offspring, spoilt, selfish, self-indulgent, unsociable, arrogant. These, at any rate, are the words which come to most Chinese minds when you mention an only child. As a nation the Chinese have always loved their children to a sickening degree, and now that they are limited to only one, they have truly gone to extremes. More than ever now, parents live for their children, and through them. The result is that these children have become despotic masters of the house. 'I rode on Daddy's shoulders and got Mummy to stretch out her arms and make a circle with Daddy's. And I said to them, "You are the sky, and I am the little sun." ' This was how, in a storytelling competition in Peking, an only child described himself— as the sun around which the planets revolve—and the metaphor has become a part of Chinese imagery.

Single children are subjected to unprecedented parental watchfulness, their every cry attended to, their every whim indulged. But the parents' constant offering of anxious assistance at the first suggestion of difficulty serves only to increase their children's dependency. China abounds in stories of single children who prove incapable of fending for themselves—the eleven-year-old boy who didn't know what to do with a hard-boiled egg because he had never peeled one for himself, the ten-year-old girl who never learnt to dress herself or tie her own shoe laces. So anxious are the parents to forestall any threat of unhappiness that when their children are assigned extra-curricular tasks like classroom cleaning, they rush to the school to do the job for them. And since the Chinese habitually equate happiness with eating, and health with plumpness, some children are literally stuffed to death. A medical director at the Peking's Children's Hospital told the press in 1986 that 800 of the children referred to her since 1980 had been twice the normal weight, and that two she saw had died of obesity.

The great hazard facing the single child is not only parental indulgence and ignorance, but also parental ambition and vanity. Regardless of the child's abilities, the parents demand academic success. That their offspring should turn out to be a child prodigy is the great parental fantasy. At the same time as they are showering their darlings with toys, parents are goading them hard to come top in class and master the violin or piano besides. A survey of parental attitudes conducted at a Peking primary school revealed that more than 90 per cent of the parents expected their children to become scholars, professors, archaeologists, artists, or to study abroad; none saw their child growing up to be an ordinary worker. It makes one think that two kinds of character will be governing China in twenty years' time: the over-achiever, and the psychological wreck.

The tyranny of the spoilt child has given rise to something new in China, the Chinese answer to Dr Spock. Previously nobody could tell the Chinese how to bring up their children, but now parenting is entering a period of transition, when folk wisdom can no longer provide all the answers. Manuals on child rearing are making their first appearance in China, and a book translated from the Japanese called *Coping with the Only Child* was eagerly snatched up and read. By 1986, some 30,000 classes on child rearing had come into being. A 'Be a Good Parent' drive attracted thousands of young fathers and mothers in one city; courses on child psychology, education, nutrition and health care drew thousands of parents in another. The authorities are keen enough to support such activities, hoping they will palliate parental excesses as well as steer people back to the traditional ideals of filial respect and authority.

Often it is not just the parents who need to go to school, but the doting grandparents too. Against that, there is the fact that the grandmother's role in the domestic scheme is diminishing. It is another sign of changing times that her help with the baby is no longer so eagerly accepted (because her methods are considered a little too old-fashioned), nor so readily offered (because she now has other things to occupy her). The familiar picture of babies being aired by their grandmothers in what look to Western eyes like bamboo supermarket trolleys with handles at both ends is beginning to fade from the city streets; and her place is increasingly taken by the *baomu*, the Chinese *au pair* from the countryside. Demand for such girls has shot up in the cities, and domestic agencies and babysitting services have mushroomed.

One reason there is such a demand for child minders is that there are simply not enough day-care centres or nurseries. In Peking, for instance, only four out of every ten children who need to be placed in one may expect to get in; while in Shanghai it is not at all uncommon for parents to queue for twenty-four hours to get their children a place in a kindergarten.

If the Chinese are recognisably Chinese because of their family upbringing, they are also influenced by those others who look after them in early life. Western visitors to Chinese day-care centres and kindergartens are often struck by their collectivist ethos; individuality, never a strong Chinese trait, is deprecated, and when children are selected for special recognition, it is in order that an example may be held up for others to emulate. The teachers try to supervise the children as much as possible, and what Westerners understand by 'free play' rarely occurs. Set beside their Western peers, Chinese children appear exceptionally self-restrained. You will seldom see thumb-sucking or nail-biting, and if you ask the Chinese child-minder questions about hyperactivity or aggression, she will most likely look at you with blank incomprehension. The simultaneous indulgence and represssion of children is one of the ways by which Chinese society develops those characteristics which, for want of a better term, we might call national character.

The Chinese pedagogical approach has been interestingly described by Gertrud Schyl-Bjurman, a Swedish educator who visited a teacher training college in Peking in 1982. Two research students were testing children in an experiment inspired by Piaget. For each they noted down only whether the children responded correctly or incorrectly for their age, or whether a child was ahead of his age level; they paid no attention whatsoever to what the children said, or to the reasoning with which they tackled their questions. This disconcerted the Swedish observer, who asked the students afterwards why they didn't listen to what the children said, since this was much the better way to understanding how a child thinks. But the students didn't understand her: that it was far more important to record each child's attainment seemed to them to be self-explanatory.

For the most part children are given few opportunities to use their creative imaginations; as far as the teachers are concerned there is a right way and a wrong way—but never a different way—to doing everything. Here is an illustration of how rigidly Chinese children are taught. In a test conducted by a kindergarten in Peking, one of the questions was, 'You are out with your parents, and you see a toy you want. Your father won't buy it for you: what do you do?' One child answered, 'I will tell father why I should have it, and then I'll ask him his reasons for not wanting to buy it for me. If his reasons are sound, then I'll give in; if not, I'll have him buy it.' The child received no score for this, because marks were given only for the correct answer, which in the teachers' opinion was 'I won't insist until father has the money to pay for it.' Another question in the test was, 'What do you do when you see your friends come to blows?' The only correct answer to this was, 'I'll tell my teachers.'

For the most part what I have described pertains only to the urban child, because in the village you would be hard put to it to find a day-care centre or kindergarten. This is yet another manifestation of the polarity in living standards between city and country. The government ordered hundreds of thousands of collective day-care centres to be set up during the Cultural Revolution, but they did not get off the ground in rural areas, and few of them survived into the 1980s. Similarly, the countryside cries out for teachers, but in a country so inadequately supplied with them, it is the poor of the remote villages who go without them first.

China is weak in that most basic element of economic development, human resources. She simply has not skilled manpower enough for what she wants to accomplish, and her leaders are all too aware of this. Speaking to a group of Central Party School leavers in 1984, Hu Yaobang observed that China's cadres were currently doubly disadvantaged, by their lack of book learning on the one hand, and their lack of practical experience on the other. His view is shared by Gu Mu, the economic planner, who said that of all the inadequacies bedevilling the open-door policy—of energy supply, tele-communications, transport and so on—he had come to the conclusion that the most dire was the shortage of qualified people.

Finding and employing able people, Deng Xiaoping himself had said, was the key to the ultimate success of his reforms. It was appalling that, of the 42 million members in the Communist Party, half had failed to progress beyond primary school, while only 4 per cent had gone to university. In fact, it is commonly supposed by the man in the street in China that an inverse relationship existed between official rank and educational attainment—the higher the office, the lower the level of education.

China is paying for her earlier squandering of human talents. The story of education is a sorry one, with a continuous decline in the proportion of students in higher education between 1960 and 1970. Politics had dominated in schools and universities, and a whole generation had grown up badly educated, if at all. During the Cultural Revolution, such was the prejudice against formal education that when a student (the famous Zhang Tiesheng) turned in a blank sheet of paper in an exam, he was instantly hailed as a national hero and even tipped as the next minister of education under the Gang of Four. Universities did away with formal entrance exams, and selected students from among 'workers, peasants and soldiers' on the basis of their class background and political soundness. Yet the system could not always be defended on grounds of equal opportunity, because the absence of academic entrance requirements made it easier for those with the right connections to win places by string-pulling. It was not until 1983 that the first PhDs ever to be granted in the People's Republic were awarded; one could tell from the average age of these graduates, which was thirty-eight, that they had mostly been undergraduate students before the Cultural Revolution.

Today the class the Chinese call *zhishi fenzi* (a term, commonly and misleadingly translated as 'intellectuals', for graduates of secondary school and above) are anything but deprecated, and to produce enough of them a distinctly elitist approach to education has evolved. Since 1977 the achievers (or the well-connected) have been creamed off by the so-called key schools (of which there were only 239 in 1983), from where they go on to universities, if they are very bright or lucky. The rest are shunted to ordinary secondary schools and they go straight on to jobs or vocational schools. The pressure to make the grade is enormous; and Shanghai, for one, has decided to phase out key lower secondary schools because children have been committing suicide under the strain, and pupils in the ordinary schools are developing deep feelings of inferiority.

The one-baby policy has made parents all the more eager that their child outshine his rivals at school. Nor is it only the parents who demand hard work of their children; it is also the teachers. The pace has greatly quickened. If teachers used to expect their pupils to learn 2000 characters by their fifth year, they now expect them to learn 3500. Children used to receive lashings of politics; now, wrote a complainant to the *China Daily* in late 1985, they are 'drowning in a sea of homework.' He went on to describe what a six-year-old boy who had started school less than three months before had to do for his homework: to write all the numerals from 1 to 10,000 in a single evening! As in a classical Chinese education, in which memory work was all important, a heavy emphasis has been placed on rote learning and exam marks, and many schools have become little more than crammers or sausage machines.

Some schools contrive to correct this bias. One school in Shanghai was forced to rethink its teaching methods when a boy it had expelled for repeatedly failing his exams went and won two prizes at an international exhibition of new inventions in Geneva. He had thought up a device for threading clotheslines on electrical wires to help his grandmother, who had trouble airing her clothes. The school he now goes to bends over backwards to nurture his creativity, providing him with space, always at a premium in Shanghai, to use as a laboratory.

In China there is no question at all of holding back really gifted children in mixed ability classes, and future Einsteins are educated separately from future shop assistants. The first place to set up special courses for child prodigies was the China University of Science and Technology at Hefei, but its example was promptly followed by a dozen other universities. Many of the first crop of students are now studying for their doctorates in the United States. In the meantime the university at Hefei pushed streaming back even further by setting up special preparatory classes for bright pupils in secondary schools in Peking and Suzhou.

The elitism which streaming by ability creates in the Chinese educational system is compounded by the fact that the students of key schools and universities come preponderantly from privileged families. There is no doubt that, while many are there through their own merit and effort, the children of high-ranking officials have far greater access to opportunities, whether it is a place at a prestigious institution or a chance to study abroad. A prime example of this is Deng Zhifang, a PhD candidate in Physics at America's Rochester University, and the younger son, it so happens, of Deng Xiaoping. (Deng Zhifang is at Rochester with his wife, who is also working on a PhD. They recently had a child, whose being born in the United States makes an American citizen of him. 'For China's supreme ruler to have an American citizen for a grandson is scandalous,' remarked a Chinese student at a British university. In China the story was hushed up.) One does not have to look far to find another example. In Stanford, as we saw, are Chen Yun's daughter and her teenage daughter, whose growing up Californian seems not to bother the grandfather, who of all China's most powerful leaders condemns 'polluting' Western lifestyles the most.

The last few years have seen an enormous increase in the number of Chinese students abroad, which a conservative estimate for 1985 put at 30,000. To be sent abroad to study in the West is to be given the most coveted of opportunities, but it is hardly the easier for that. For some students, the rudest culture shock is to find that, in sharp contrast to China, where everything is decided for you, no one tells you what to do. For others, the obvious discrepancy between what their ideological conditioning tells them and what they discover for themselves can be deeply unsettling. Led to expect cruel income disparities in a capitalist country, as well as vice at every corner, a recent arrival in London was never more relieved than when a friend took him to see a slum in Manchester and showed him a working-class pub offering lunchtime striptease. When he phoned to tell me about it, I couldn't help thinking of something Wen Yuankai had related. It was when he went to listen to jazz in New Orleans. 'The music instantly set off a conditioned response,' he later related, 'and I thought that at any moment a Mata Hari would walk in through the door and bewitch us all—because that was what my 30 years of education had told me to expect.'

I am told that, depending on where they happen to have studied, students are left with very different feelings about the capitalist West. 'No one who goes to the United States,' I have been told again and again, 'is left in any doubt that America is best; they're as sold on the American system as those who studied in the Soviet Union in the 1950s were on the Russian. On the other hand, people who study in Japan almost always end up hating Japan and the Japanese. It is only the ones who study in Europe who come away with anything like a balanced view of capitalism and the West.'

Whatever may be their view of the West, there are few to question the usefulness of knowing a foreign language; and the study of English particularly, a compulsory secondary school subject, has become all the rage. The first British woman to become a household name in China is probably Katherine Flower, who taught English in a widely popular TV programme called 'Follow Me', a joint production by China Central Television and the BBC. The programme, which had an impact unimaginable in Britain, made a star of Ms Flower; and whenever she appeared in the streets, her fans would fall over each other for the privilege of talking to her and trying out their newly acquired English phrases. The sequel, a twenty-eight episode series to be called 'Follow Me to Science', is scheduled to finish filming in 1987, and is likely to prove even more of a success, since it combines Katherine Flower and English with a still greater enthusiasm, science.

The craze for learning English is part of a larger zeal for self-improvement. A recent public opinion poll, which questioned the wishes of several thousand unmarried young people in Changsha, Chairman Mao's old home, showed that far more people would rather devote their spare time to acquiring knowledge than to dating or making money. Evening schools—offering subjects ranging from English, acupuncture and business management to dressmaking and disco and ballroom dancing—have become rapidly more numerous in the cities, attracting particularly people in their 'thirties, whose schooling had been interrupted by the Cultural Revolution, and who feel that they badly need to catch up. Many such schools are frankly money-making organisations, whose high charges have come in for much press criticism. Among the offenders named was the Qianjin (Progress) Evening School in Shanghai, which charged a swingeing 400 yuan a term for its course of TOEFL, the Test of English as a Foreign Language. It was an exorbitant sum for people whose monthly income was no more than 100 yuan. What is more, by offering high wages to their staff, these schools were encouraging moonlighting by teachers; in Shanghai, the educational authorities complained that some secondary school teachers were taking on as many as thirty hours of evening classes a week, with the result that their normal teaching suffered.

The purpose of the students flocking to these schools is, in most cases, just as utilitarian: it is to acquire the paper qualifications necessary to a widening of their career horizons. This is why there has been such a mania for diplomas. One day, these people hope, all this spare-time study will pay off, in promotion, in higher pay, or in better career opportunities. The economic reforms have sharpened the lines of competitiveness in Chinese society, and shifted the criteria by which people are marked out as special. The days when you could rise to high office without a secondary school certificate look to be numbered; what kind of people will the modernisation drive throw up if not a class of well educated administrators and professionals?

As in other domains of planning, China's approach to education is to start from a given target rate of economic growth and then ask what amount of resources will be required to reach that goal. Her planners believe that by 1990, China will need to have doubled her number of skilled people from 10 million to 20 million. How is this to be achieved, given limited funding? As always, the first step was to bring about a change in the leadership: the hidebound Ministry of Education was abolished and replaced by a supra-ministry State Education Commission headed by Li Peng. Then a three-part plan, spelling out the areas where efforts and funds were to be directed, was unveiled in the spring of 1985.

The first aim was to make nine-year compulsory schooling universal. This is a mammoth undertaking. More than a quarter of China's people, something like five to six times the size of Britain's population, are barely literate, and two million teachers will have to be trained before one can expect *any* real improvement in primary and lower secondary school education. What is more, the means of improving the calibre of the teaching profession—which has suffered the worst that low pay, unappealing living conditions, low public esteem, rigid political control and overcrowded classrooms could do to it—do not lie ready to hand, for it is not as though the State could greatly increase its spending, though teacher training colleges and teachers have been promised more money. In the end it was the schools themselves which found a way: in keeping with the get-rich-quick spirit all around, they took it upon themselves to let some of their classrooms and office space, and used the rents to increase staff wages and benefits. They might almost have flowered into estate agents, had their local governments not declared the practice irregular.

It is unusual for China not to fix a date by which a target is to be reached, but no timetable has been set for the introduction of universal compulsory education in the poorer and more remote regions of inland China. This is being realistic: one can scarcely apply to the sleepy backwoods the standards of the coastal cities. Some places have not even been touched by the hand of Mao Zedong's revolution, let alone Deng Xiaoping's. This is borne out by an astonishing social survey which recently came out of Guizhou, one of the country's 'wildest' provinces. There, in the township of Yangwang, it was discovered that two private schools of the kind which clan organisations or local officials used to sponsor in the old days had been set up.

Yangwang had had such schools since at least the Manchu dynasty, but they were forced to close in the early years of the New China. Yet old habits die hard in China, and in the early 1980s, after a gap of twenty-nine years, back they had sprung. The pupils, all boys, range in age from fourteen to twenty. The two teachers, both in their 'fifties, come from a long line of old-style private tutors. The textbooks are as one would expect in schools of this kind (though not in a country which had been under communist rule for more than three decades). They are the books which formed the basis of Confucian teaching throughout imperial Chinese history, classics like the *Mencius* and the *Analects*, the *Book of Odes* and the *Spring and Autumn Annals*. Some of the books are freshly hand-copied, others are hand-me-down and faded with age. Exactly as in the old days, the desks and benches are brought by the pupils from their homes, as are the brushes and the inkstones. Each pupil pays his teacher 15 yuan a year in school fees, as well as sixty catties* of rice and two baskets of charcoal. The teacher, for his part, sets the noses of the boys to the grindstone of ancient literature seven and a half hours a day, 240 days a year. The boys are expected to memorise their lessons and recite them, inability to do so being punished with caning—or in some cases, by being made to skip lunch or stand in front of an altar to Confucius. Each boy bows before this altar as soon as he arrives at the school in the morning, and also before and after each recitation. In the afternoon he practices calligraphy, just as Chinese schoolboys have done since antiquity.

All this would have seemed extraordinary, were we to think that Maoism had come to grips with Chinese tradition's extreme tenacity. But 2000 years of history cannot be wiped out in just one generation, and the township of Yangwang was, it seems, never in any danger of losing its links with

* One catty = 1·1 lb.

antiquity. In faithfully reproducing the curriculum and discipline of the old-style school, the teachers are not being subversive. They are only imparting to their pupils what they themselves learnt, and they probably believe in all sincerity that theirs is the only kind of education worth having. The schools have the full support of the parents, who happen to be mostly local dignitaries—cadres and village elders and even an earth-diviner or two. Education is still something of a luxury here, beyond the reach of humbler folk, and it was Deng Xiaoping's rural reforms, and the prosperity they created, which brought the schools into being.

Elsewhere the responsibility system and the surge of family free enterprise have worked to frustrate the aims of the educational reformers. In a situation where the more hands you have, the better off you are likely to be, child labour is perhaps inevitable, and all over the country there are girls under sixteen being kept at home by their parents, to help around the house or work in family factories. Between 1978 and 1981, the proportion of school-age children at school actually fell, and the State Education Commission reckoned that there were three and a half million girls being kept from school in 1985. In one factory I visited, in southern Zhejiang province, I found that the children were not even local, but had been drafted to work there from neighbouring villages.

That they were mostly girls is not surprising either. It is their fate to live in a country which still frankly holds females inferior. In schools and universities, males predominate, the male—female difference widening as one progresses up the educational ladder. The science departments of the country's most prestigious universities are practically male preserves. This is as you would expect, when neither the teachers nor the students themselves regard women as the equal of men. I remember asking a male physics teacher, whose mixed class I came upon in a Chinese secondary school in 1983, how many of his best pupils were girls. 'None,' he answered. 'Physics is after all a very difficult subject.'

Many girls who might have done well at university get shunted into the technical stream. Here much expansion has occurred in recent years. There is an appalling shortage of middle-grade technicians in China, and the second of the three aims of educational reform—the extension of secondary technical education—is intended to correct this deficiency. In certain Chinese cities a large number of vocational training facilities has quickly come into being in recent years. But this is not so much the result of direct government action as a response to demand. Many vocational schools have appeared as, with economic reform and the decentralisation of State control, more and more people seek and find jobs outside the government labour allocation system. As the unemployed have become the self-employed, and as enterprises have begun to exercise a degree of autonomy, so the demand for vocational skills has expanded. Parallel with this trend, joint sponsorship of vocational courses between the educational authorities and various commercial or industrial concerns has evolved. An example of this are the so-called Hilton courses in a vocational school for tourism in Shanghai—these being programmes for training people who, if they prove satisfactory, might subsequently be taken on by the sponsoring hotel.

There has also been a tremendous effort to develop alternatives to the conventional system of higher education, from non-residential part-time schools to correspondence colleges. One such form of education, the Radio and Television Universities, has evolved rapidly. Though begun largely as an indigenous enterprise, these universities have since received help from several quarters abroad, from the World Bank to Britain's Open University. 'A courageous attempt' to meet China's special needs is how a lecturer at the Open University has described them; and it is true that they are an admirable venture, narrowing the enormous gulf between supply and demand, and transcending State budgetary cheese-paring. More courageous still are the correspondence courses set up by groups of private individuals. One such group I interviewed consisted of a clutch of university lecturers and retired women operating out of two rented rooms. No correspondence college could be more admirable; starting up on 600 yuan the lecturers had made by giving private tuition, it was teaching thousands of students (a handful of them serving sentences in prison, I was told) within a year.

The third aim of the educational reforms is to loosen the government's control of higher education. Under a new deal which drew heavily upon experiments conducted in Shanghai's Jiaotong University, universities were given more say in their own day-to-day running, whether this was a question of how funds should be allocated or what subjects to include in a course of study. So long as they fulfil the intake targets set by the State, universities may now decide on student admissions themselves. Here and there a new system of tying salary to job title, rather than to seniority, has been tried out, in a bid to diminish the tyranny of age and give younger lecturers fairer chances of promotion. In 1986 a plan to make students sing for their supper was tried out in a number of institutions. Instead of free lodging and tuition, the scheme applied a means test, awarding grants to hard-up students and low-interest loans (to be repaid once they start working) to the better-off ones.

To most Westerners Chinese universities are still hardly more than boarding schools, where the undergraduates are treated like minors and subject to rigid rules and regulations. You can get ticked off for growing a moustache. You are not allowed to marry. One of the most telling of all student demonstrations is the one staged on the Peking University campus in late 1984: it was to protest against 'lights out' at 11 p.m. 'Reforms give students freedom to flourish', read the headline of a story on Qinghua University in the *China Daily* in November 1985. But the freedom turns out to be small beer, consisting only of the right for a student to pursue courses and activities outside his or her own curriculum (provided that he or she has earned the requisite number of credits), and the right to decide which of several lecturers giving the same basic course he or she would rather listen to.

One would expect to find many grievances among China's university students, whose living quarters are cramped (six or seven to a room measuring 4 square metres at Peking University), the food abysmal, and the queues for meals endless (only seven dining rooms for 12,000 students at Peking University). And indeed one of the most widely publicised events to have occurred in 1985 was a wave of student unrest in the autumn. On September 18, the 54th anniversary of the Mukden Incident (with which Japan began her occupation of Manchuria and, in the view of many historians, sowed the seeds of the Second World War), students in Peking pasted up wall posters and took to the streets in what was said to be the largest student demonstration in a decade. Student frustrations also came to a head in Chengdu, in southwest China, and in the northwestern city of Xian two Japanese visitors were even physically assaulted. The students were protesting against the Japanese Prime Minister's visit to the Yasukuni Shrine, but their outburst at what they would presently denounce as Japan's 'economic aggression' against China was to become mingled with other grievances. One was the canteen food, a running cause of student disgruntlement, hard hit by the inflationary effects of the price reforms. Another, so some observers say, concerned the initiators; these were gilded youths who felt aggrieved because their parents had been ousted from power and they had lost the perks that go with high office in China. The offspring of the upper crust are often the most cynical, because they are the ones with the insider's view of Party politics and corruption.

Restlessness among the students grew with the passing months. As yet another anniversary loomed—that of the December 9 Movement of 1935, in which students clenched fists, shouted 'Down with Japanese imperialism!' and demanded that the Kuomintang and communists form a united front to oppose Japan—the authorities took steps to nip another revolt in the bud. Everything was done to deflect the students' energies and dampen their passions. Party officials made the rounds of the nation's universities, lecturing to students and soliciting their support for the government's policies. A meeting to commemorate the December 9 Movement brought together students, lecturers and the old-timers who had taken part in the movement itself, and who readily declared what patriots they were, how loyal to the Party and its principles. The students did hold a rally in the Square of Heavenly Peace, the historical scene of demonstrations in Peking, but it was a tame enough gathering, ringed around by the police.

But will China be able to avoid the fate of other Asian societies (South Korea and Taiwan spring immediately to mind), where rapid economic and social change coupled with limited political liberty has thrown up ominous tensions, rising expectations, and student demands for democracy? The answer, as student unrest erupted in China's universities at the end of 1986 and the beginning of 1987, is a resounding 'no'.

The demonstrations began in Hefei, then spread to about a dozen other cities, among them Shanghai and Peking. They may be seen as the price of Deng Xiaoping's reforms, part of the larger struggle of his policies, which have opened a chink in a hitherto closed society, have initiated profound economic change and whetted people's appetites for political change as well, and which do not benefit all citizens equally, giving rise to conflicts between the State and individual interests. The interests expressed by the student rallies are familiar enough. Some of the marchers were protesting against rising university fees. Others were clamouring for the freedom of the press; the right to name their own candidates to the provincial Party congress instead of having to accept Party hacks; for less bureaucracy; accelerated change; and democracy. At the Shanghai rallies, marchers carried banners portraying the Statue of Liberty and a Chinese dragon bound in chains.

But Chinese students have only the haziest notions of what democracy really means, and the responsibilities that it entails. They may think they were serving a constructive purpose for China, but their protests have put the reforms at risk, because they may impel the authorities to a course of suppression, and provide the conservatives in the Party—who think Deng Xiaoping's reforms have gone quite far enough already—with an excuse to call a halt to further liberalisation. Students have failed to grasp that democracy has to be built upon a free economy, and it is precisely for a freer economy that Deng's economic policies, if carried to their logical conclusion, are headed. When the unrest first began, Wen Yuankai was visiting Hong Kong from Hefei. I spoke to him there, and he was initially of the opinion that the student movement would help to accelerate the reforms. Subsequently, when it persisted and grew more intense, he said that it might well retard the restructuring of the economy.

The police who moved in to break up the rallies showed remarkable restraint, and those who believe that nothing of importance happens in China without design thought they detected Deng Xiaoping's guiding hand behind the movement—at least in its very earliest stages. Later, as the official line hardened, as some of the regime's most outspoken critics were expelled from the party, as Hu Yaobang came under fire for his failure to deal decisively enough with the protests, and as the student unrest was subsumed into a larger struggle over political reform within the Party, those observers whose minds are more attuned to the stop-go rhythms of Chinese politics found it difficult to avoid an acute sense of *déjà vu*. Among the country's rulers, stability and unity have always been the great Chinese dream. Quelling dissent, the leaders said, would ensure a stable environment in which to continue their experiment with the economy.

The unrest died down, but it was no change of heart by the students, who mirror their generation and the age with their rejection of ideology. No longer do young people accept with such docility the dictates of the Party. The sense of cynicism and boredom which pervades classes on political theory is palpable. These are people who were only about ten when the 'calamitous ten years' drew to a close. For them the early years of revolutionary endeavour are only so much unreal history; in nothing is the generation gap greater than in the view people hold of the communist revolution. To the younger generation, there are more absorbing things than the history of the Communist Party: when graduation approaches, for example, there is the all-important question of where one will be assigned work.

The Chinese university is like a State-run factory in that its products, the graduates, are sent only to State jobs, or kept for the use of the ministry or province which happens to run the university. Nothing worries the students more than the thought of ending up in the sticks—in outbacks like Tibet or Xinjiang (Chinese Turkestan). And even for those lucky enough to be given work in the big cities, there is no guarantee that it will be in the desired organisation or in their speciality.

There has been much debate of late on what has fashionably been called the 'floating of talents'—in other words a labour market. There is no doubt that the practice of assigning people to jobs with little regard for their preferences and qualifications on the one hand, and the needs of prospective employers on the other, is very unsatisfactory, and the idea of allowing skilled professionals to 'float' to places where their qualifications can best be used has been mooted. The issue is one which the educational reformers can scarcely ignore, concerned as they are to husband the country's scarce human resources. As part of the educational reforms, it has indeed been decided to allow students more say in their careers after graduation, and universities have been told to try and match speciality with job and to arrange for the graduates to meet their prospective employers beforehand. But no sooner had the reform been introduced than it was rescinded. In the summer of 1986, it was discovered that though the reform had suited the students well enough, it had left the State sector—the key industries and government projects in the remote backward regions—critically short of graduates. So students were again told to put their country's interests before their own, and comply with the planned placement system.

No case is quite like another, and rather than generalise, it may be better to relate the story of a real student, who sums up many of the qualities of his generation. He is an orphan from a poor rural backwater in Hunan province, part of that first batch of students to enter university on their own merits after the Cultural Revolution. His subject was pharmacology, his speciality Chinese herbal medicine. It was a branch of learning with which he already had some familiarity, because the grandfather who brought him up was a traditional Chinese doctor.

But he did not do well in his first two years at university; he was far too hopelessly in love. She was in the same class, and though she was much too grand for him—her father was the deputy head of their department, its sole assistant professor—he simply could not help himself. Of course there was no question of dating her, nor did she give him any encouragement. They did go out once in their second year, on an outing to the botanical gardens, ostensibly to pick specimens. But her nonchalance hurt him, and he vowed to put her out of his mind.

His work soon improved, and people began to look up to him. In his fifth year he left to do his 'internship' at a hospital. To his surprise, he was given a book by the girl as a parting gift; it was a story called *Love Must Not Be Forgotten*, and it bore the inscription 'Care to continue our interrupted outing?'Of course he did, and the two paired off. But his room-mate, a country lad from the same county as he, deflated him by saying he had only become more eligible because he was the very pick of his class, with a good chance of being assigned to work in a top hospital.

His grant of 13 yuan a month, supplemented by the 10 yuan his grandfather sent him, was not enough to pay for his food at the hospital; but his girlfriend would help by slipping him some of her own money. Later he became a regular guest at her house. She suggested they got engaged. His future seemed assured, because even without an influential prospective father-in-law his chances of being allowed to remain at university were good: he really could contribute to Chinese pharmacological research, an area in which both Chinese and Japanese specialists have been energetically working, but which has as yet yielded no theory.

Then his grandfather died, and he all of a sudden felt he had to go back. This meant parting from his fiancée, because no Chinese girl in her right mind would voluntarily forgo her urban registration and go live in the countryside. But when he thought of his native village (where it was more than seventeen miles to the nearest clinic, and thirty-four miles to the county hospital) he was certain he should go back and take his grandfather's place. Hardly any of his fellow-students could understand his reasons, and some suggested that he would do better to ask for a posting to a real backwoods like Qinghai or Tibet if it was honour and money he was after. At least there would be heroism in it, as well as a hardship allowance.

Back in Hunan, he was asked if he wouldn't prefer to work in the county seat, where conditions were so much better. The commune health clinic, too, tried to keep him. He was the only bona fide university graduate around for miles, so why should he want to bury himself in the country? Nobody who got as far as university would return to work in the sticks except as a punishment, so his own native villagers satisfied themselves that he had done something wrong, perhaps even committed a crime. As for the precise nature of his crime, it was rumoured that he had 'slept with the daughter of a distinguished professor'. It was not until they heard him praised on the radio that they thought differently.

For a year and a half, from late 1982 to early 1984, he tended the sick. Was he heroic? He didn't think so. He did join the Party, but it was not to get ahead. At heart there still lurked some idealism. He did not give up his hope of beating the Japanese at herbal medicine research, however. So when a clinic opened in his hamlet, and another doctor was sent to replace him, he set off once more for Peking, there to take an exam for postgraduate study. His fiancée, in the meantime, had married, and the man she had married was his former room-mate.

If he does get taken on to do research one day, what kind of working life can he expect? To see what the future holds for him, one has to explore the lot of the Chinese academic and his place in society. You see only one facet of the life of the Chinese learned profession in the teaching institutions. There is the official academe, dominated by the Chinese Academy of Sciences and the Chinese Academy of Social Sciences, and when one talks of the think tank in China, one has in mind the research organs under the jurisdiction of these bodies. The doors of these organs bear high-sounding titles—Institute of High Energy Physics, for example, or Institute of Marxism-Leninism and Mao Zedong Thought—but behind them poor working conditions can prevail. As recently as November 1985, an investigation into the conditions of work in the Biophysics Research Institute showed that half the time, research scientists were doing the job of laboratory assistants: a scientist whose project used extracts from pigs' hearts travelled thirty miles a week to buy them; another killed his pigs himself to extract the blood required for his experiment. 'It is not that we dislike killing pigs,' he said, 'it's just that we waste a lot of valuable time which might otherwise be spent on the research project.' Nor were these two scientists in any way exceptional: of the young to middle-aged research scientists questioned, some 70 per cent complained that their skills were not utilised fully.

Yet, partly because of the traditional Chinese reverence for scholarship, and partly because the times demand it, the savant now occupies a potentially honoured place in society, his learning harnessed to the political and economic purposes of his country. In China many intellectuals work inside the system, not outside it; some of them are very close to the sources of power in Peking, incorporated into the business of the State somewhat like Confucian scholars in earlier days. They are theorists of government and society, and therefore men of public significance. In the old days they were elevated above the masses, their long fingernails symbolising their disdain of physical labour. Mao, who had been cold-shouldered as a young man at Peking University, hated their kind. 'The more you learn,' he once said, 'the stupider you become.' Nor was there much love lost between the intelligentsia and the millions of unlettered country men who, after years of guerrilla warfare in the backwoods, became Party officials and cadres in the new China. So intellectuals have had a hard time of it, branded the 'stinking ninth category' in the Cultural Revolution and punished for their superiority by being made to clear pig-sties or lavatories. After all, to reverse the ancient Chinese proposition that 'He who works with his mind rules; he who works with his strength is ruled' lay at the heart of the Communist Party's policies. And it has for long been understood that students and scholars should be 'both red and expert', and that to advocate 'expertness first and redness later' was to deny the supremacy of politics, a fundamental principle in education and life.

Though prejudice against intellectuals persists in some quarters, a trend towards the redefinition of their social status is apparent. A law has been drafted to protect academic activity from outside harassment, and to clarify the relationship of learned societies to the Party, government and industry. The Double Hundred theme—first struck as we saw by Mao in his call to 'Let a hundred flowers bloom, let a hundred schools of thought contend'— was re-aminated in the summer of 1986. In all this it is useful to remind ourselves that it has ever been the intellectual's role to fulfil two functions in society—to think up theoretical schemes for those in power to carry into practice, and to concoct theories that will legitimise people's exercise of power after the event. These two functions the Chinese savant has now resumed.

One intellectual who enjoys enormous prestige, and whose ideas and interests happen to support the top leadership's, is the anthropologist Fei Xiaotong, whose checkered career parallels those of many of his calling and generation. Short and sprightly, Fei is well into his 'seventies; silenced for decades, he has only now come into his own, teaching and supervising the kind of research which won him so much recognition in the 1940s.

Fei is one of the most westernised of China's intellectuals, having been educated in missionary schools in China and then in England. He first studied sociology at Peking's Yanjing University, where the atmosphere was distinctly American and where, for a term, he had the eminent Chicago sociologist Robert Park (whom he said he worshipped) for a teacher. At Qinghua, Peking's other famous university, Fei studied for an MA in Anthropology with the Russian scholar S. M. Shirokogoroff. His third mentor was the great Bronislaw Malinowski from the London School of Economics. Fei was deeply influenced by Malinowski, who supervised his PhD; and Malinowski in turn warmed to him, styling himself 'your affectionate uncle' in his letters. Fei was later to preface a book he wrote about his second visit to Britain in 1946 and 1947 with the words, 'I love England.'

When he returned from London in 1938, it was to the southwest of China that he made his way—the coastal region, including his native southern Jiangsu, being already under Japanese occupation. Fei devoted himself to teaching, pioneering field studies, and to writing for both the academic audience and the general reader. He acquired an international reputation, and his work was published in England and the United States.

All the while the situation in China worsened, with war and unrest added to the pressures of social change and rural poverty. It was probably difficult not to become politicised at such a time, for a social scientist who not only had views on what to do about the sorry state of the villages, but who expressed them publicly in the press. Fei was no Marxist, but one did not need to be a Marxist to see that the Kuomintang was not the best government for China. His second visit to England had left him with an enormous enthusiasm for the welfare state; he had taken eagerly to the Labour Government's policies, and he viewed socialist principles admiringly—even dreamily. But he was above all a Chinese, who believed that China ought neither to modernise in the American way nor go the way of the Russians; rather the Chinese should, he wrote, 'seek for our own society a way which will be suited to our own tradition and environment'.

It might be supposed that, as a leading proponent of rural development, Fei would have the ear of China's new communist masters, whose bases of support lay first in the countryside, and who rode to power on the back of the peasantry. This, however, was not the case. Under the new regime, China was to be developed in the Soviet way, with Stalinist central planning and priority given to heavy industry. Fei was heard to say some strange things—that he had urged a second-rate kind of development for the Chinese because he had underrated the power of the people to achieve real industrialisation once they were united. The only true science of society being Marxism–Leninism, sociology as a discipline, banned in the Soviet Union, was expunged in China. Fei was offered responsibilities in ethnographic work among China's ethnic minorities, but then came the Anti-

Rightist Campaign and the Cultural Revolution, and people like him, who had had such intimate links with foreign 'imperialists', were as good as finished. 'In a way', writes his American biographer David Arkush, 'There was symbolic truth in the published catalogue of the University of Michigan's Asia Library, which says he died in 1975.'

But with the great turn-around in Chinese policy in the late 1970s, Fei Xiaotong's much maligned views were honoured again. Both Fei and sociology were dusted down and restored to their rightful places. He was one of the judges at the trial of the Gang of Four; he revisited America; he was made director of the new Institute of Sociology in the Chinese Academy of Social Sciences; his books were reprinted; and he accompanied Hu Yaobang when the Party general secretary visited Britain on Margaret Thatcher's invitation in 1986. By a paradox of history, his proposals for reforming the rural economy, but forward in the 1940s, were found to be ideal for the Chinese countryside of the 1980s.

Fei's PhD dissertation for the London School of Economics—published as *Peasant Life in China: A Field Study of Country Life in the Yangtze Valley*— was an investigation of Jiangcun ('Yangtze Village') in his native southern Jiangsu province, and it was to the scene of that early endeavour that he repeatedly returned in the early 1980s, to conduct his new studies on the changes in the rural scene. Long ago he had written, 'An analysis of culture is the basis of planned reform.' Now he is back in the field again, more than ever the pundit of rural reform.

Neither in the 'forties, nor now, was Fei advocating the revival of old fashioned handicrafts; he was no Gandhi, promoting home cotton-spinning. He recognised the need for modern technology, but he did believe that other patterns of industrialisation than the one offered by the West were needed for China. His critics thought this sentimental of him: while most people looked to the urban factory, he looked to the country.

There does seem to be a nostalgia for pastoral values in Fei Xiaotong, even now. He once wrote, 'I am still turned to the countryside; my character and prejudices are still traditional. I cannot feel at ease in the tumult of Shanghai or the night life of Hong Kong. I seem unable to get rid of the ideal of life of one raised in Suzhou: a silk gown, satin shoes, and leisure in a teahouse.' Today, he is the country's chief exponent of the southern Jiangsu and Wenzhou models of development. When he revisited Jiangcun, and other small communities in southern Jiangsu, he was heartened by the thriving village industries. Here, he thought, was the kind of industrialisation he had been propounding all along. His long essay, setting down his reflections on what he saw, was entitled simply *Small Town, Big Issue*.

# 10

# WRONGDOERS

In the winter of 1982, during a visit I made to an aunt of mine in Hangzhou, her eldest daughter, my cousin, returned from the backwoods where she had been rusticated during the Cultural Revolution. My cousin's appearance proved brief, however, because although she had asked to be reunited with her family in Hangzhou, permission for her transfer had not yet been given by the authorities, and she was only in Hangzhou for a short visit.

When it was time for her to leave, I went to see her off at the railway station. I was amazed at the amount of luggage she had, and quickly supposed that she had used her time in Hangzhou to stock up on things hard to come by in the small county town in which she lived. But some of the things she was taking puzzled me: bottles of well-known wines and spirits, lengths of silk fabrics, at least four thermos flasks, and large quantities of cigarettes. Later I asked my aunt why my cousin needed such luxuries, when by all accounts her life in the country was extremely simple, not to say primitive. It turned out that the goods were not for my cousin at all, but for the local Party secretary who had it in his power to authorise or to thwart her transfer back to Hangzhou. They were a bribe, in other words.

This is only one of countless examples that illustrate the seamier side of life in China. I could just as easily cite the case of Weiwei and her husband, the childless couple I mentioned in the last chapter. Weiwei did not get to see a gynaecologist by playing by the rules, because that would have been far too slow, if not downright unfruitful. She used what is commonly called the 'back door'. A distant cousin, the recipient of many gifts from Weiwei's father (including, I discovered, the duty-free American cigarettes that I used to give him!), knew a pathologist at the hospital where the gynaecologist worked. And since that pathologist owed Weiwei's cousin a favour, and had at the same time done the gynaecologist a good turn, he was easily persuaded to arrange an appointment for Weiwei to see the gynaecologist ahead of the queue. What was more, the gynaecologist took far more pains with Weiwei than if she had entered as a total stranger by the 'front door'.

The personal connections exploited by Weiwei, her cousin and the pathologist, which led to the unlocking of the back door, are called *guanxi* in China. Chinese society is a web of such connections, each based on obligations and favours, and not to have them is like not having *blat* in the Soviet Union. The butcher will not put a cut of lean pork aside for you; your wife's old classmate at the cinema will not see to it that you get seats to the latest foreign movie; the bunks in the overnight boat will all have been taken; the surly receptionist at the guesthouse will insist there are no free rooms.

It is much more than an old boy network, when the society in which such connections operate is one where almost everything is bureaucratically allocated, and a large number of consumer goods, not to speak of luxury items, are scarce. In such a society, the people who control the distribution of scarce goods and services—the storekeepers, the shop assistants, the clerks who man the ticket counters, the taxi-drivers—are invested with enormous power. Even the casual visitor has to submit to this power system, feeling it in the petty tyrants who decline to notice you trying to catch their attention through the guichets, in the taxi-driver who refuses to understand that you are in a hurry and are desperate to catch a taxi. Each of these people rules over something he doesn't own, and from which he derives, not direct monetary benefit, but a power he can exercise in his relations or transactions with others.

All this adds up to fertile opportunities for corruption. Often enough the mere offer of a cigarette will turn an unheeding functionary into an instantly attentive one, but equally often one has to resort to one's network of *guanxi* or, like my cousin, to bigger bribes. In China one is always having to use irregular channels, because the regular ones are so clogged by red tape and bumbledom. 'Networking' infects the character of social relations of China on a grand scale, and though many a *guanxi* rests on bonds of true friendship, one is often left wondering how far one is valued for oneself, and how far for one's power or usefulness.

If people do not trust each other very much in China, it is also because they have seen how, come a political campaign, yesterday's confidant can become today's informer, betraying one's innermost thoughts to those who could use them as fodder for denunciation. The mass campaigns, the eradication of the private sphere by an insistence on the political character of all human relationships, and the setting of one group of citizens against another in the name of class struggle have left a legacy of suspicion, hatred and cynicism. They have left family ties stronger, but loyalties more ambiguous. The state of distrust and dissembling in which many have existed through the years has left a long trail of deep immorality, so that on the whole the Chinese now behave badly. Furthermore, the experience has persuaded a younger generation that for getting what you want out of life, nothing beats a good set of *guanxi*. These young people have seen enough unscrupulous, two-faced time-servers win not to set much store by probity themselves.

People who argue that *guanxi* and 'back-door' transactions are a characteristic of socialist countries have only to point to *blat* and its counterparts in other Eastern bloc countries, but those who say that they are historical symptoms would not find it hard to cite examples either. Social relations between Chinese individuals or families have traditionally been guided by a sort of mental balance sheet of favours rendered and received—'If I give a gift and nothing comes in return,' pronounces the Confucian classic *The Book of Rites*, 'that is contrary to propriety; if the thing comes to me, and I give nothing in return, that also is contrary to propriety.' The Chinese have always counted on their favours being returned, no matter how long it takes; and an element of 'you scratch my back and I'll scratch yours' has sustained Chinese exchanges all down the ages.

If the mandarinate of old was corrupt, so is the Party cadredom of today. The Chinese have always equated officialdom with corruption. 'After three years in a position of authority,' goes one of the old Chinese sayings, 'even an upright official is enriched.' It would not be going too far to say that, far from altering the pattern expressed by the saying, the present system of privilege, built on the principle of 'to each according to his official position', enshrines it.

Some abuses are petty, like the use of one's influence to get one's undeserving son a place at a university. Some are more serious, like the use of one's office for personal gain or for doing down an enemy. Nobody can be altogether certain which abuses are punishable and which not: the law (of which more later) is fuzzy on many points, and much depends on whether the perpetrator is highly placed enough. The ones at the top of the Party hierarchy enjoy a grand immunity, and China is full of stories of local Party bosses behaving criminally during the Cultural Revolution and getting away with it.

The people who most notoriously exploit this immunity are the *gaogan zidi*, a name to raise many hackles. Though the phrase only means 'offspring of high-ranking cadres', in the popular conception *gaogan zidi* are a reprehensible breed, pampered, arrogant and very often criminal. Their swagger, and the ingratiating way in which the rank and file responds to them, have provided a theme for a number of plays and stories. One of the best known of these is *What If I Were Real*, a play staged by the Shanghai Drama Company (and shown to a restricted audience on account of its controversial nature) in 1979. With a nod to Gogol's *The Government Inspector*, the play shows how well a humble young man does out of impersonating the son of a prominent cadre.

What gave the play added plausibility was the real-life case of Zhang Longquan, a young man who had the run of Shanghai because he pretended to be the son of Li Da, Deputy Chief of Staff of the People's Liberation Army. His story began with the difficulties he had in obtaining a ticket to see a popular production of *Much Ado About Nothing*. As a way out of his difficulty, he hit upon the idea of passing himself off as a *gaogan zidi*. The theatre responded obligingly—and so did almost everybody, Zhang

Longquan found, as he continued his deception into the highest circles of Shanghai society. Soon he was going about in a chauffeured limousine, and everywhere he went there were sycophants to fawn upon him. He was exposed when his neighbours reported him, but not before he had revealed the sickness in Chinese society. Upon his arrest he was supposed to have said, 'My only crime is that I am not the son of So-and-so. What if I really were his son?' These remarks were widely repeated in Shanghai, where in the popular mind Zhang was turned into something of a folk hero.

When Chinese Marxists talk of social classes, they talk of workers, peasants and the bourgeoisie. But the significant social divisions in Chinese society are not these. They are the ones which separate the privileged from the underprivileged, the ruling from the ruled. One of the most interesting changes to have flowed from Deng Xiaoping's reforms is an alteration in the structure of rights in Chinese society: it is not only position which opens doors now, but also money. The *guanxi* network has been overlaid by a cash nexus, and there has emerged a new social distinction, that of rich and poor, to complicate the scene. The change is welcomed by those who, debarred from certain privileges by reason of their humble social position, may at least now gain them by monetary means.

Of course the classes overlap, and all too often the privilegentsia and the moneyed are one and the same. There is much more room for private enterprise now, and Party and government cadres are often better placed than the rank and file to engage in it. Hundreds of thousands did, until a ban was placed in early 1986 against 'commercial involvement of the children and spouses of leading cadres' (the term 'leading cadres' to be understood to refer to those, active or retired, above the rank of county magistrate or People's Liberation Army regimental commander). In Hong Kong one is always hearing rumours of top Chinese officials stashing away their ill-gotten gains in foreign bank accounts, and fewer Chinese export orders would have been won by the foreign trader if he had not greased some official palms. The Chinese appetite has grown too, with expanding contacts and trade: a Japanese trader I once spoke to went so far as to say that he preferred doing business under the Gang of Four, 'because in those days people were pleased enough with pocket calculators and TV sets; now it has to be cars and computers.'

In early 1986 a nationwide crackdown on corruption was launched with considerable publicity, with the authorities undertaking to catch not just the small fry but the big 'tigers'. It was Party rectification, on a grand scale, of errant officials and their guilty relatives. The Party media were full of exposés of nefarious activities, and to go by the newspaper headlines one would think that corruption had seeped into every corner of the vast bureaucracy. But it has to be remembered that campaigns in China are often an occasion for one faction in the top leadership to discredit another, or even to wipe it out. It is tantalising to see the new clean-up drive as having fateful consequences for the balance of power between the reform camp and the leftist-conservative camp. For it was a vicious affair, shot through with factional conflict, growing ever more vicious the higher it went up the Party hierarchy.

We shall never know the true scale of corruption in China, and how it compares with countries like India and Indonesia. The Chinese public believes it to be rampant, applauding the Party each time it indulges in one of its periodic orgies of self-recrimination. Hu Yaobang once listed the things he thought wrong with Party officials, but no one present at the speech would think he was hearing anything new: 'Party cadres are', Hu said, 'double-dealing, agreeing with the Central Committee's policies in public and disagreeing with them in private. They use their official positions for private gain and string-pulling. They raise the cultivation of useful connections to the level of art, and go in blatantly for gift-giving and bribery. Instead of admitting their own mistakes, they use their authority to frame and take revenge on innocent people. They resort to deception; there are people who go in for personality cults in the Party, but equally there are people ready to pander to them, doing nothing but toady these past few decades. Finally, they go to extraordinary lengths to evade responsibility.'

The anti-corruption campaign got off to a ferocious start with the conviction and execution of two *gaogan zidi*, Hu Xiaoyang and Chen Xiaomeng, in Shanghai. They and four other young men, it seemed, had between them individually raped or gang-raped six women, and attempted to rape, seduce or indecently dally with forty-two other women. (For 'rape', as I suggested once before, one must sometimes read 'seduction'; men accused of sexual assault or immorality in China frequently turn out to have been guilty only of having slept with a larger than usual number of women, not necessarily without their consent.) These young men had apparently been doing this for some years, living only for the gratification of their sexual passions. The place where it all happened was Chen's private dance hall, a dimly lit room on the first floor of the building where he lived, and to which young women—not all as innocent as had been made out, one would guess—were lured. Because Hu and Chen were the sons of two VIPs—the chairman of the Municipal People's Congress, and the former deputy Party chief of propaganda in Shanghai—their execution was a sop to the public hatred of the privileged and their immunity. There, the authorities seemed to be saying, we *are* delivering on our promise to strike at the children of bigwigs. The affair was given much publicity, with the two men, their heads bowed and arms bound, paraded before a crowd of several thousand spectators, and shown on television being driven off to be shot. The people of Shanghai were driven into transports of delight.

Other heads rolled as the campaign proceeded. The Party fell upon Zhou Erfu, a seventy-two-year-old writer who misbehaved when, as the vice-chairman of the People's Association for Friendship with Foreign Countries, he went on a trip to Japan. Against the advice of the Chinese embassy in Tokyo, Zhou had visited the Yasukuni Shrine, the military cemetery so distasteful to the Chinese, who can only think of it as a symbol of Japanese wartime atrocities. But what capped his indiscretion was Zhou's prurience. He had not only availed himself of certain services in the red light district, and bought Japanese aphrodisiacs, but he had watched a pornographic film in his hotel room, and further 'compromised national dignity' by asking his woman interpreter to help him understand the Japanese dialogue. The Party's central discipline inspection commission sacked the hapless writer from his job and expelled him from the Party; this caused a stir because Zhou was the first person of ministerial prominence to have been expelled from the Party.

Still, to outside observers the excitement of the campaign owed much more to the revelations which touch the top leadership itself. One of the most startling exposés to come out of the campaign was the case of Mrs Fu Yan, the head of an import–export firm and the daughter, it turned out, of Peng Zhen, the politburo member and chairman of the standing committee of the People's Congress. By taking a bribe of a dollar for every ton of coal she sold below the official rate, she had earned $300,000 in kickbacks. Another of the more surprising victims the campaign claimed was Hu Shiying, the son of no less a personage than Hu Qiaomu, the Party ideological watchdog. Not only had the younger Hu made off with part of the fees he had collected for a correspondence course (on law, ironically) which never materialised, but at least sixteen girls had come forward to accuse him of having trifled with them sexually. As 'rape' can be punishable by death in China, we may, a Hong Kong periodical tells us, start thinking of Hu Shiying in obituary terms. But he was to be released from house arrest upon the fall of Hu Yaobang—one more indication of how far China still is from the rule of law.

Also brought to book was Ye Zhifeng, who was given a seventeen-year jail sentence for 'revealing State secrets' to foreign car exporters. She is the daughter of the vice-chairman of the standing committee of the People's Congress, and one of those people whose arrogance forfeits all one's sympathy. It was a French car exporter who reported her, for pocketing a 'commission' for a deal which subsequently didn't come off. Upon investigation, it was found that she had done something more: she had tried to help a Hong Kong exporter sell cars to China by informing him of impending import policy changes and by advising him to backdate a contract to circumvent such changes. Of courses she was rewarded for her help; among other bribes she received an air conditioner from the Hong Kong businessman. Her partner in crime, a young man who is said to have directed the whole affair, was executed.

The man in the street was ecstatic when they got Liu Shikun, the renowned pianist and the former son-in-law of the redoubtable Marshal Ye Jianying (last seen in these pages retiring from the politburo). As a celebrated concert pianist and a relative of one of the country's top families, Liu did not lack opportunity for travel abroad—nor, it seemed, for gold speculation and drug smuggling.

Rumours of corruption approach the very apex of national power. There is substance to these rumours. We hear of Zhao Ziyang's son, Zhao Dajun, making a fortune in Shenzhen. We hear of one of Hu Yaobang's sons heading a big corporation. We hear of Chen Yun's son using—and losing—public funds in a joint venture with a Japanese concern. We even hear of Deng Xiaoping's son-in-law running an investment firm in Macao. Of course they may be doing nothing venal, or even wrong, and nepotism may have nothing to do with it; but still one cannot help finding it anomalous, when they are so closely allied to the sources of power and protection, and it is enough to be So-and-so's son to be a success.

The increase in the temptations to corruption, brought about by the recrudescence of the profit motive and the open door, perhaps indicates a return to form, for revolutionary rectitude is not as deep as it may have appeared to foreigners who visited the country in the 1970s. Certainly there is no lack of what the Chinese call 'economic crimes', from fraud and peculation to smuggling.

A survey of the recent crime scene in China might well start with a man known as Moneybags Du, as bold a swindler as ever appeared in China. The fifty-three-year-old Du was a humble clerk in the Road and Highway Bureau of the southern coastal province of Fujian before he decided to go into business. He hadn't a penny to his name, but this did not in the least deter him. Within ten months he was richer by about $70 million. How had he done it? By playing upon people's greed and gullibility. Claiming to have close connections with investors in Hong Kong, Taiwan and other overseas Chinese, he had signed bogus contracts, set up dummy companies, and had had dozens of organisations, including the Bank of China and a number of government bodies, scrambling for his bribes. Besides speculating in foreign currency, he engaged in large-scale smuggling and profiteering, colluding with some crooked Hong Kong businessmen, and diverting merchant vessels to berths controlled by his cronies. It took a special squad of a hundred cadres to catch Du and all his accomplices, so grand was the scale on which they had operated. When news of the scandal broke, it shook the whole of Fujian province; the hoodwinked officials were flabbergasted. The *People's Daily*, the Party paper, was suitably reproving:

'Some of our Party members have completely disarmed themselves ideo-logically,' it said, 'sold their honour for money, forsaken their communist spirit and the Party's goal and programmes, and degenerated into sinners.'

Often in China crimes are committed not so much for personal gain as for the good of a work unit or locality. Whole departments or villages may be involved. The Hainan Island affair, it will be recalled, was one such case: there the predominant motive was to enrich a laggardly area, and little money actually ended up in the leaders' pockets. In other cases, as part of a long-standing conflict between Us and Them, the State is cheated of its taxes so that there may be more money left for an enterprise and its staff bonuses.

A greater rise, by far, than that of any crime in China is the increase in serious larceny (the word 'serious' designating any instance in which the stolen amount exceeds 1,000 yuan). Gone are the days when a foreign visitor to China could leave his belongings unattended, in the assurance that nobody would think of touching them. Now there are thieves about in the hotels where foreigners stay. The twenty-five-year-old Duan Xiaohua, a tourist guide for the China Youth Travel Service in Shaanxi, was one of the most remarkable. He concentrated on hotel rooms, obtaining the keys to them from receptionists by posing as a Japanese tourist. He was well-dressed enough to be plausible, and his imitation of a Japanese accent was always persuasive. It was four years before the police were on to him; by then he had successfully pulled off thirty-one burglaries, seventeen in his home town of Xian, and fourteen in Peking. The son of a veteran Party official, Duan had the help of his two brothers, and an indulgent supporter in his mother, an architect. He is sure of an entry in the annals of crime in China because, to return all the stolen articles to their foreign owners—the traveller's cheques, the foreign exchange certificates, the cameras, watches and cassette tape-recorders—the Xian and Peking police had to seek the help of Interpol.

So rapidly has larceny proliferated that a new industry, a private security service, has come into being to deal with it. In Canton, China's busiest centre of private trading, hundreds of uniformed security agents may now be seen patrolling the markets and guarding office entrances, most of them ex-servicemen trained in legal procedures and the martial arts. They are called 'private bodyguards' by Canton's citizens, and the name is apt because they are directly hired by their clients to protect them from theft and other harms. Many of the crudest and most unsavoury men in China are to be found in the free markets of the larger cities, and fights frequently break out between shoppers who protest against overcharging and private vendors who are nothing but grasping, unlicensed profiteers.

Another great consumer grievance is the tyranny of scalpers, who buy up tickets for railway sleepers and terrorise passengers into paying extra for them, or who exact a fee for a place in the queue. Many of these are young and jobless, people of the underbelly of society, who often work together in small gangs, and who can be sinister and dangerous. In transport, as in most other services in China, supply falls critically short of demand, so the proliferation of scalpers has been inevitable, especially as people are now travelling far more, for business or pleasure, than ever before.

The lifting of economic controls is open to countless abuses, and the new entrepreneurship all too often flowers in criminal ways. One of the commonest ways of being cheated these days is to be sold a fake. The papers are full of such cases. In one, the purchasing agent of a food company in the southern coastal province of Fujian had sold more than 20,000 kilogrammes of fake monosodium glutamate ('gourmet powder') before anyone discovered that the product was actually a sham mixture of sugar, salt and starch. In another, tons of aluminium ingots were passed off for silver in Hebei province. The racket, involving whole townships and villages, had the blessing of at least twenty-five government and Party officials, who must have thought there were graver crimes than helping to create rural industry and to enrich the local populace and themselves.

From time to time reports of immoral goings-on appear in the papers. The existence of prostitution may not particularly strike the innocent stranger, but the seasoned traveller will attest to it as a fact. China is very far from reviving the sing-song house—it is many years since socialism chivvied the pimps and madams into obscurity—but there are always women willing to sell their sexual favours for money. This is truer of Canton, with its relative uninhibitedness, its streams of business visitors and its proximity to Hong Kong, than of any other Chinese city. Periodic crackdowns excite the city, where taxi-drivers have been known to be sent off for 'reform through labour' for being procurers or for using their cars as brothels-on-wheels.

Occasionally one reads of crimes of passion, and of people being knifed or poisoned in some sexual connection. At other times one hears of people lashing out at each other in a bust-up, and of one or more men being killed in a brawl. It has lately been noticed that the violent side of Chinese behaviour can be greatly aggravated by drink. Though the Chinese seem in some periods of their past to have been very fond of alcohol—the drunken poet is a compelling historical figure—they are nowadays not generally thought of as topers. Drink in China is not the scourge that it is in the Soviet Union, and one sees few drunkards in the streets of Canton or Peking. But still it is a release from the day-to-day humdrum for many, and an absolute must at banquets and dinner parties. It does not threaten the country with a possibility of widespread alcoholism, but it does seem to contribute to crime.

This was found to be the case in Qinghai, the province in China's wild west to which criminals are regularly transported. A branch office of the Public Security Bureau in Xining, the provincial capital, gives these figures for the proportion of offences committed under the influence of drink in 1982: 40 per cent of the 471 criminal cases handled; 70 per cent of the 327 breaches of public order. A very large number of the offenders were found to be young people and, of these, 60 per cent were found to have been affected by drink.

It is among the young that the rising crime rate in China has been the most alarming, the breakdown of public morality most obviously extreme. What causes the public security authorities added anxiety is that the youthful law-breakers are getting younger and younger. Of course juvenile delinquency in China is nowhere near as common as it is in many Western countries, but it is the sharp increase that the authorities find unsettling. At first sight this is a consequence of unemployment, but while it is true that the jobless are obvious mayhem fodder, in recent years children not yet out of school have increasingly contributed to the crime figures. Indeed, it was the finding of an investigation by the People's University that many begin their life of mischief at eleven or twelve, reaching the peak of their juvenile criminal careers at fifteen, sixteen or seventeen.

The commonest juvenile offences are said to be robbery, rape and hooliganism (which covers many kinds of unruly behaviour, from vandalism to starting a fracas in a public place). In the spring of 1986 I visited what was called a 'disciplinary institution for young criminals' in Chengdu, Sichuan's provincial capital, and was told by the wardens that the 800-odd male inmates were being held there for robbery, theft, rape and manslaughter. The chief warden at the Chengdu reformatory impressed me by saying that there was no simple answer to the question of why his young charges took to crime, though he laid some of the blame on bad upbringing and unsatisfactory relationships with parents and teachers. I was told that social scientists and psychologists were amassing data to try and explain the rising tide of delinquency in China, and to discover the conditions that produced it. He struck me as being thoughtful, or perhaps more honest, than Ruan Chongwu, the then new Minister of Public Security, who said in a published interview in 1985 that one of the reasons for the rise in juvenile delinquency was that 'the corrupt ideas and pornographic video tapes and books creeping in through Hong Kong, Macao and other channels are poisoning the minds of our youth'.

Both Ruan Chongwu and the chief of the Chengdu reformatory were agreed, though, that education was the ultimate social weapon, and that by its use better moral standards could be achieved. It is entirely in the spirit of Marxism to presuppose that man is wholly conditioned by the circumstances of his existence, and to deem his virtues to be the product of ideal conditions of life and not of his own free will. The reformatory devotes many hours to 'moral education', lessons on how to become a better man. The aim of the enterprise, summed up by the phrase *ganhua rencuo*, is to help a misguided person change by persuasion and example, and to bring him round to acknowledging the error of his ways. Seeing themselves as social engineers, the wardens only consider their jobs done when the guilty are truly contrite. But the system is also designed to raise an inmate's fitness for the workforce, and this implies teaching him a useful skill or vocation. He will usually have done badly at school, habitually playing truant or dropping out altogether, and the reformatory continues an inmate's interrupted education.

Some of the boys were in for 'reform through labour', a criminal sanction requiring that charges be laid and the accused brought before a court. Others were undergoing 're-education through labour', an administrative penalty imposed by the Public Security Bureau without recourse to the courts. Their ages ranged between fourteen and eighteen. They looked fresh-scrubbed and disciplined to a man. The rate of recidivism was said to be low, at 5 per cent. In cell block after cell block, I saw spotless dormitories, each with fourteen neatly made-up bunk beds; in one I glimpsed four or five picture postcards and a pin-up of a Hong Kong songstress, Xu Jie, on a far wall. The wardens admitted with pride that, as reform schools went, this was certainly one of the most agreeable. Prisons are a different matter. To go by a place like Gongdelin ('Virtue Forest'), a gaol-cum-mandatory shelter for beggars and vagrants in the northern outskirts of Peking, they are ghastly hell-holes, crowded, dirty, and brutalising. Similarly, inferno yawns behind the gates of the detention centre in Shanghai's Huangpu district, where a chillingly ingenious method is practised for breaking a newcomer in. He is simply thrown into a cell where a bunch of hardened criminals—the toughest, most pugnacious and most vicious hooligans in the centre—await him.

When the law operates in China, it operates implacably. In 1985, Deng Xiaoping is said to have told a group of officials, 'I have killed a batch of people.' This was a chilling reference to the wave of executions which swept across the country in the summer of 1983, in the wake of a massive anti-crime crackdown. It is well known how executions are carried out in China: the victims are taken to a field, their hands are bound and they are told to kneel down, and then a shot is fired into the back of the neck. Excepting people under eighteen and pregnant women, the death penalty is to be applied to those who commit 'the most heinous crimes', states the criminal code of the People's Republic. One example of 'heinous' crime is that of a thirty-five-year-old farmer in Shaanxi province who was executed in 1986 for dismantling thirty-four electric transformers used in irrigation and selling the parts for scrap, thereby damaging acres of crops. What perhaps compounded his crime was that he had been arrested before—he had served a twelve-year sentence for stealing railway equipment—and should have known better. What matters, the law strongly suggests, is repentance; nothing will undo a criminal more than obduracy.

The formal Chinese criminal code only came into being in 1980; previously a quote by Chairman Mao could be the ultimate arbiter of correct behaviour. Party bosses could, and did, act arbitrarily and without accountability. During the Cultural Revolution the legal system was as good as extinguished. In any case, it had not occurred to many Chinese that theirs must be a society subject to the rule of law, and it is only in recent years that the idea has come into the forefront of public debate. A body of laws is being hammered out, and though the Chinese socialist legal system started life with a Soviet stamp, it has now moved closer to Western jurisprudence. The trend is inseparable from the changes taking place in China's trade and economy, and it was her pursuit of an open door policy, for instance, which set the pace for the rapid codification of her commercial law.

Hand in hand with the construction of a legal system suited to new needs goes a programme to publicise it. This is uphill work: in traditional China law was merely a code which told the people what not to do, and what punishments would ensue if they disobeyed. As for civil matters such as marriage and inheritance, they were generally settled by the old traditions. The law was enforced in a Confucian manner, differentiating in its scale of punishments between the two basic classes of society, the noble and the mean (or the Confucian 'gentleman' and the 'small man'), and recognising the demands of family ethic and filial piety, so that sons could be pardoned for killing their father's murderers, and a man sentenced to death might have his sentence commuted if he had to look after aged parents or grandparents. The Chinese are now trying to create a contemporary system out of an order that has always been based upon older values. Not long ago an old man was astonished to find himself arrested for murder; he had killed his son, whose habitual thieving and fighting he had repeatedly failed to curb, in a fit of anger, and he had not thought it particularly wrong to have done so, for wasn't he the father, and hadn't he performed a public service by ridding society of a troublemaker?

A further obstacle faced by the law as it tries to develop its own independent existence in China is the supremacy of the Party. Real law recognises no exceptions; before it all citizens are equal. The system which prevails in China is not this impersonal law, but a kind of socialist legality: people are subject to written law, but at the same time they are subject to certain rules for applying these laws, and these can vary with the category of people, with the interests of the Party or even of the nation, with the Party directive operating at any given moment or the ideological campaign running at the time, or simply with circumstances. The years ahead are likely to see a strengthening of the judiciary, but it will prove hard to set the absolute authority of the law above that of the Party. In both criminal and civil cases, Party discipline has all along superseded judicial procedure, and different standards have always applied to Party and non-Party members.

Still, better times have come for the courts and the procuracy, which until recently were little used in the criminal process, this being administered almost entirely by the public security apparatus. Public security officers in China seldom feel themselves to be just crime fighters; they are peace-keepers, guardians of the socialist order. They are part of the reach of Party and government into the daily life of every Chinese citizen. It is with the police that births, deaths, and changes of residence are registered; it was the police, too, who issued the ration coupons needed to buy grain, cloth, cooking oil and other necessities.

Around the authority of the police is assembled a whole range of control mechanisms, from neighbourhood committees to informers and busybodies. No one escapes supervision: put a foot wrong here, and a member of the neighbourhood committee, usually a prying, middle-aged woman, will report you; put a foot wrong there, and an entry will be made in the dossier kept by your workplace. How to rationalise the maintenance of social order is something the Chinese instinctively know, from their long history of sophisticated political administration, and there is not much that Lenin or the KGB could teach them.

Police action was little inhibited by rules and regulations, before the codification of law. It is no exaggeration to say that public security officers could punish trouble-makers as they pleased, by pinning on them the tag of 'counter-revolutionary'. In theory the authorities no longer have so much leeway; but under the new laws political dissenters may still be arrested for 'counter-revolutionary' activity, and the quashing of poli-tical opposition continues to lie near the heart of the public security apparatus.

On a May day in 1983, a thirty-nine-year-old man called Qu Youyuan was declared an enemy of the people and arrested by public security officials. Qu published an 'illegal' poetry magazine called *Eyes* in the northeastern city of Changchun; a vehicle for political protest, this ran for four issues before it was suppressed by the provincial government. The authorities, reviewing the evidence they had collected on Qu, branded him a counter-revolutionary. What else, they must have asked themselves, could be said about a person who wrote such lines as these?

The seeds of Marxism–Leninism
Mutated
In this ancient soil.
Into what did it mutate—
Socialist feudalism,
Socialist autocracy,
Or socialist fascism?

Qu Youyuan knew that trouble was bound to come. Far from being cowed though, he told his colleagues on the magazine, 'I'm not as timid as you are when I write; I'm prepared to go to gaol.... If I'm banned I'll just go down to the countryside and castrate pigs. I've got my knife ready.' Publicly and privately, Qu had made no bones about his distaste for China's ruling class, the vast bureaucracy which he termed 'the new exploiters, the new parasites' who live by the blood and sweat of the people. It is not so much Marxism that repels him, more the Communist Party which it inspires, and which, once it has seized power, degenerates into a privileged ruling caste of oppressive cadres. All single-Party regimes, Qu claims, are counter-revolutionary; and while it is commonly made out that the horror of the Cultural Revolution was an aberration, Qu insists that, on the contrary, it was the Communist Party at its most expressive. None of the most reprehensible protagonists, Qu observes, 'from Lin Biao and the Gang of Four down to the Party secretary of the rural production brigade, was not a Party member'. And nothing, he reckons, 'has wreaked more suffering on the Chinese people than the Communist Party'. It is up to poets to raise their voices for the people, because 'their eyes are the clearest'; it is for art and literature to assault tradition and feudalism, the battle against which, in Qu's opinion, could only be won through a bourgeois democratic revolution.

The word 'democracy', along with terms like 'autocracy' and 'bureaucratic feudalism', had marked the vocabulary of the dissident movement which flowered in China in 1978–79. This was a time of lively debate and excitement, of rising hopes, and, finally, of almost total silence. The movement was brought into being by the righting of the official denigration of an earlier protest, the Gate of Heavenly Peace Incident of April 5, 1976. The incident, which began with tens of thousands of people gathering spontaneously to honour the cherished memory of the late Zhou Enlai, and also to express their hatred for the Gang of Four, had ended in rioting and mass arrests. Deng Xiaoping, yet to emerge completely from political limbo, was blamed for the disturbance, but no sooner had he regained power than the sentences passed on the rioters were revoked. The rioters were no counter-revolutionaries, it was declared, and this reappraisal of the popular demonstration gave a fresh impetus to the burgeoning dissident movement.

The movement found a focus and emblem in a long, grey wall—the closest such wall to the Forbidden City—near the Xidan intersection in downtown Peking. This, the famous Democracy Wall, was where political posters went up, crowds gathered, and 'underground' magazines were sold. It was where the manifesto 'The Fifth Modernisation', later to be translated and published in dozens of books in the West, appeared, signed by one Wei Jingsheng, a one-time Red Guard employed as an electrician in the Peking public parks administration. By the Fifth Modernisation Wei meant democracy, the only goal which, in his opinion, gave the Four meaning. 'Freedom and happiness,' he declared, were what people wanted to achieve with modernisation; they wanted to be masters of their own destiny and, without that fifth modernisation, all the others were illusory. To publicise these ideas Wei and a friend edited a mimeographed paper they called *Explorations*, one of about fifty-five such papers which circulated in Peking.

People like Wei Jingsheng were the nearest China came to having dissidents, so they were made much of by foreign reporters. When Wei Jingsheng was arrested in the spring of 1979, and tried six months later, his having consorted with foreigners, and spoken to one of them of China's war with Vietnam, was held against him. He was found guilty of 'counter-revolutionary crimes of a serious nature', and sentenced to fifteen years' imprisonment. His appeal was denied. 'You have read it yourself', the prosecutor said. 'It is decreed in our Constitution that there is freedom of belief. You can believe or not believe in Marxism–Leninism and the Thought of Mao Zedong as you wish, but you are absolutely not permitted to oppose them. . . .' Amnesty International protested, but Wei Jingsheng could not be left at liberty. Despite some support from abroad, Wei remains in solitary confinement in a prison near Peking. It is another seven years to the end of his sentence, and his mental health is already said to be seriously deteriorating.

Also behind bars or in labour camps are many other prisoners of conscience. One of the most prominent of these is Xu Wenli, editor of the *April Fifth Forum*, a periodical named for the Gate of Heavenly Peace Incident. Born the son of a Red Army doctor in 1943, and the devoted father of a daughter named after Qiu Jin, a famous Chinese woman revolutionary, Xu is by no means opposed to Marxism, or to the régime for that matter. He is one of those people who would protest at being described as a 'dissident', for that would imply opposition to the State, and he objected only to the doctrinaire Maoist elements in it. He didn't think he had any quarrel with the reformers, the group led by Deng Xiaoping; and neither open opposition to Marxism nor naïve demands for human rights would win much sympathy from him. Yet the views he aired could easily be seen as subversive, however confused they might seem to more realistic minds— the setting up of a proletarian two-party or multi-party system 'under the conditions of socialism'; the establishment of an organisation, with perhaps its head office in Hong Kong, to link up Taiwan's democracy movement with the mainland's and to work together for the unification of China.

If there continues to be a democracy movement in China, with so many of its activists behind bars, it is lying very low. But it is not entirely dispersed, and a group of Chinese students, led by one Wang Bingzhang, has come forward to carry it on abroad. Wang had completed a combined course of study for an MD and PhD at McGill University when he announced in New York in November, 1982 that he was remaining in the West to continue the fight. The group held its first international representative conference in New York a year later, and fifty-three delegates from across the world attended. Wang and his fellow-organisers claim to be in touch with an underground network in China, and a magazine they publish, *China Spring*, is full of articles purportedly written by insiders. Wang even claims to have sympathisers in the public security apparatus in Peking; it was with their help, it seems, that a 241-page self-defence Xu Wenli had written in prison was smuggled out of China to New York. The chronicle, plus some letters Xu had written to his wife and daughter, saw the light of day in the pages of *China Spring* in 1985–86, and no sooner did this happen than Xu was punished with solitary confinement in a windowless cell.

What did *Eyes, Explorations, April Fifth Forum, China Spring* and all those other 'unofficial' journals press for, as they sprang one by one into being? Democracy, one reads in their pages, human rights and political pluralism. Yet there is no very clear conception of what these words mean, and if the democracy movement is to be remembered for its idealism and courage, it will also be remembered for its innocence and naïveté. Certainly there were moments when Chinese dissidence, or at least some segments of it, seemed naïvely to idealise the American system, equating material prosperity with democracy and addressing open letters to President Jimmy Carter (one of them suggesting that he intervened on behalf of any Chinese citizen arrested for exercising the right of free speech). Speaking to some anonymous dissenters in 1982, I was uncomfortably reminded of the unquestioning faith in the immense capabilities of the American political system of the immediate post-war period. But equally there were times when Chinese dissidence seemed to assume Russian forms, speaking in voices which could just as easily have come from a *samizdat* journal. At the same time the movement was true to Chinese tradition in its concern with the political roots of China's stagnancy, and with the question of the form of government best suited to her advancement towards modernity.

This is a familiar concern, reaching back at least a hundred years. Some of the most impassioned thinkers then had concluded that China could not afford liberal democracy, and that to achieve national strength and unity of purpose, and to survive in the ferociously competitive century upon which she had entered, she had to plump for enlightened autocracy. Chinese traditional preferences are against the democracy movement, the preference for a strong ruler to 'keep the ring' while competing interests fight it out among themselves, the preference for order and conformity. To the traditional Chinese view, the important question about dictatorship is not so much how far it will hold the country back as how securely it will keep it together. (One can make a case out of Hong Kong for the idea that the Chinese are not natural democrats; there, as we saw, many leading citizens have made it all too clear that they have little time for democratic reforms, seeing political plurality and competitive elections as unhelpful to the continued booming of the economy.)

The notion of a plurality of interests, as well as being alien to Chinese tradition, is at odds with the historical materialist view that conflicts in society are reducible to a basic clash between a progressive class and a reactionary one. The progressive class having triumphed in China, there is no longer any justification for more than one interest in society; this one interest is represented, as part of its historical mission, by the Communist Party. The idea of social harmony, of the absence of irreconcilable interests, is essential to the theoretical justification of the existence of the Party leadership, which is that it is able to rule in the interests of all. China would fall apart as a nation, her rulers insist, if it were not for the authority of the Party. The last thing they want is a Chinese version of the Polish Solidarity movement.

The Party's primacy is deemed unchallengeable, and whoever is not with it is against it, or in league with an external enemy. The idea of the likes of Wei Jingsheng defying the Party with impunity is intolerable. Whatever happened, Deng Xiaoping asserted, the Party's primacy must never be questioned. To underline this, he laid down 'four principles' for everyone to follow. Presently to be written into the preamble of the 1982 Constitution, these were the proletarian democratic dictatorship, Marxism–Leninism and Mao Zedong Thought, Communist Party leadership, and the socialist road. As for democracy, it was the 'disciplined and orderly' socialist kind that China should aspire to, and not the liberal bourgeois variety. In any case, the Party's view was that the people were not yet fitted to run their own affairs, and that it knew best where their highest interests lay.

Democracy Wall was closed at midnight on December 7, 1979. A water truck arrived an hour later to hose it down. At the wall were two soldiers, a policeman, and a number of foreign journalists, including the BBC correspondent Philip Short. He reported that fifty municipal street cleaners, men and women armed with scrapers and old-fashioned twig brooms, worked until 4 a.m. to scrub it clean. But there were places where the ink had come off and soaked into the grey brick.

Still, the quelling of dissent did not herald a return to Maoist witch-hunting. China's leaders have pledged an end to 'class struggle', and this is reflected in the new definition of 'counter-revolution'. The shift may not be apparent in the description of 'counter-revolution' in the new criminal code, which has it as any act 'endangering the People's Republic of China committed with the goal of overthrowing the political power of the dictatorship of the proletariat and the socialist system'. This is vague enough, it is true, and the words 'endangering the People's Republic' can be stretched to include any form of opposition the Party wishes to suppress. All the same the meaning which 'counter-revolution' has today is a far cry from what it had in the heyday of the class struggle. In those days, a bizarre method for delimiting counter-revolutionaries or class enemies prevailed, a quota system under which the political leadership simply decided what proportion of the Chinese population was counter-revolutionary, and gave the figure to the Party and the police to fill. For a very long time, the ratio of people to class enemies was set at 19:1, so that every twentieth Chinese was by definition a class enemy. The effect of this may easily be imagined: concerned to meet their quotas, the authorities simply apprehended whoever they pleased, no matter now innocent or loyal. Gross violations of human rights were commonplace, and the temptations to them persist among many activists to this day.

Since then, the Party leadership *has* tried to lessen conflict and discontent, and to liberalise the system slightly. Under a set of political reforms adopted in 1980 to adapt the system to the economic changes, elections were held, delegates voted to county people's congresses, some forms of democracy (if not its substance) were introduced to the Chinese people for the first time.    The trouble is that, in their attempts to lessen Party control, the reform- minded leaders often succeed only in accentuating the resistance of other more conservative power-holders, and end up having to harden their line against all antagonism or defiance, whether this stems from threatened vested interests or democratic activists.

Be that as it may, the top leaders have periodically admitted in public that China could not be a modern country until she had made herself democratic, though when they spoke of political reform, they seemed only to have had administrative reform in mind. They certainly did not mean the kind of political change urged upon them by those they condemned as 'bourgeois liberals'. One of these, Fang Lizhi, the astrophysicist the international press has called the Chinese Sakharov, has said that in China 'the very ABCs of democracy are unknown'.

Fang Lizhi is a courageous and admirable person, a hero among China's political dissidents and students; but one wonders, from his answer to a question put to him in an interview by the former China correspondent of *Der Spiegel*, if even he understands the relationship between democracy and economic development very well. He was asked, 'Is democracy really a necessary condition for the development of a country? States like Taiwan, South Korea, Singapore and the crown colony of Hong Kong have made enormous economic progress without being true democracies.'

His answer, to my mind a very unsatisfactory one, was, 'First of all, in the countries you named there is far more democracy than in China. Secondly, those countries are under American protection, and the US wish their economies to develop. In the case of China things are different. Moreover, in China it is particularly difficult to separate economic from political democracy.' The level of political discourse in China, even among her intellectuals, is not that high. But this is not to deny the value of what Fang Lizhi does: the Chinese leadership can hardly be reminded too much or too often that 'Man should be allowed,' as Fang Lizhi put it, 'to criticise his leaders without fear.'

Will the Chinese populace be given more than just a nibble of political liberty in the forseeable future? I asked three thinking Chinese what they thought. One, a sceptical political scientist who has emigrated to Britain, said that he was not optimistic, because democracy is so alien to Chinese tradition. Another, a cousin who lives in southern China, set much greater store by it. 'Without political change,' she said, 'the economic restructuring will be stymied.' My third informant, a one-time student activist and enthusiast of competitive elections, began by saying that the expiry of the democracy movement had taught its supporters to moderate their aspirations. I then asked him what kind of freedom he wanted to see in China. 'The kind they have in Yugoslavia,' was his modest answer.

# 11

# FREE EXPRESSION?

Sometimes it is hard to believe that it has been eight years since a 'thaw' occurred in the Chinese arts scene. In the spring of 1986, a Chinese writer I had better not name turned down a request I made through a mutual friend for an interview; he was afraid that it would land him in trouble with the political authorities to talk to a stranger from a foreign country. This is not a reaction one often gets from writers today, some of whom are all too eager to talk to foreigners. But the man I had asked to see had been a victim of the Anti-Rightist campaign of 1957, persecuted and silenced for twenty years for doing no more than accept Mao Zedong's invitation to 'let a hundred flowers bloom'. And that experience for him has not receded into history, but haunts him still.

His is an uncertain profession. There are writers and writers, and which category one falls into is decided by the State. One recognised writer I know draws a fat salary and spends seven months of the year on the Peking-Euro-American conference circuit. By contrast, another writer could be a non-person. In between are those who are neither 'official' nor 'non-official', neither fully recognised by the State nor entirely discredited by it. How one fares in the profession depends on the kind of work one produces, one's relationship to magazine editors and, above all, on the climate in the wider political arena.

The heat is turned on and off for writers, depending on the political climate. These alternations are intertwined with the stop–go approach the top leadership takes to the economy and other policy areas, and are ultimately traceable to the balance of inner-Party power. The fate of a piece of contentious writing is bound up with that balance, and a writer could be banned one minute and back in print the next. As one writer put it to me in a recent interview. 'There is actually no clear policy on the arts. What appear to be the vagaries of cultural policy are really the swings of the political balance between left and right, though both groups are agreed that there should be limits to the scope of permissiveness, and no-go areas into which we writers mustn't venture. Whenever unwelcome change appears to be on the way, be it a decline in the moral tone of society or a rise in the divorce rate, we artists are always the first to take the rap for it.'

Since 1978 the fortunes of writers have fluctuated. With the rise of the dissident movement in the autumn of 1978, something akin to *samizdat* surfaced in China. Much new writing saw the light of day in unofficial journals. The most famous of the mimeographed literary magazines to spring up was *Today*, which ran to all of nine issues before the Public Security Bureau ordered it to stop publication. *Today* represented the literary impulses of a new generation of writers—of whom the buzzword 'emergent', liberally applied in the economic sphere, has been used by Chinese critics. What its contributors proposed—that a poem or a novel is first of all a thing in itself, not necessarily to be approached through politics—is taken for granted in much of the world but was almost revolutionary in China. Other writers had sounded the note of rebellion before them, but this was something different from a challenge to authority or an exposé of the practice of corrupt politics. What these people wanted was the right to artistic truth, privately and individually pursued.

When the public voice of the dissenting movement was silenced by official suppression, the poets and short-story writers were put on the defensive too. Though some were later accepted into the literary establishment, others remained in limbo. A number of these came under attack in the campaign against 'spiritual pollution', an exercise which, as we saw earlier, sent liberals and controversial writers into retreat. Poets who emulated European modernist techniques were particularly subject to abuse, for the literary community was dominated by a generation of writers who, with few exceptions, had produced dull or Party-line works themselves and who were not favourably disposed towards adventurous or new writing.

The campaign went off the boil in the spring of 1984, and by the start of 1985, a breath of liberalism was in the air. The fourth congress of the Writers' Association was convened; and Hu Qili, speaking on behalf of the Party, assured writers that their freedom of expression would be guaranteed. This was the first time in thirty years that such a promise had been made by the Party, so the undertaking was not without significance. But would it herald great days of self-expression and creativity? Among writers wariness persisted, as well it might; they had learnt from bitter experience not to take the Party at its word. Some had not yet got over the Anti-Rightist campaign, let alone the one against spiritual pollution. When the dramatist Wu Zuguang (whose opera greatly impressed audiences at the London International Festival of the Theatre in 1985) made an impassioned speech about all that had happened to his wife, who had urged him not to speak his mind at the meeting for fear of possible repercussions, he struck a deep chord.

Now a writer herself, his wife was one of China's most popular stage actresses. When Wu Zuguang was branded a Rightist, a high-placed official offered her a choice between divorcing her husband and joining the Party. When she chose to stand by her husband, she was labelled a Rightist 'for internal purposes'. Why internal? Because the theatre, or more pertinently the box office, wanted her to go on acting. So a distinction was drawn between the life before the footlights and life backstage; no sooner had the applause died down than she was emptying spittoons, tidying up, and cleaning the lavatories. And it was understood that whoever felt like insulting or abusing her could go right ahead, such being the lot of those who bore a political stigma. Worse was to come when the Cultural Revolution unfolded. She was physically assaulted by the theatre director, which, together with the hospital's mistaken diagnosis, left her half-paralysed for life. A person more prone to despair might have opted for suicide. Many writers did—quite how many nobody knows.

Such experiences are not easily forgotten. The summer of 1986 saw the thirtieth anniversary of the Double-Hundred movement; and though, as we saw, thinkers and artists were invited to express themselves freely, memories of what happened the last time have not dimmed. Nor is it only the unpredictability of Party policy that engenders inhibitions. However sincere may be the Party's proclamation of creative liberty, one can never assume in China that the leadership has merely to announce a policy for every cadre to carry it out in the way intended. The same policy, implemented by different cadres, can end up very differently. None of this was helped by the fact that the arbiters of literary questions, Hu Yaobang and his secretariat, felt none too at home in the realms of art and literature. To a closed gathering of Party cadres in April 1985, Hu gave his reasons for hesitating to pronounce on cultural policy: 'First, my unfamiliarity with the situation: I simply haven't read or seen many of these works; nor, quite frankly, do I have the energy to concern myself further with such matters. Secondly, literary and artistic matters are really beyond my ken, and I can say little about them that would pass muster. Third, these days one hesitates to make policy statements, because of the reverberations that are set off the minute the Central Committee says anything. You make a statement, and instantly it's all over the country that "The reins have loosened, loosened! Things will be easier now." You make another, and you're immediately greeted with, "That's torn it. They've tightened up, tightened up! Things aren't too good now."'

There is also the fact that what a writer understands by creative freedom is not necessarily what the authorities understand by it. To me it seems quite clear from Hu Yaobang's remarks what *he* meant by it: 'We haven't gone back on our word,' he maintained. 'Do you see any writer being labelled a Rightist? Or charged with being anti-Party or anti-socialist? No.' To Hu Yaobang, it seems clear, liberty of expression simply meant that writers would no longer be subjected to the more flagrant harassments of the Maoist period. In no way does liberty of expression imply an end to censorship, or to that practice which is usually translated as 'criticism' and which is perhaps better rendered as 'censure'.

As for the workings of censorship, they are familiar enough. Plays can be closed down, books can be banned or placed under an indefinite embargo, publishers can be dissuaded by fear or intimidation from handling a suspect title or author, manuscripts can be edited and altered beyond recognition. In China a writer doesn't even have to come into direct conflict with the censor to be hindered from following his own heart and instincts. Chinese writers are sometimes their own best censors, skirting external curbs by exerting internal controls on themselves. Great Russian literature has been created under conditions of external unfreedom, but no masterpiece can be produced by someone who lacks internal freedom. In Chinese writers the instinct towards independent thought and creation is often blurred by a spirit of conciliation. I don't mean that they live in ingratiating compromise with the cultural officialdom, but the Chinese intelligentsia tend to operate within the system rather than in opposition to it. It is part of their heritage to understand the importance of what is popularly termed 'backstage support', in other words patronage; and Chinese creative writers know that a work that would normally be considered too hot to handle can sometimes be published if it has the right backing.

Besides patronage, Chinese writers try for independence through the use of red herring: a writer publishes a spate of the tamest and most stereotyped short stories, say, and then, when no one is looking, slips in something more genuine and controversial. He becomes adept at detecting his opportunity, lying low until, with the next ideological U-turn, he judges the time right to make himself heard. Yet another method is for him to muffle his message, so that it finds expression in only a hint, an undercurrent, or even a sort of code to which only other writers or people in the know hold the key. This obliqueness makes much Chinese writing unreadable to the uninitiated reader, but it is what gets it into print.

No one better embodies the complex relationship of the artist to the State, the ambiguities of loyalty to Party and fellow writers, than Wang Meng, an ex-Rightist. In the summer of 1986, he was made Minister of Culture, an appointment he had at first resisted, on the grounds that bureaucracy and writing don't mix. To co-opt an erstwhile rebel into power is of course to remove his sting and to enlist his following, but not all writers give the appointment so dark a meaning. In Wang Meng, some of them think, they will have a spokesman, 'a hot line to the top leadership'. How that hot line will work, and whether it will help or hinder creative writing, still remains to be seen.

In China, as elsewhere, censorship often achieves the opposite of what is intended. All that the censor succeeds in doing by banning a book is to lend resonance to its author's words. Paying a piece of writing the compliment of persecution, the censor turns it into something important. What is more, censorship creates publicity abroad, where dissidence holds a strong appeal for many people, interested in writers only so long as their works are banned. They equate the politically risqué with the good; meanwhile, better voices go unheard.

Being controversial at home enhances the chances of recognition abroad, but while seeing advantages to being translated and written about in European languages, Chinese writers are understandably anxious to be judged for themselves; for to see a writer as a dissident, they feel, is to see him as an opposition figure instead of a literary one. The wish to be read beyond the frontiers of their own country goes hand in hand with a wish to be judged by wider standards than those of their own backyard. Sad to say, the works of Chinese writers do not fare all that well, set alongside those of many other countries—or even those of Taiwan's writers, for that matter.

Yet some writers are impatient to see their national literature become a part of world literature. Indeed, nothing would please them more than to see a Chinese awarded the sort of international recognition which the Nobel Prize for Literature, for example, confers. The Nobel Committee has never awarded the prize to a Chinese writer, and there is no pretending that Chinese pride is not hurt when, year after year, they see it go to another country. (The Committee knows this, and it is no coincidence that one of its newly elected members is Göran Malmquist, professor of Chinese at Stockholm University and one of the world's finest translators of Chinese writing.) 'To go into the wider world' is an expression often heard nowadays in Chinese literary circles, and though Chinese writers are carried by the fervour of their hopes beyond the sober limits of actual possibility, it is still true that for the first time since the founding of the People's Republic, it may be said that they are making a start. The playwright Gao Xingjian, last seen in these pages staging *Bus Stop* in Peking, told me in the autumn of 1985 in Durham, to which he had been invited to a conference, that: 'In five years, provided a reasonable degree of creative freedom prevails, you will see something good and important come out of China.'

Looking back at the Cultural Revolution, one feels it ought to be documented in some panoramic Tolstoyan unity. It is certainly an epic theme, so sweeping in kind and scale, so terrible in its violence and effect. There are millions of Chinese who, thinking back on it, must feel as though they were looking through a window at a scene of endless pain and sacrifice, across whose surface there confusedly moved a nation in torment, displaying those characteristics of its condition—mutual suspicion, mutual hate, mutual calumny and persecution—which even now no one fully understands. 'How could we Chinese do such things to each other?' they ask. How did the revolution, won so painfully over the years, degenerate into palace intrigue and tyranny under Chairman Mao and the Gang of Four?

Chinese writers certainly ponder these questions, but I think it will be some time before they can clarify their views. The hate, the betrayals and slander of that grisly time would not surprise someone like the Soviet novelist and philosopher Alexander Zinoviev, who has said, 'Communism is above all a society of people who behave badly', and who designed the dust jacket of one of his books to show two snarling, half-choking rats grasping one another's throats, their paws clasped in a handshake, their tails tied in a knot. But of course no Chinese writer would go as far as that. In some writers, the question of what lay at the bottom of the atrocities has become fused with ideas about humanity, something which they feel has been eroded by the ideological insistence on viewing man always in terms of his class nature. The most interesting full-length work of fiction to deal with this idea is the novel *Stones of the Wall*.* This is by a literature teacher in Shanghai called Dai Houying, and it was brought out by a Canton publisher in 1980 after it had been rejected by several others, instantly causing a stir. Dai's view, compellingly expressed in an afterword, is that Marxism and humanism were not incompatible; and it showed how crude was the Chinese dogma, how doctrinaire the reactions of its guardians, that such a view, long taken for granted by the majority of European Marxists, should cause so much controversy.

Yet someone who aired it would still be considered bold, for all that a thaw had occurred in the literary scene. It took somebody of the stature of Liu Binyan to voice it unequivocally and publicly, in 1979: 'Good people punishing good people, people injuring their own—this is what "class struggle" meant in those years.' And it came, he went on to say, of not putting man first: stamping out human nature meant not the appearance of godly nature, but the spread of animal nature.

Some kind of interpretation of the Cultural Revolution did come blazing out of its aftermath, in the thaw of 1979 and 1980, a period which many Western observers see as the Second Blooming of the Hundred Flowers in Chinese fiction ('flowers' is a constant Chinese metaphor for literature). This fiction, compared to what had passed for literature before, was arresting in its candour and its closeness to expressing heartfelt emotions. Before the lid came down on them, tales of suffering poured out, their authors writing, for the first time in years, about broken lives and families the way they (and not the Party ideologues) saw them. The injuries done to the characters by the Cultural Revolution being their main theme, these works were called 'scar literature'.

If some of these stories seem too much on the edge of emotions—tears welling up in the eyes on every other page—they struck a responsive chord in their readers, who knew it all to be true, the wreckage of lives, the

* Dai Houying, *Stones of the Wall* (tr. Frances Wood, London 1985).

injustices and the suffering. The authorities tolerated this fiction so long as everything could be blamed on the Gang of Four, but it was not long before the subject-matter widened, and the uprush of expression was staunched by an official clampdown.

It makes one think that it is useless to demand that China produce a Solzhenitsyn, because who is going to start a massive novel when there is so little certainty that it will get published or slip through the ideological mesh? Chartering a big boat for a tempestuous sea requires confidence. Instead of the single big novel of Dostoyevskian quality and dimensions, what one finds is a wealth of short stories and novellas. The short story predominates in China, a natural enough development in a literary scene just awakening from a long period of uncreativity, where one would expect the first steps to be taken in a form of limited range. The short story, moreover, suits Chinese purpose, being essentially a form which deals with life's victims, the injured and the alienated, and the quashing of aspirations by cruel circumstance.

Nor should one try, just yet, to look at Chinese literature as the creative use of language rather than as an outlet for feelings and preoccupations. The Chinese practitioner of fiction has always been obsessed—not too strong a word—with China and her social realities; add to this the obligatory infusion of political subject-matter and socialist realism over the past forty years, and you have a literature where content is all. The long established realist approach to fiction is difficult to shake off, and literature is still a very good place to look if you want a true record of what happens in society. It is an approach which Chinese writers will no doubt outgrow, but in the meantime they have taken up more adventurous themes. Elsewhere I have already referred to women writers tackling the risqué topics of extra-marital love and divorce. Other issues explored in fiction were bureaucratic corruption, individualism, the generation gap. In late 1985, a writer called Zhang Xianliang even went so far as to deal with life in a labour camp and sexual impotence.

Zhang Xianliang's novella, *Half of Man is Woman*, could scarcely fail to provoke controversy, and this was perhaps its purpose. No Chinese writer had written of sex so explicitly before. The literary establishment at home viewed him with disapproval, but critics abroad honoured him, inviting him to America and proclaiming his work to be a breakthrough. His novella shows how, beneath the routines of life in a forced labour camp, sexual urges fester; women prisoners, positively bursting with frustrated desire, are seen throwing themselves at the men. Man is shown to be at the mercy of his instinctual drives and, at the same time, shown to lose his human qualities—including the capacity for tenderness and love—because he has been forced to live a life in which his innermost impulses are dammed back. The hero never quite recovers from his spells in labour camp; making love for the first time in years, he discovers himself to be sexually impotent, robbed of the deepest responses of his nature. Zhang Xianliang is an experienced writer, and had come into prominence before he published *Half of Man is Woman*. But for my taste there is too heavy a sense of striving for 'fine writing' in his prose, and I felt it was not entirely bitchiness or bigotry which made some critics dismiss him as a hack.

It is not only in subject-matter that Chinese writing has changed in the last eight years or so; the writer in China is also tackling new styles. It is only European writers who talk of the death of the novel; to the Chinese, as to the Latin American novelist, the idea would make little sense. Why, the novelist in China is just starting to get into his stride; a literary scene sadly impoverished through lack of contact with the ideas of the outside world has just seen a burst of vitality unknown in the creative history of the People's Republic. It is not just that writers are no longer confined to black and white themes of revolutionary triumphs, super-heroic peasants in conflict with revisionists; it is that an atmosphere has evolved in which some experimentation with technique and language has come to be done. For a time after the opening to the West, black humour, stream of consciousness, and other Western styles were all the rage. Chinese writers gravitated towards these, to them new, literary devices with all the enthusiasm of innocents and discoverers treating themselves to forbidden sweets. After all these years of being isolated from the literary life of the outside world—even that of the Soviet Union was closed to them for two decades—they desperately wanted to wire themselves into the main circuit again.

It became fashionable to have read Virginia Woolf, Camus and Kafka. (Kafka was enormously popular; one hardly needs to read further than this opening sentence in *The Trial* to know why: 'Someone must have been telling lies about Joseph K, for without having done anything wrong he was arrested one fine morning.') Translations appeared, from Proust to Marguerite Duras to Joseph Heller. The avidity with which these authors were read betrayed how starved the Chinese were of new ways of thinking and being. Then there were protracted debates on whether modernism was quite right for China, with polemical articles appearing in the *People's Daily* and literary magazines. What modernism meant was none too clear to its critics, and their obvious confusion made one of its practitioners, Gao Xingjian, pronounce the whole exercise a non-debate. Nevertheless, questions such as 'Is there necessarily a link between modernisation and modernism?' were thought worth the generous yardage of print devoted to their elucidation, and literary theoreticians and polemicists who could scarcely compose a readable sentence were seriously suggesting that the writer ought not to remain enclosed in the impenetrable world of his own subjectivity, his duty being to translate into terms understood by the mass of readers the reality that lies about him.

Behind the new writing and its forays into modernist techniques, there reared the whole phalanx of literary conservatism, supporters of the out-of-date, has-beens and older critics trying to keep the world as they had known it. The new writing was said to smack of the pursuit of things foreign. Yet it would be impossible for these writers merely to bring tradition up to date, and following European forms is only part of their foraging for new ways of expressing their approach to the world.

Literary historians might find the forays into experimental writing not altogether unfamiliar: sixty years earlier, there had been the intellectual flowering of the May Fourth movement, when students marched and workers downed tools and new forms of literary expression were tried out. That period saw the creation of a new literary language and the birth of western-style fiction. Surveying the literary scene today, it is difficult to avoid the impression that Chinese writers are retreading the path taken by their grandfathers. There is the same fascination with the West. There is the same questioning of Chinese tradition. (In Chengdu in the spring of 1986, the poet Ouyang Jianghe subjected me to five hours of brilliant invective against Confucianism and Daoism [Taoism]—which he found, if I understood him correctly, irresistibly beguiling as philosophies but utterly repellent in their popular, vulgarised forms.)

To question tradition's worth is not always to reject it, however. Many writers and critics have come to believe that the sources of renewal lie ultimately in their own heritage. Two words you often hear today are *xungen* and *fansi*, 'roots seeking' and 'reflection' (or *nachdenken* in its original Hegelian derivation); these describe a tendency which runs through the work and purposes of certain artists, in some cases diffusely, in others more explicitly. Yet a complementary trend is a looking towards foreign models. This is a time of change and experiment, and far from ending with European modernism, the search is widening. Gao Xingjian told me when we spoke in Durham that Chinese writers were finding an example in Latin American authors; he named Gabriel Garcia Marquez, Mario Vargas Llosa, Jose Maria Arguedas and Jorge Luis Borges, among others. In Latin America, as in China, a *social* conception of man predominates; there, too, writing is a difficult vocation, one which impels its practitioners to social and political commitment.

Here is how a British Sinologist, John Minford, writes of the new generation of writers and artists: 'It searches for inspiration in the West, but finds time and again that the modern West has drawn its own inspiration from the ancient Orient. Familiarity with Ezra Pound and imagism leads unexpectedly to new explorations of classical Chinese poetry and poetics.... A knowledge of abstract expressionism leads back to the more uninhibitedly abstract styles of traditional calligraphy and painting.... College students in China discover Gary Snyder's poetry, Jack Kerouac's *The Dharma Bums* and the novels of Herman Hesse, and find themselves pointed back to Zen Buddhism, Daoism and the *Book of Changes.*'

Answering a question about the stages of his development, the poet Bei Dao described how, from a sense of frustration and anger at politics and a wish to carve out a quiet corner for himself, he came eventually to feel a dissatisfaction with mere social protest. 'What we had not done,' he realised, 'was to dig at the roots of the flaws in national character, the ones which made our civilisation stagnate for a thousand years.' One way of getting to know one's own culture better is by being receptive to the ideas of others. While some writers have wondered if they have over-modelled themselves on the West, Bei Dao takes the opposite view. 'On the contrary,' he said, 'I think we are still insufficiently acquainted with the West; we should learn and draw from Western poetry still more. It is only by doing this that we shall discover things of worth in our own culture.'

Reading and talking to China's younger writers, I have been struck by how much they are preoccupied by the national historical personality. Even Gao Xingjian, for all his indebtedness to Artaud and Beckett, is no exception. The big novel he was working on when we spoke could scarcely have had a more Chinese ring. The themes revolve round a view of two cultures, one centred on the Yellow River basin, the other in the Yangtze. 'When we think of the dawn of Chinese civilisation,' Gao said, 'we think of the neolithic culture which arose on the banks of the Yellow River. But there was a parallel prehistoric culture in the south, a Yangtze civilisation, if you like.' The novel ambitiously ranges from those times down to our own, and it would not surprise me to learn that one of its concerns was the ancestry of those characteristics which lie at the bottom of China's unhappy recent history.

At first sight Gao's ideas for his novel seemed original and interesting, but when I thought about it later, I found that it was something more. Gao's concern reflects a trend, one which, as I pointed out earlier, the Party leadership itself started when it pronounced the Cultural Revolution to have had 'feudal' features and complex historical causes. Those Chinese writers who suppose the roots of their national tragedies to lie, not in Marxism or Maoism, but in the heart of darkness in the national character, have something in common with those Russian intellectuals who believe Soviet political ideology to be consistent with Russian cultural tradition. Against such a writer as Solzhenitsyn, for example, who argued that the political ideology 'bears the entire responsibility for all the blood that has been shed', there are those who, like Sakharov, see contemporary Soviet politics as only too clearly a manifestation of ingrained Russian qualities. The conclusions at which the new generation of Chinese writers have arrived will be familiar enough to Sakharov, who said, 'I don't accept that Russia preserved her well-being up to the twentieth century. I consider the slavish, servile spirit which existed in Russia for centuries to be the greatest misfortune, not an indication of national well-being.'

These are the sketched outlines of the literary scene. For a more detailed view, we have to narrow our focus to individual writers. Rather than swamp the reader with difficult Chinese names, I shall merely select six of the most famous. Two are men who made their mark in the 1950s, and whose youthful impulses, fuelled by the ebullient years of revolutionary success, were dampened by the Anti-Rightist campaign. The other four are young writers whose consciousness was formed by the Cultural Revolution, and whose voices we are hearing for the first time.

Wang Meng we have met already, in his role as the new Minister of Culture. He has fallen out of favour with Western observers of the Chinese literary scene because he has 'sold out' to the establishment. Still he has not always been so respectable. He had won a moment of fame, brilliant if all too brief, with a story he published in 1956, when he was only twenty-one. Like other writers of his generation, Wang Meng was much influenced by Russian example, and his story was inspired by a Soviet novel by Galina Nikolaeva, *The Manager of a Machine Tractor Station and the Chief Agronomist*. Wang's story dealt controversially with bureaucratic apathy and corruption, not a good subject to have tackled just a year before the Anti-Rightist campaign: it doomed him to a twenty-one-year exile among the Uygur tribesmen in China's far west.

When, with the thaw, he re-entered the literary stage, it was not without a suggestion of subversiveness either. He was the first writer to attract wide public attention for his experiments with Western literary techniques, and when he incurred censure, it was not so much for his subject-matter as for the ambiguity and foreign flavour of his language. When the term 'stream of consciousness' was applied to his writing, it was to suggest that he was trying to be new-fangled. Few Chinese writers had so consciously manipulated language. This concern with words shows in his descriptive passages, which piles onomatopoeia upon alliteration, adjective upon adverb, with a prolixity bordering on overkill. One of his devices, using strings of Chinese ideographs displaying the same root element, makes one think of the kind of visual effect which e.e. cummings created with his typographical tropes. Though his writing does, here and there, achieve some striking cinematic effects, Wang Meng embroiders the text too much, and what he does is artful but not art.

Out of the same generation has come Liu Binyan, to whom there is a touch of Upton Sinclair and Ralph Nader. His work straddles fiction and journalism, and is usually classed as reportage, his method of documentation being the visit paid, notebook in hand, to the locale where his story is to take place. Much of it is legwork, digging, and reporting; especially reporting of the muck-raking kind. He is very bad news to work units or Party functionaries with anything to hide, because he has made it his business to expose bureaucratic corruption, ineptitude and injustice. He is quite aware that he treads a tricky path, but he is a man of singular courage, and he believes that if one openly declares what is wrong with Chinese society, who the evil-doers are and who its victims, then perhaps the injustice and misery will by degrees diminish a little.

As a genre reportage flourishes in China, where large numbers of readers prefer it to pure fiction. To many the force of its findings would be weakened by the distracting packaging of art. The success of reportage is perhaps not remarkable, in a country where fact is so often stranger than fiction. Asked why he doesn't write more fiction, Liu Binyan gives as one of his reasons the drying-up of his imaginative powers by the 'super-actuality of Chinese life'.

Examples of the kind of writing he does can easily be found in European literary history: Orwell's *Down and Out in Paris and London*, for example, or any of the tell-it-like-it-is pieces of American New Journalism. But though he had read a great deal of American and European reportage, Liu Binyan's chief debt is to the Russians. This has something to do with his age and experience: when he published his first controversial story, *At the Building Site of the Bridge*, it was in 1956, not long after he met N. Ovechkin, who came to China with a Soviet journalists' delegation. The following year, after a visit to Poland, Liu spent some days with Ovechkin in his home. He came away much admiring the Soviet writer, whom he saw discharging the useful function of a 'scout' for the Party; one who, by making the results of his independent investigations known to the public, raised issues which might otherwise have escaped the notice of the leaders.

Liu Binyan has been privileged enough to be an accredited journalist with the national Party paper, the *People's Daily*, which gave him an entrée to institutions everywhere. But he acted altogether independently, honouring at all times the 'Party conscience', something loftier than unquestioning allegiance to the prevailing orthodoxy. The distinction between the Party as it is and the Party as it should be is one that he still insists on making today, with more than the implication that the one falls short of the other. If by doing so, he discomforted the political bosses, he did little to mollify them when he published his diary and a work of reportage called *Another Kind of Loyalty*.

In *Another Kind of Loyalty*, a true tale of two men, Liu Binyan exalts those who, at whatever cost to themselves, speak out against the wrongs perpetrated by the régime. Such men are few and far between, because it is the goody-goody type, the blindly faithful and obedient conformists who thrive in China's political climate. One of the men was openly opposed to Chairman Mao's rabid denunciation of the Soviet Union, where he himself had profitably studied. The other is a dedicated employee of the Shanghai Shipping Institute, continually subjected to unjust persecution by a higher-up, an unsavoury character who reappears in Liu Binyan's published diary. The persecutor is one of those out-and-out opportunists who built their career on enthusiasm for whatever political campaign was afoot, whether it was to denounce Rightists or Deng Xiaoping. At the shipping institute, Liu Binyan finds him still sitting pretty. To many readers of this story, the question that springs immediately to mind is, 'How could he, unless it is because we are still not curing the ills of society?' The maladies of an earlier age persist, Liu Binyan is saying, the wrongs go unrighted, the innocents still suffer.

The considerable stir the publications provoked went beyond the offices of the Shanghai Shipping Institute, and at a stroke Liu Binyan found himself in bad political odour. His implied criticism of the Sino-Soviet split in the 1960s, which Deng Xiaoping had been all for at the time, had not apparently gone down well. Magazines in Hong Kong urged courage upon him, and one of them ended an article with the words, 'Liu Binyan, China needs you!'

And so China does, to judge by the sackfuls of letter he gets from troubled people. His life and work offers in Chinese literary history the case, perhaps unique, of a man who is at once a writer, an investigative reporter, and a champion of the wronged and helpless. Since 1979, when he published his ground-breaking *Between Man and Monsters*, a true story told in the form of fiction, of bureaucratic corruption in a northeastern province, he has travelled extensively, bent on using his searching intelligence, his energies, his persuasive prose and his moral courage to challenge every kind of injustice, to make Chinese society a little less wasteful of lives, ideals and ability. He receives so many pleas for help by letter and telephone that he has scarcely time to press on with his writing. Yet he responds to them as to a call of duty, only regretting he has not the means to be of service to them all. If what he does endangers his person or position, he is, as he himself wryly puts it, 'past caring'. Silenced for twenty-two years as a Rightist, he has more than once looked death in the face. What stopped him from taking his own life, he said, was the thought of all those other lives which might be wasted.

In much of the world this may sound heroic. Not in China, where the possibility of being persecuted or imprisoned has confronted the writer for generations. The moral fervour and grandiloquence which a Western audience would find embarrassing has a place in such a society, and only bigotry or cynicism could prevent our admiring both what Liu Binyan does and the spirit which sustains his work.

Part of that spirit contains, even now, a strong strand of Marxism. Constantly challenged as it must be, the faith of younger years in the Communist Party continues to suffuse his writing. He is painfully aware of his inability to reconcile China's practical realities with his faith that Marxism would make it a better place for everybody. His diary records an inquiry he received at a lecture he gave to a group of student journalists; how would he explain, the inquirer asked, the untruthful reporting of the Chinese press for the past thirty years, when journalists were wanting in neither true Party conscience nor integrity? While he was lecturing, another student penned a question to him: 'The *People's Daily* has an unwritten rule: a good reporter is necessarily a good Party member, strongly imbued with the Party's spirit. What is the inherent connection between this principle and the untruthful reporting of major historical events?'

What Liu Binyan goes on to write in his diary strikes with some pathos. 'I replied to neither query,' he says, 'because I am none too sure of the answer myself. I have still to find the answer to another question—why, in the spring of 1985, there should be two Chinese simultaneously raising such a query.' The Party was to give him still greater cause for painful reflection at the start of 1987, when it expelled him from its ranks and effectively silenced him.

If Chinese society is rich material to Liu Binyan, it offers as much to Zhang Xinxin. Here and there in this book I have drawn upon her *Chinese Lives*, one of the most interesting works to appear in China in recent years, written in collaboration with one Sang Ye. An ex-soldier, ex-nurse and a student of film and drama in her early thirties, Zhang Xinxin is without doubt the most accomplished Chinese woman novelist I have read. But *Chinese Lives* is oral history, not fiction. In it, a hundred Chinese men and women talk about themselves. The method she uses recalls Studs Terkel's, and that writer's *American Dreams: Lost and Found* is a work that she explicitly acknowledges.

Here are a hundred specimens of humanity, some of them injured, unhappy creatures, some self-satisfied ignoramuses. They speak in an authentic vernacular, rich, individual, spontaneous. 'We're friends, so don't you go and make a fool of me, see? My good looks have given me enough trouble as it is ...' begins one story. To record the lives and thoughts of all these characters is, in some measure, to define what it means to be Chinese at the present time. No one who seeks to know what makes the ordinary Chinese tick could afford to ignore this work.

Another star is Acheng, of all Chinese novelists the least self-conscious and the most convincing. He broke upon the literary world with his prize-winning *The Chess Master*, a tale of startling maturity. It tells the story of educated youths rusticated to State farms, one of them a Chinese chess addict named Wang Yisheng. The narrator meets him on the train taking the youths to the countryside, and they tell each other their life histories. If Wang is aware of a need for a richer basis for living than mere eating and drinking, then chess is what fulfils it. Later, Wang turns up at the farm where the narrator has been put to work, and is introduced to Ni, the scion of a cultured family and a chess enthusiast. Wang wins Ni's admiration by beating him at chess. Ni succeeds in entering Wang's name for a chess tournament at the county town by bribing a district official with a family heirloom, an ebony chess set dating from the Ming dynasty. But Wang declines the challenge, preferring to take on the winner and the runners-up privately, after the matches have ended. He plays against all nine of these at once, winning game after game. Against the champion, who has gone home, he plays blind chess, every move being relayed by bicycle to and from the champion's home. A throng of villagers gathers. The tension mounts. Then, when the last game is being played, the champion turns up himself, to ask Wang if he would agree to a face-saving draw. He is an old man, a throwback to the hermits of history. He says he takes heart from Wang's genius, because he sees it as signifying the survival and continuity of Chinese heritage. Wang, on the point of collapse, is raised to his feet and away to where he and his friends are putting up for the night, in a haze of milling crowds and torches.

No Chinese work of fiction I have read shows greater dramatic compactness and intensity. Acheng's mastery of language is the source of much of the intensity; and what makes him so satisfying to read is that his style is not the consequence of radical departures in new directions but rather the full use of the potential inherent in established methods. Acheng's unselfconsciousness would be remarkable in any novelist, let alone one who is writing his first work of fiction.

Acheng is a writer of the 'roots-seeking' school, a master of home-grown styles. He has said that it is only when a Chinese writer has thoroughly steeped himself in his own tradition that he may communicate with the wider world. Not so much in *The Chess Master*, but in Acheng's other works, critics find tinges of mysticism; and some say he is most truly himself when he expresses Daoist thoughts, as in this passage from *The Chess Master*, in which Wang Yisheng tells the narrator about the old man who helped him perfect his chess:

What was wrong with me, the old man said, was that I was too keen to win. If my opponent were too eager to win, he told me, I should use soft methods to work a change in him, and while I was changing him, I should be creating my opportunity to defeat him. Softness isn't weakness. It's containing, drawing in, holding. By holding and changing your opponent you draw him in to the strategy you're evolving. And to create this strategic situation you do everything by forcing nothing. To force nothing is the Way. That's the changeless nature of chess too: try changing it, and it won't be chess. Not only will you lose, you won't be able to play at all. You can't go against the nature of chess.

My own reaction, upon reading Acheng's story, was to wonder if it hadn't also a slyly and subtly subversive meaning—which is that in China it is ultimately always the old men who have to win.

A writer of an altogether different kind is Bei Dao. Like Acheng, Bei Dao was born in the year the People's Republic came into being, in 1949. In his time he has been a Red Guard, an employee of a construction company, and an editor at *El Popola Cinio*, China's Esperanto magazine. He is chiefly a poet, one who, in the words of David Pollard, professor of Chinese at London University, 'is capable of being ranked with Mandelstam'.

But he has also published a handful of short stories and a novella, *Waves*. This did not appear in its final revised version until 1981, but it had been widely circulated in hand-copied form among the country's young people, for whom he was already a celebrity. The story is concerned with the profound bewilderment of those who face a world gone mad; in such a world, one is glad to be a lunatic. It depicts the so-called 'lost generation', young people who think their lives wasted by the Cultural Revolution, and who have been left broken in spirit, confused, disillusioned, and untrained for any profession. Where there might have been youthful hopefulness, there is only cynicism and emptiness. The novella was completed in 1974, two years before the fall of the Gang of Four, and it is that time of disintegration, when things seemed out of joint and inexplicable, that Bei Dao evokes. In this scene, where a young man (the narrator) and woman (Xiao Ling) come upon a derelict temple in the hills, Bei Dao looks at the times wryly:

> We step inside the main hall, and into a faint odour of must and decay. Through the gloom, a shaft of sunlight falls upon the long slender hand of the Buddha facing us.
>
> 'Hello, Goddess of Mercy,' Xiao Ling shouts like a child, and from somewhere in the dimness there comes a muffled echo.
>
> 'It's Sakyamuni,' I say.
>
> 'An Indian?'
>
> 'Yes.'
>
> 'Well, Mr Sakyamuni, welcome to our country. But do you have a passport?'
>
> 'He has the scriptures,' I say.
>
> 'We've enough of those in our country. Break a commandment, and you might find yourself packed off for reform-through-labour.' Abruptly Xiao Ling turns to me and asks, 'Are you interested in religion?'
>
> 'You can't not be: it's a kind of religious atmosphere we've been living in these years.'

The author attempts technical devices which allow him to record multiple viewpoints, and to achieve a narrative structure which moves forward and backward with a fluidity which captures the sense of time as it is actually experienced in human consciousness. All this is familiar to readers of modern European literature, but apparently Bei Dao's *Waves* was written before he had been exposed to such writing. *Waves* is seen by his Western admirers to be a remarkable achievement, and in some ways it is. How splendid it was that he could write like this at all in 1974, when it would have been too much to expect that anyone should produce real novels instead of propaganda fables. But when his European champions praise his fictional writing, one feels they are being more enthusiastic than, for the good of his work, they might be. Perhaps they should limit their enthusiasm to the fact that, reading him, one feels a sense of encountering something new in China. It would be wrong to complain that this feeling had no artistic basis whatsoever, but it should still be admitted that his accomplishment is great by Chinese standards rather than international ones.

Another of his much praised pieces of writing is a short story about writer's block, *Moon on the Manuscript*. The approach is again highly subjective. The effect of the story is somewhat mannered, but the emphasis on the individual's loneliness, the sense of being haunted by private thoughts and emotions, the product of a unique train of association which can never be communicated to others by social gestures—all these are marks of a modern sensibility, something rare in China. I am not surprised that many Chinese readers find his work difficult to understand: the idea that one is lonelier than ever in a crowd must seem utterly baffling to a race who are never happier than when they are surrounded by hordes of people.

Another short story, *13 Happiness Street*, uses Kafkaesque ambiguity to good effect. A child whose kite gets caught in a tree vanishes mysteriously. The tree, which stands near a walled compound bearing the address 13 Happiness Street, is felled for no apparent reason. The hero investigates, and through successive barricades of bureaucratic unconnectedness, suspicion and arbitrariness, arrives at the conclusion that he must discover what lies behind the high walls of 13 Happiness Street. He finds a chimney, and climbs it to look over the walls through his binoculars. When he descends, he finds an unidentified stranger, already glimpsed once before in the story, waiting for him. He is spirited away to a lunatic asylum, and when he looks about him, he realises that he is at last inside the walls.

It was as the practitioner of a new kind of poetry that Bei Dao first made his name. His poetry is new in the sense that it incorporates modernist techniques but also in the sense that when it first appeared, nothing as good or as intelligent had been seen in the People's Republic before. The school of verse of which he is the leading practitioner is dubbed Misty Poetry. Using techniques associated with the modernist movement in Europe, Misty

Poetry is, as John Minford writes of it, 'the first real experimentation with poetic language within China since 1949. This poetry has an authentic inspiration and passion. If there is an alternative culture in China today, this is its voice. It speaks for its generation, and over and above that for the rediscovery of the poetic pulse of one of the world's great literary traditions.' But it has repelled some of the old guard: 'weird', one critic uncharitably called it, a poet himself.

The appeal of Misty Poetry to many young Chinese readers when it first appeared was instant and strong, giving voice as it did to a range of emotions which had been waiting for an expositor. Yet one cannot pretend that it is all admirable; some of it is facile and adolescent, if deeply felt and moving. (Try as one might, it is hard to respond to the sophomoric sensibility of Shu Ting, the best known woman poet of the school.)

But the new poetry had a catalytic power. Following its appearance, a number of regional groupings sprouted, so that one has to make a distinction nowadays between the northern and southern schools. Voices still younger than Bei Dao's are increasingly heard. Even within the original coterie itself, there have emerged new subdivisions. One of these is epitomised by the young Yang Lian, who now has a following of his own. With his un-Chinese, bard-like long hair, Yang Lian looks the poet that he is. He deals with things in a large way, and the mould in which he pours his thoughts is the long and prodigious poem-cycle.

One of his main preoccupations is the inferiority of the present to the past. He clearly feels the allure of classical tradition, a subject on which he spoke with almost bewitching articulacy when he visited me on a brief trip to London in the summer of 1986. As an expression of his relationship to history one can take these lines from his personal statement on his calling as a poet:

> The hoary century deceives its children
> Everywhere leaving puzzles
> Snow on stone, to touch up the furbished filth
> In my hand I clutch my poems
> Call me! In that nameless moment
> Wind's small boat bearing history scuds
> Behind me—shadow-like
> Pursuing an ending

It is people like him who will revivify Chinese culture, under whose accretions of decay, Bei Dao tells us in his poem *The Old Temple*, there is yet life—

The silenced chimes
form cobwebs, spreading annual rings
between splintered columns
without memories, a stone
sends an echo through the misty valley
a stone, without memories
at a time when a path wound away here
dragons and strange birds flew off
carrying the mute bells under the eaves
once a year weeds
grow, unconcernedly
not caring if the master they submit to
is a monk's cloth shoe, or a breeze
the stele is chipped, the writing on its surface scuffed
as if only in a conflagration
could it be read, yet perhaps
with a glance from the living
the stone tortoise in the mud will come back to life
and crawl out across the threshold, bearing its heavy secrets

# 12

# MINORITIES

Strictly speaking the term 'Chinese' designates a nationality rather than a race, and if one were pedantic one should always say 'Han' instead of Chinese, if what one means is the predominant race in China, rather than a minority group like the Tibetans or Mongolians. A large number of China's inhabitants are not Chinese at all, but belong to pockets of other cultures which have historically existed beyond the frontiers of Chinese colonisation—or above them, in the hills.

As Chinese civilisation spread outwards from its cradle in the Yellow River basin, it absorbed more and more aboriginal cultures along its expanding borders; and there are now fifty-five racial minorities in China. Though they make up less than 7 per cent of the total population, in absolute terms they number no fewer than 67 million people. The racial mix contributes colour and variety to Chinese life, but it also adds to the obstacles in China's progress towards modernisation. Areas of minority settlement are rich in natural resources, and cover over half of China's land, but they are generally far-flung and underdeveloped, and on the whole their inhabitants live poorer and ruder lives than do the Han Chinese. As in other countries, the issues of racial justice, cultural integration and economic advance are intertwined in China, and how to improve the minority's lot technically and economically without depriving it of its cultural identity is as much of a dilemma here as elsewhere.

The temperaments and customs of these peoples are very different, and some are better assimilated to the dominant Han culture than others. Although the Chinese Communist Party has penetrated the whole of China, one has only to see a Yi tribesman from southwest China, for example, to realise how far some minorities are from being moulded into new socialist men. The Yi (or Lolo, as he was once called) may not, as he used to, make a living out of growing and selling opium, or exist in a rigid caste system of patrician landowners and servile tenant slaves, but he probably still believes in sorcery, and looks as though he might lunge out at any passing traveller from under the folds of his voluminous felt cape. The Lolos were highway robbers well into recent times, and when the Red Army crossed their territory in 1935, in the course of the famous Long March, it did so safely only by buying its way through. A couple of decades earlier, a British War Office agent who hazarded a survey of the area had his body sent back chopped in half.

The proud and striking figure that the Yis cut is also a reminder of the time when they and the Chinese constantly fought each other. A French missionary who had lived much of his life among them blamed this on the Chinese, whom he thought had 'even less spirit of assimilation than the English' and were much readier to kill and massacre than to ally. The Chinese belief in their cultural superiority was indeed absolute: Chinese civilisation or savagery was how they interpreted the alternatives of the human condition. The conviction that the closer one drew to Chinese manner and thought, the more civilised one became, dates from the earliest times. And even if one tried to believe otherwise, one had it from no less an authority than Mencius that the evidence was all to the contrary: 'I have heard of man using the doctrines of our great land to change barbarians,' he had written, 'but I have never yet heard of any being changed by barbarians.'

The Chinese seldom bother to hide their racial prejudices, but official policy towards ethnic minorities, enshrined in the Constitution, opposes 'Han chauvinism'. At the same time, it is evident that feelings of 'local-national chauvinism' will not be allowed to ride high. The ethnic minorities are to be brought in step with the Chinese materially. This need not imply cultural conformity. However, there is no question that should a clash arise, cultural individuality must submit to unity of authority. It would not do for any of the areas of minority settlement to chafe at the control of the central government, and the Constitution explicitly forbids actions which 'instigate their secession'.

'Equality, unity and mutual assistance', is how the Constitution charac-terises the relations between China's races. This is of course an ideal, not at all easy to approach in practice: the interests of 67 million minority people are bound to be secondary to the interests of 936 million Hans. But it is also true that much is being done to redress the racial injustices of an earlier period, and that more than just lip service is being paid to the idea of letting the minorities run their own internal affairs. In this official attitudes differ sharply from those of the Cultural Revolution, when 'class struggle' and condemnation of all things old and traditional combined to place minority customs and practices in serious jeopardy. In one case in Inner Mongolia alone, no fewer than 16,000 people were persecuted to death.

From the very first the People's Republic of China set up autonomous administrative areas wherever minority communities were concentrated. There are five autonomous regions, on an administrative par with provinces: Inner Mongolia, Xinjiang (Chinese Turkestan), Guangxi, Ningxia, and Tibet. Every minority, regardless of population size, is represented at the National People's Congress, the highest organ of State power: even the Hezhen, at 1400 the smallest minority people in China, send a delegate. What is more, the minorities are allowed to send more delegates than would have been the case if representation were to be based on their proportionate size in the total population. A law passed in 1984 provides for various safeguards of minority interests, stipulating that the head of an autonomous area be a member of the appropriate minority, and granting local organs a measure of flexibility in adopting policies. Economically, the autonomous areas have been given, if not a free hand, at least much leeway in adapting government plans to local needs and peculiarities. And being poorer than most provinces, the autonomous regions receive substantial subsidies by the State. In 1983, for example, a total of 5600 million yuan was pumped into the areas predominantly inhabited by minorities. All in all, the authority of the organs of self-government has greatly expanded in recent years.

It is part of the aims of China's minority policy to create, by training, a governing corps of cadres, specialists and administrators. The pre-eminent instrument of training and indoctrination are the Institutes for Nationalities, of which there are now ten in China, including the Central Institute in Peking, the archetype. The courses offered are the usual academic ones, but one need not doubt that ideology forms a large part of the content. Here minority students absorb many Han ways and manners, along with technical and managerial skills. The institutes have by now produced tens of thousands of educated cadres, but many more will have to be trained, if the proportion of minority cadres is to reflect the proportion of minorities in the population. The government does what it can to step up the educational development of the minority communities, and schools and children there enjoy several kinds of preferential treatment. In proportion to their intake, for example, secondary schools receive larger State stipends for the support of minority pupils than are awarded for the Chinese; and minority students have greater access to grants, free tuition and textbooks than do Chinese ones. In some circumstances entrance requirements for admission to universities are lowered for minority candidates, and it is a matter of policy to favour a minority candidate from a Han area over his equally qualified Chinese competitor.

Ethnic minorities are also linguistic minorities, and only the Hui and the Manchu, among China's non-Han population, speak Chinese as their first language. The others speak a total of more than sixty languages, certain ethnic groups using more than one tongue. Multilingualism on this scale clearly poses problems for the government. Whether or not to make provisions for non-Chinese speakers to be educated in their own languages is a far from straightforward matter: to some, such provisions may indicate respect for minority cultural identity and integrity, while to others they may appear to be an attempt to isolate minorities from each other, from the dominant culture, from possibilities of advancement, and from international literature and other contacts. The Chinese approach, though, is not one of 'divide and rule', because it is broadly bilingual and pressures for all to learn the lingua franca, the standard speech known as *putonghua* (or Mandarin), remain strong. (Nor is it only the minorities who feel this pressure: speakers of Cantonese, Shanghainese and other Chinese dialects, too, have to learn *putonghua*, which is as different from their own speech as French is from English, before they can function as full members of Chinese society.)

At the same time the position of minority languages in China is healthier than it has been for years, and no one can pronounce with any confidence the doom of any of them. The Chinese now admit that, instead of rushing into the reform of minority written languages in the 1950s, they should have left well alone. A case in point was the attempt to replace the Arabic alphabet of the Uygur and Kazak scripts with Roman letters. Heritage proved stronger than government demand, for no sooner had the political climate relaxed than the old script was back in use again. The government of the Xinjiang Uygur Autonomous Region was obliged to authorise the use of the Arabic alphabet, and today the *Xinjiang Daily* is printed in two separate editions, one in the new script, the other in the old.

The Minority Languages Department of the Central Institute for Nationalities in Peking offers courses in Mongolian, Tibetan, Korean, Kazak and Uygur, while at the other nine institutes one can study the languages of the region in which each institute is located—so that Vietnamese, Thai and Lao, for example, may be studied at the Guangxi Institute, while Tibetan and Yi are offered at the Southwest Institute. There is now more teaching of minority languages in schools than there used to be; and publishing and broadcasting in minority languages has greatly revived. The official policy is certainly not one of linguistic unification (or subjugation, depending on one's point of view), though there is no doubt that competence in the majority language is essential for upward social mobility.

There are at present no systematic attempts to suppress, as a first step to Chinese-style modernisation, such other expressions of ethnic identity as diet, dress, festivals, rituals and taboos. Embroidered ethnic costume, festivals, folk song, folk dance—these are not only harmless enough, but an attraction to tourists. For the most part the State steers clear of tampering with folk ways, provided that they are 'healthy'. 'Unhealthy' mores are those which 'tend to retard production and cultural development'—the butchering of cows as sacrifices to ghosts, for example, or the practice among some minorities of prohibiting men from engaging in rice transplanting and women in ploughing. In the end, it is assumed, the unhealthiness will wear off, as the practitioners of such customs become more and more advanced ideologically.

But Chinese officialdom would be affronted indeed, if anybody had suggested that they did not respect minority folk ways. Aren't the local governments authorised to give minority people holidays on their respective feast-days? And aren't arrangements made to cater to their special diets—beef and mutton for the Moslem Huis, parched rice for the Mongolians, *tsampa* (parched barley flour) for the Tibetans?

Minority heritages are not about to be Sinicised, reports Colin Mackerras, a scholar who has made a special study of the performing arts in China. He notes a return to certain forms of traditional culture in recent years among the Uygurs of Xinjiang. A visit to the region in 1982 left him with the impression that music, song and dance, the minority's traditional forte, have undergone a radical change in the way in which they are organised; the most obvious, he notes, is the new professionalisation. The performers are no longer so many amateurs: they undergo more rigorous training, and at the same time their social status has risen enormously. Of course the boundaries of their art are defined for them by Party cadres; yet the surprise is that the theatrical activities in Xinjiang can justly be described as flourishing because, and not in spite of the Party's concern to direct local arts into channels of new organisation. Obviously the better organised the activities are, the easier it is to control them, but Colin Mackerras's impressions from observing the school where future troupe members are trained were that the trend was clearly towards encouraging the Uygurs to dominate and determine almost all of the form and style, and part of the content of their own arts. He found that the teachers were more and more members of ethnic minorities, though the Party's concern to achieve racial equality is not entirely disinterested: as Mackerras puts it, 'Any régime which treats artists well can begin to win over not only the performers but also the people who enjoy their art.'

As evidence that central government policies are flexibly applied to minority peoples, population control is often cited; Chinese officialdom claims that the minority groups achieved little or no population growth in the old China, and that some were even on the verge of extinction. Since 1949, however, the combined population of China's minorities has doubled, and in recent years, the ratio of minority people to Hans has increased (though not all minorities grew at the same rate, and some have actually declined in number). One reason the birth rate grew so much among some groups is that the government policy on family planning has always been watered down for the minorities. The degree to which policy is relaxed varies with the size of the minority and with the region. Restrictions on family size are altogether waived in the case of minorities with exceptionally small populations, and in the case of minorities living in Tibet, Inner Mongolia and Xinjiang, the three areas located along China's inland borders. In more populous autonomous areas, minority couples are allowed two or even three children each, and are subjected to lighter penalties than the Chinese if they exceeded their limit. Even in the more crowded cities, minority couples may have two children if they wish. Paradoxically, minority people often take more readily to birth control than do the Chinese, because they are not nearly so obsessed with producing male progeny, and some of them are matriarchal societies.

The Chinese Marriage Law does not apply equally to all the races. In one modification of the law, the legal minimum marriageable ages of twenty-two for men and twenty for women are lowered to twenty and eighteen for certain ethnic communities. In another, marriages between collateral relatives by blood (up to the third degree of relationship), prohibited everywhere else, are tolerated in the Liangshan Autonomous Prefecture, whose inhabitants, the Yis, are allowed to get away with it. The Chinese do recognise that different cultural norms prevail, but concessions to such differences go only so far: no Moslem Uygur, for example, may divorce his wife simply by telling her so, whatever may have been the practice all down the years. Nevertheless it often pays to be a member of a minority, and not a few cases of intermarriage occur on account of the minority's special privileges; it has not escaped many Chinese men that the best way to circumvent the country's strict family planning policy is to take a minority woman to wife. Chinese officialdom is none too sympathetic to such marriages, but government policy is neither to interfere with, nor encourage, them. Marriages between Han Chinese and ethnic minority are not thought a particularly good thing because the onslaught of Han culture is massive enough as it is, and the government does not want to see the lesser races slide rapidly into Chineseness.

Yet the minorities *will* grow more and more Chinese. As the economic gap narrows, so will the cultural ones. The modernisation of China, if it is to occur, will make the modernisation of her people certain. The chief questions are, how quickly and with how much compulsion. In the 1950s and 1960s the Chinese tried to hurry things along by sending hordes of Han cadres, technicians and qualified people into the minority areas, but the present policy is to achieve local recruitment; and in line with this policy, there has been a sharp reduction in the number of outsiders being sent to work in the autonomous areas. It would not be true to say that the Chinese presence is unobtrusive. But there does seem to be an effort to refrain from overwhelming the natives.

One concern of the Chinese emperors remains to this day: the subjugation of the Mongolian steppes, Central Asia and Tibet. These are borderlands, thinly populated and difficult to defend.

The Mongolian steppes had been under the domination of Chinese emperors for centuries, but in 1911, when the last of China's dynasties came to an end, the Mongols in what is now Outer Mongolia (the heart of Mongol land) asserted their independence. Tsarist Russia, which had designs on Outer Mongolia, managed through a series of treaties, and by way of economic and political penetration, to establish a protectorate over the territory. Later Outer Mongolia lost its 'autonomy', a Chinese army re-occupying its capital in 1919, when Russia was too embroiled in civil war to defend it. But the Russians presently came back, and in 1924, the Mongolian People's Republic was established, becoming Soviet Russia's first satellite, with a capital at Urga, now renamed Ulan Bator, or Red Hero.

Chinese rule was oppressive. Certainly there were Mongolians who thought the USSR the lesser of the two evils, and preferred domination by Russians to engulfment by the Chinese. Today the Mongol tribes are separated from their brothers by a sensitive political border, and though the Sino-Soviet quarrel seems to be past its worst, still there always exists the possibility of a threat to Chinese security from Outer Mongolia, and a shift of allegiances by the Inner Mongols.

Long before the Chinese communists took over, Chinese settlers were in the majority in Inner Mongolia. Today the Chinese far outnumber the Mongolians, who constitute only 13 per cent of the population. What is more, Chinese immigration changed the character of the grasslands, turning them over from pasture to arable: Chinese farming instincts, as well as Mao's obsession with grain, had seen to that. But now there has been a change: the Mongolian herdsman has been encouraged to engage in stockbreeding by what is called a 'double contracting' system, whereby pasturage is contracted to individual households, and livestock sold on an instalment plan.

Allowing the Mongolian herdsman to come into his own is of course part of the general relaxation of agricultural policy, and need not imply a concession to tradition. What does suggest such concession is the recent renovation of Genghis Khan's tomb in western Inner Mongolia, at the Ejin Horo banner in the Ordos highlands. The tomb houses the coffin of the Khan, though not his body, which was buried secretly in the steppes sometime after his death in the thirteenth century. In 1984 the government allocated funds for the restoration of the tomb, at which grand celebrations, complete with cow and sheep sacrifices, are held each year.

There is little feeling of nationalism in Inner Mongolia, but such is not the case in Xinjiang, Chinese Turkestan. Xinjiang, which is Chinese for 'the new frontier', is important to China for at least three reasons. Its borders march with those of Soviet Central Asia, it covers a sixth of China's land mass, and it contains no less than 80 per cent of China's mineral resources. But Han command of the region is not fully accepted by all of Xinjiang's inhabitants, six-tenths of whom are not even Chinese. The population of Xinjiang is a patchwork of Uygurs, Hans, Kazak, Huis, Mongolians, Kirgiz, Taijiks and even Russians, with Uygurs predominating.

Hemmed in by the Pamirs, the Karakorum, the Altay and other mountains,

Xinjiang is unlike any other territory in China, partly because of its deserts and oases, and partly because of its cultural identity. The Uygurs, whose autonomous region it is, are a Turkic people, historically subject to the influence of Islam and, for a time, of the Soviet Union. One is not surprised to hear of defections to Soviet Central Asia, where the Turkic-speaking inhabitants of Xinjiang would feel themselves to be amongst kinsmen, where there has not been a Cultural Revolution, and where on the whole the people enjoy a higher standard of living. The Russians trained some of these defectors, it has also been rumoured, and sent them back to subvert Chinese rule in Xinjiang.

Though many Uygurs ask for no more than cultural independence, there still run currents of nationalism in Xinjiang. It is hard for the casual visitor to detect any stirring towards secession in Xinjiang, but a foreign diplomat Colin Mackerras spoke to in Urumqi, the capital, claimed to have met someone who frankly espoused independence 'with no ifs and buts about it'. Certainly the news which reaches Peking from faraway Xinjiang can sometimes be disturbing. In the spring of 1980 it was reported that a skirmish between the minority populace and the People's Liberation Army in Aksu, central-western Xinjiang, left several hundred soldiers and civilians dead and wounded.

One great grievance the Uygurs feel is the continual use of Xinjiang for China's nuclear tests. Although the testing site, Lop Nor, is in the north-eastern corner of the Gobi Desert, the protestors claim that the effects have spread to the string of oases which skirt the desert to the south, and where eight-tenths of the Uygur population live. If this seems a large distance for the radioactive dust to carry, there are the violent sandstorms and high winds which sweep across the Gobi Desert. Though Xinjiang is famous as the land of the centenarians—of whom there are no fewer than 856, including a 102-year-old Uygur peasant who has married thirty-eight times—there are numerous reports of early deaths from cancer. The locals blame this on the nuclear tests, citing as added evidence cases of deformity among newborn babies, lambs and calves. As still further evidence, they quote the suspension of imports of Xinjiang's prize produce, Hami melons and grapes, into Hong Kong. Chinese officials, on the other hand, maintain that the safety precautions were adequate, and said that fears of health risks had been laid to rest by tests carried out in both China and Hong Kong, which showed the fruits to have been free from radioactive contamination. Nevertheless, on a quiet Sunday morning in December 1985, some 200 students from Xinjiang protested against the government's nuclear pro-gramme by staging a demonstration at the Square of Heavenly Peace in Peking. The incident was unprecedented, for no anti-nuclear demonstration had ever been reported from China before.

Behind the demonstration lay other grievances, a mood of historical opposition to Chinese rule, and a feeling that the amount of local say granted was niggardly. For all that the governor is an Uygur, ånd half the leading posts are held by Uygurs, one could not claim that Xinjiang was a self-governing region, when the first secretary of the Party Committee is a Chinese. To add insult to injury, the Chinese had replaced the enormously popular governor with someone who did not look as though he was capable of standing up very firmly for the minorities' interests. The Chinese might argue in their own defence that they have subsidised the region very heavily, but the locals are not persuaded that Xinjiang's considerable natural resources are not being exploited for the good of the undeserving Chinese.

The domestic tension in his corner of China might be worse, were it not for the easing of the international strain along the frontier. Border trade between Xinjiang and the USSR, resumed in 1983, has increased by leaps and bounds, and a railway linking the Chinese region to the Soviet Republic of Kazakhstan is being built to facilitate its further expansion. Peking and Moscow have even conferred over the possibility of re-opening the Central Asian lap of the ancient Silk Road, so that foreign tourists who wish to retrace the route by which silk, gold, glass, amber and precious stones flowed between China and Rome may do so, crossing with relative ease between Western and Eastern Turkestan.

Domestic and international politics are linked, too, in the Chinese handling of Tibet, of all autonomous regions the most extraordinary, the most obdurate, and the most nationalistic. Because it borders India, Nepal, Sikkim, Bhutan and Burma to its south and southwest, Tibet is of strategic importance to China. To both India and China, it is the country in between, a factor in the evolving of neighbourly relations. Historically Tibet is doomed to come under the sway of the surrounding powers, and it was as a frontier country which lay at the limits of India that Tibet became, for a time, bound to the influence of the British Empire.

The British were concerned to ward off the Russians, whom they suspected of having designs on India by way of Tibet. A British armed expedition under Sir Francis Younghusband marched on Tibet in 1904, persuaded that to defend British interests against Russian incursion, the Tibetans must be brought to heel. It was an inglorious invasion, beginning with a massacre of 600 to 700 Tibetans by the imperial force. It ended ingloriously too, with the signing of a treaty which obliged the Tibetans to agree to a British presence in the Forbidden Land, and to deal with no foreign power without British consent.

In theory Tibet owed allegiance to the Chinese emperor, represented in Lhasa by resident Chinese officials called ambans. The Tibetans did not enjoy anything like nationhood, but after the collapse of the last Chinese dynasty the ambans were evicted and Tibet was for all practical purposes self-governing. It was the Dalai Lama, the incarnate manifestation of the Bodhisattva Avalokitesvara, whom the Tibetans revered as their spiritual and political head. Yet when the Chinese communists entered Tibet in 1950, they did not think themselves invading an alien country. Nevertheless they found themselves resisted. The United Nations was appealed to, and absorption of Tibet into the People's Republic was only peaceably achieved by the Chinese agreeing to certain guarantees, including the guarantee to maintain the status, functions and powers of the Dalai Lama.

Afterwards, life went on almost exactly as before in some parts of Tibet. But this was not so in the places where Tibet and China met. Trouble was bound to come, for it was against every communist instinct to let the rich landlords and landowning monasteries be. The Tibetans naturally rebelled, and in 1956 there began the first of a series of uprisings against Chinese rule. Later it was revealed that the CIA had a hand in fostering the resistance movement, smuggling out young Tibetans for training in Taiwan and the USA, and supplying modest amounts of money and weapons. In March 1959 a revolt broke out in Lhasa itself, the Chinese troops came and put it down, the Dalai Lama fled to India followed by thousands of other Tibetans, and when the disturbance died away, the Tibetans found themselves faced with all the familiars of communist rule—land redistribution, denunciation meetings, ration systems. It was the end of the old order, the system in which authority over all matters, clerical and secular, emanated from the Buddhist lamas in their monasteries.

Still it was not until the Cultural Revolution that the systematic destruction of Tibetan society truly began. If there were desecrations of holy places in China, there were desecrations still worse in Tibet. The monasteries, whose mysterious and stuffy interiors felt as though no fresh air—let alone the improving breath of socialism—had been admitted for centuries, were a sitting target. Sadly but hardly surprisingly, the people who did the destroying were mostly Tibetan themselves, subjects in their masters' image, youths who had grown up under the wing of the Chinese Communist Party, and who probably preferred not to be identified with what they felt to be Tibetan atavism.

Nothing comes to Tibet without a time lag, and its emergence from the trauma of the Cultural Revolution was later than the rest of China. In 1979 it was over the worst, when a group of Tibetan exiles representing the Dalai Lama freely toured their homeland as guests of the Chinese government, and were greeted so emotionally that even their Chinese guides were reduced to tears. But the turning point really came with the visit of Hu Yaobang in 1980. It was then that new policies, kinder and more generous, were announced.

Policy is one thing, its implementation at every level is another; inevitably there were local officials who chafed at the change. There was no pleasing everybody. Some foreign journalists noted the restoration of old monuments like the Potala Palace with approval; others expressed nostalgia for the beautiful battered façades, now gaudily masked by new paint. The expansion of educational facilities (Tibet is the only area of provincial status to provide free education for all children) is welcomed by some observers, but decried by others as a means of Han indoctrination. Yet even the Dalai Lama, whom the Chinese have tried hard to woo back from exile, concedes that things have improved.

One does not have to be in Lhasa long to discover the devotion that ordinary Tibetans still accord the Dalai Lama: children, for instance, still wear lockets holding his image. Many older people easily accepted the Mao cult because their minds were attuned to the notion of the god-king. Among such a people, the return of the Dalai Lama is certain to be cataclysmic. Nor will the effect be felt only in Tibet: half of the four million Tibetans in China live outside Tibet, in settlements scattered across four Chinese provinces. The Dalai Lama has sent three delegations, one led by his own sister, to Peking to discuss the future of Tibet and the possibility of his return; but China will never agree to independence of the sort that he demands as a condition of his return.

An address by the Dalai Lama to a subcommittee of the US Congress in September 1987 (calling for, among other things, the withdrawal of Chinese authority and an end to human rights abuses) proved a prelude to the most violent Tibetan–Chinese clash to have occurred in Tibet since 1959. On China's national day on October 1, Tibetan nationalism burst into the open with a riot near Lhasa's Jokhang Monastery. Though the true figure may well have been larger, the official account put the loss of lives at twelve, six Tibetan and six Chinese. Dozens of people were injured, and the riot was followed by two more demonstrations by monks protesting against the arrest of their fellows and calling for independence.

Though the Chinese might argue otherwise, the behaviour of the Tibetans was much like that of all those people who had fought for independence in the European colonial empires. Across the world public opinion sympathised with the Tibetan cause, and what made it all the more galling for the Chinese was that the anti-Chinese resentments had flared up at a time when, in their eyes at least, a start was being made on compensating the Tibetans for the terrible abuses of the Cultural Revolution.

Financially, independence is not viable at all; Tibet's economy would collapse if the central government were to stop its subsidies, which currently make up some 98 per cent of Tibet's budget. Although the State already pours more money into Tibet than into any province or autonomous region, since Hu Yaobang's visit still more funds have been made available for the region's development. Tibet is an expensive place to develop, so hard is it to get to, so lacking in infrastructure, and so harsh in the conditions it offers its inhabitants. To the thorny question of how it could immediately begin to pay its way, no better answer has been found than tourism.

Generations of Europeans have felt Tibet's seduction: the snow peaks soaring five miles above sea level, the summit of Mount Everest rearing above the Himalayas, the blinding blue sky, the resplendent shrines. It is a country like no other, with an atmosphere so rarefied that one has to exert one's heart to move far more than one does lower down. To many minds it is a land of mystery, tantalising above all in its impenetrability. No wonder the tourists have come. They have come in increasing numbers, since Tibet opened its door in 1980; and regional projections are that by the end of the century, 200,000 tourists will visit Lhasa annually.

In 1985 the modern Lhasa Hotel opened, complete with oxygen supply equipment and close-circuit television (it was not until the end of the 1970s that Tibetans got their first TV sets); a year later an agreement was signed to hand over its management to the American hotel chain the Holiday Inn. Built at a cost of 100 million yuan, it will be joined by many others. Upon Tibet the tourist trade looks set to fall like a blight. It has plenty of sights to offer. There are few spectacles to beat those acts of devotion which give Tibetan worship its exotic fascination—the prostrations of pilgrims who edge up to the temples on their bellies like inchworms. And for a more chilling thrill, there is the Tibetan 'sky burial' rite, the age-old practice of dismembering the bodies of the dead and feeding them to vultures to hasten the souls to their next incarnation. The authorities know that the Tibetans hate the rite to be observed, so they have planned to build a special hillside lookout for tourists to watch it through telescopes—no matter that this is in appalling taste, and just as insulting to Tibetans.

A great misfortune, not just in Tibet, is that the authorities have not grasped how corrupting tourism can be. They feel only satisfaction at the rapidity with which Tibetan children have learnt to blow kisses at the tourists, and the readiness with which young monks in lamaseries say 'hello' and 'bye-bye' in English. Economics has overtaken politics, and as buildings go up and more scenic areas open, it is difficult to avoid the conclusion that Tibetan culture, which has survived the worst that Maoism and force could do to stamp it out, has been left to be killed by tourism.

Every morning the devout stand in line to enter Lhasa's Jokhang Monastery, muttering their prayers and pressing their foreheads to the feet of the Buddha and to the *hada*, the white silk scarf with which the statue is hung. All day long the pilgrims pass, twirling prayer wheels beneath flapping prayer flags. Step inside a Tibetan home, and there around stand all the tokens of the creed: Buddhist shrines, butter lamps, holy water and portraits of the Dalai Lama. Church and State may no longer be virtually synonymous, as they were in pre-communist days, but no one who visits Lhasa can fail to notice how resilient religion has proved, and how cohesive a force it still is in Tibetan society. The decade of suppression, it seems, has only served to give it added strength.

This appears to be true of other faiths too, and many Western onlookers believe they are witnessing a religious revival in China. Certainly there have been many official pronouncements on the freedom of religious belief in China, one of the liberties guaranteed by the Constitution. To forestall any suggestion that this is at odds with Marxism, it is repeatedly argued that religion is not something which can be completely done away with just yet. This is because, dialectically speaking, religion is a product of history, one which will not wither away before communist society has advanced to a certain stage. That stage not having yet been reached, it would be jumping the gun to expunge religion, though this is not to say that religion is not superstition, to Marxist minds, something that will die out in time with better ideological education.

But organised religion is tolerated up to a point only. One reason the Chinese so abhorred lamaism was that it had become a ruling force, and it is only countenanced now because the lamas have been stripped of their temporal power. With the priestly caste's hold on government broken, there is not so much reason now to suppress the faith. Nevertheless the authorities remain wary: there is the powerful pull of the Dalai Lama, representing a sort of resistance in exile, and demanding the return to the unity of Tibetan race and heritage. There is also the fact that religious habits die hard in Tibet, and too much clinging to old ways could obstruct the course of modernisation.

Yet Tibetan Buddhism does not pose as great a potential threat to the authority of the Party as that other faith practised by minority races, Islam. All over China there are adherents of the Moslem faith, congregating in mosques and paying their obeisances to Allah. No fewer than ten of China's ethnic minorities are Moslem, and one count puts the number of functioning mosques at 15,500 in Xinjiang alone. If there is a revival of religion in China today, it is in Islam, above all, that it is manifested the most clearly. Islam is resurgent in the world, and in China, too, one senses how hard it will prove to break the Moslem from his creed and heritage.

Of the ten minorities professing Islam—Hui, Uygur, Kazak, Tajik, Tartar, Salar, Kirgiz, Ozbek, Dongxiang and Bonan—the first two are the most numerous. The Huis are something of an anomaly, because all that really distinguishes them from Han Chinese—whose language and physical traits they share—is their religion: they are a cultural rather than an ethnic minority. But the Chinese justify their separate classification on the grounds that they have been a distinct people historically. Today's Huis fuse three different ancestries: the Moslem Arab and Persian traders who came to trade and eventually to settle in China in the seventh century, the Arab and Persian migrants from Central Asia at the time of Genghis Khan's western expedition in the thirteen century, and assorted peoples, including Hans and Mongols, who converted to Islam.

The Huis have their own autonomous region in Ningxia, to the south of Inner Mongolia, but they are scattered all over China, and there is scarcely a Chinese city without its pork-free Moslem restaurant. One way in which Moslems were persecuted during the Cultural Revolution was to be made to rear pigs, but such cruelties are a thing of the past now, and in factories, hospitals, schools and offices, Moslem staff are given an extra subsidy to meet the higher cost of eating at a Moslem restaurant if the canteens at their place of work do not offer fare proper to their religion.

To see the comeback of Islam in all its vigour, one must go to Kashgar, a city which seems more Middle Eastern than Chinese. The trading hub of southern Xinjiang, Kashgar was where caravans used to arrive from points as far as Hamaden and Samarkand. Today, thousands of devotees come to worship at its Id Kah Mosque on a Friday, presided over by Sadi Haji, a mullah in white turban and gown. Sadi Haji, as his name suggests, has been on a pilgrimage to Mecca. So, recently, have 2000 other Moslems from China, despite the fact that diplomatic relations have not yet been established with Saudi Arabia. These pilgrimages, suspended throughout the Cultural Revolution, were resumed with the assistance of the Moslem World League, but the Chinese government has also helped, providing the pilgrims with foreign currency and allowing them to take out duty-free goods, including silks, fabrics and art objects, to sell along the way.

All these are the outward signs of devotion, but much religious activity in that corner of Xinjiang goes unperceived, kept by the faithful as a secret from the world. The sect which bears the name *ishan*, a Persian word used to mean 'teacher' or 'guide' in Turkestan and an order regarded as synonymous with Sufism, is outlawed in China. A document issued by the Party propaganda department in 1980 makes this more than clear: 'With the consent of Uygur cadres, and Uygur and Kazak religious leaders,' it said, 'the reactionary Ishan faith was banned.' The faithful, it went on to say, are 'not to be allowed to resume their activities', and 'any kind of such illegal activity is to be strictly prohibited'. Yet there are recusants against this ruling, and just as the sect went underground during the Cultural Revolution, to show itself openly the moment policy was relaxed, so there are people carrying on the tradition still, particularly among the Kirgiz nomads of Turkestan. Investigations have been conducted in Xinjiang to ascertain their numerical force, but the secrecy which shrouds these people makes this very difficult. There are only estimates for selected places; at one of these places, Yarkant (Shache) county, the proportion of Ishan followers has been put at 90 per cent.

Introduced by followers from Central Asia, Ishan as an organised faith rooted itself in Xinjiang at the start of the seventeenth century. There, dervish monasteries, called *khankah*, were quickly established in Kashi,

Shache, Turpan and Hami counties, where their influence may still be felt today. The first decade of the People's Republic saw the dispersion of the monasteries for safety's sake to remoter regions, beyond the direct authority of the State. There, beside the tomb of a saint, and above a mound of desert sand, they re-established themselves. They are threadbare places, but numinous to the faithful, in whose hearts, observed a Chinese investigator who visited some in 1982, they remain 'sanctified places of infinite mystery'. Take the one to the east of Yingjisha, which is nothing but an adobe, shabby both inside and out. All around lies desert. Inside, one sees only two cauldrons. From these a consecrated maize gruel, as deeply cherished as holy water, is ladled out to those who come to worship there.

The faith is disturbing to the authorities for several reasons. It is arcane, and it seems to exercise what seems to them to be a dark and unearthly hold on the imagination of its believers. What is more, it is a strict and hierarchical order. The ishan's authority over the followers is absolute, and the rank of leader is transmitted from father to son. None of these characteristics make it welcome to a communist régime, which is on guard against class, any challenge to its authority, and hereditary succession. Its intimate links with Sufism makes it further suspect, for the overwhelming majority of Chinese Moslems are of the Sunnite Sects, while the Shi'ite notions by which many of the early Sufis were powerfully influenced include the idea of the Mahdi, the spiritual and temporal leader who will one day appear to restore the supremacy of Islam over ungodly forces. The Chinese are not likely to forget, after all, that Moslem insurrections have punctuated their history up till quite recent times.

Islam and lamaism have a significance beyond religion in China, a political and racial significance stemming from their identification with particular minority groups. This is not true of Buddhism, whose adherents are largely Chinese and do not raise any spectre of militant nationalism. During the first decade of communist rule, nine-tenths of the monastic population were made to return to lay life, but many have come slipping back, dusting themselves off as they re-don their robes.

For a glimpse of how Buddhism fares today, one might do worse than to visit Putuo Shan, an island in the Zhoushan archipelago, off the coast of East China. There are four sacred Buddhist mountains in China, and Putuo Shan, by tradition the sanctuary of the Guanyin Bodhisattva, the Goddess of Mercy, is one of them. It used to be said of Putuo Shan that 'there is no building not a temple, no man not a monk', but the People's Liberation Army requisitioned most of the monasteries in the 1950s, the island being a frontline area facing Taiwan. Yet here, as elsewhere, the military presence is receding. Temples are being restored, and money spent to upgrade the island's facilities as a holiday resort.

A régime bent on economic progress would not be investing in religious pursuits unless they brought it productive dividends. This Putuo Shan does, in two ways. One is tourism. The other is performing rites for the souls of the dead. If my own relatives are anything to go by, there are many Chinese émigrés who are prepared to pay as much as 20,000 yuan to have services conducted for their dead kinsmen in China's re-opened monasteries.

The purpose of these services is to conduct the souls of the dead across the vast ocean of suffering into which Buddhists believe we are cast by our sins when we die. This has to do with the doctrine of *karma*, which holds that living creatures go through an endless cycle of rebirths, and the order into which they are born in the next incarnation—whether man, animal, hungry ghost or a lost spirit in hell—depends on their conduct in the present existence. The rites of redemption, once started, could last for up to forty-nine (seven times seven) days, with the monasteries providing not just the monks but the full panoply of sacrificial offerings, from food to paper joss money.

The price paid by those ordering these services—mostly rich ladies from Hong Kong and Southeast Asian countries—varies with the type of ceremony. The most elaborate, the Masses for the Souls on Sea and Land, are the costliest. Putuo Shan was not quite up to performing a full-scale mass when I was there in 1984, but it did offer lesser services. The one I came upon was called Filling the Burning Mouths (of thirsty and hungry ghosts); it was ordered by a number of devotees who had come specially from Hong Kong to have it performed in Putuo Shan, in the belief that they would acquire merit thereby.

But it would be wrong to suppose that Putuo Shan receives only overseas pilgrims. I climbed the steps to the highest temple in the company of native pilgrims who ascended the staircase by prostrating themselves at every third step, their hands clutching joss-sticks and their necks slung with the yellow cloth bag traditionally carried by Buddhist pilgrims.

They were mostly women, and mostly old; but there were some very youthful pilgrims among them. One of them, a pale-faced young monk, had only just taken holy orders: the twelve small round scars, burned into his bald head to signify his monkhood, were still fresh-looking. He came from Wutai Shan, another of the sacred Buddhist mountains. He told me that monks like him received a monthly allowance of ·15 yuan each for their living expenses, and that his day consisted of cleaning, sutra-chanting and meditation. He was doing the rounds of China's more famous monasteries, on a kind of Buddhist equivalent of the grand tour. It struck me that in the old days, when it was the custom for those who had just taken their vows to spend a couple of years monastery-hopping across the country, he would be called a 'cloud water' monk. Like those monks, my informant enjoyed free accommodation in any Buddhist monastery.

The monk told me he knew many young men getting ready to swell the ranks of the clergy. It seems there is room for more recruits to the clerical profession in China, because the government has decreed the restoration of 146 major temples across the country, and there has to be enough monks and nuns to man them. In 1985 the famous Jade Buddha Temple in Shanghai graduated its first batch of trainees, novices aged between eighteen and twenty-two. In 1984, the first school of higher education for nuns, the Bhiksunis Buddhist Institute, opened in the outskirts of Chengdu, the capital of the western province of Sichuan.

I spent half a day at the Bhiksunis Institute in the spring of 1986. Cloistered behind faded pink walls, thirty-seven young nuns sat in a classroom listening to a lecture on philosophy. Their shaven heads and loose gowns gave them a boyish, sexually ambiguous appearance. Some of them looked too spirited for so withdrawn and disciplined a calling. Though their behaviour is governed by 500 rules—they are, for example, not supposed to smile; they are to go about with downcast eyes; and they are to step aside when they come face to face with a stranger—I got the impression that everyday life was not really as strict as all that. It is probably a little like being at an English boarding school, where one is only allowed out on Sundays, and only in pairs. The girls are even allowed to watch television, as long as the programmes are of an improving sort. However, music is strictly banned because it arouses desire, and the central notion in Buddhism is that life is suffering, that suffering is brought on by desire, and that desire can be banished by following the Buddhist rules for right living.

Soon after 11.30 a.m. the student nuns lined up for lunch, bowls in hand. They sat on wooden benches in rows and maintained an absolute silence as rice, soup and a green vegetable were ladled out to them. An air of solemnity pervaded the proceedings, and the end of the meal was marked by a reciting of scriptures. Later, in the dim recesses of a chapel, I glimpsed two nuns absorbed in their meditation. Outside on the porch an immensely old nun, toothless and stoop-shouldered, hobbled past. She was followed by two young country girls, who had come to enquire about the possibility of taking the veil. She led them to the head of the institute, the Venerable Bhiksuni Long Lian, who gave them an elementary book on the Buddhist faith to read.

I later engaged the Venerable Long Lian in conversation. I wanted to know how the students were selected, and what induced them to become nuns in the first place. 'We received 1000 applications for admission from eight provinces,' she told me. 'The short list was made up of those who had the support of their own temples; the candidates were then selected by competitive examinations.' The girls receive a monthly stipend of 20 yuan each from the government, and undertake four years of academic study— just as they would at a university. Buddhist history and religious cultivation form an important part of their course, but yes, they have to study Marxism–Leninism too—'After all it's all philosophy.' As for their motives for taking the veil, I was told that family tradition had a lot to do with it: many of the girls came from homes long converted to Buddhism. 'Of course there are negative reasons,' added Long Lian, 'like being jilted or crossed in love. But we don't accept them into our order unless we are sure of their dedication and piety.'

The convent could only be visited with the permission of the China Buddhist Association, an official organisation through which the government keeps an eye on the religion, for no religion, in its opinion, is without its objectionable side. With Buddhism, the authorities are on guard against superstition, into which Chinese religious practices shade off all too frequently. But they can never altogether extinguish it—the popular faith of the Chinese peasant is a rich jumble, with Buddhism mingled with Daoism, myth with Confucianism, beliefs in ghosts, magic and the evil eye reaching back to the earliest convictions of Chinese antiquity. Judging by the crudely cyclostyled copies of *Huang Li* ('Imperial Almanac') I found offered for sale by street vendors in some Chinese cities in 1986, people still believe in lucky or unlucky days for their proposed actions.

It was upon this native tradition that foreign missionaries tried to graft Christianity in the nineteenth and early twentieth centuries. Though the missionaries were expelled in 1949, accused of being spies or worse, their influence remained; and one of the more remarkable things to happen to me in China in 1985 was to be given an Easter egg. All the statistical indicators of the state of Christianity in China, both Protestant and Catholic, are pointing up. Between 1980 and 1983, for example, churches re-opened at the rate of four or five a week in China, and well over a million copies of the Bible were distributed. When the Archbishop of Canterbury, the Right Reverend Dr Robert Runcie, visited China at the beginning of 1982, he heard the Chinese Christian Church described as 'a patient slowly recovering after a long and dangerous illness'. When he returned in December 1983 to take, as he himself put it, 'the pulse of the patient', he saw promising signs of 'continued recovery and renewed strength'.

The gloomiest of Christians could scarcely watch the reconsecration of the historic Cathedral of Our Saviour in Peking, the largest cathedral in northern China, without taking heart. It is Christmas Eve, 1985; and here is a grand Wagnerian march playing, as Bishop Michael Fu sprinkles holy water outside and inside the Gothic structure. The bells peal. The choir sings. There up the aisle the procession is moving, with trousers showing beneath surplice and cassock, and Bishop Fu at its head in lacy white and gold. Light shines from candles and chandeliers. Pink flowers bedeck the tabernacle. The congregation, mostly elderly women with their heads wrapped in shawls, have not seen its like for twenty-seven years.

The cathedral suffered some damage in 1900 when Britain, France, the United States and five other powers sacked Peking and relieved the several thousand Chinese Christians barricaded in the cathedral during the Boxer Rebellion; one of the stone tortoises in the cathedral's two side pavilions lost its head then. But it was in the batterings the cathedral took in the

Cultural Revolution that the other tortoise lost its tail, and the building its stained glass windows, its steeples, and its statuary. When, in 1982, the city government decided to restore the cathedral, the repairers had to rely on people's memory of what it was like, and it was only when a couple produced a photograph of their wedding in the cathedral some thirty years ago that they were able to restore some of the stone statues.

But at least some of this religious boom is deceptive. The Catholic Church in China is presided over by the Patriotic Catholic Association, and the only kind of Catholicism tolerated in China is that represented by this official body. Each of the other great faiths in China has its own government-sponsored organisation—the Buddhists the China Buddhist Association, the Moslems the China Islamic Association, the Protestants the China Christian Association—but the word 'patriotic' is used only of the Catholics. This has to do with the fact that the Chinese Catholic Church was forced to break with Rome as a condition of its survival. The Holy See having sided with Taiwan, to answer to Rome is to be disloyal to the People's Republic. The government in Peking claims, not unjustifiably, that relations between China and Taiwan are none of the Vatican's business, but in this case ecclesiastics are indissolubly mixed with politics, and though there have been many signs of rapprochement in recent years, full communion with Rome still awaits the resolution of the Taiwan question.

It is a historically conditioned view that the Chinese take. The sympathies of foreign missionaries a few generations back, they say, lay largely with the 'foreign imperialists' and the 'reactionary/oppressive Chinese government'; they did not lie with the progressive opposition. Since, to Peking's mind, one could only be patriotic if one sided with the progressives, Chinese Catholics were not patriotic. To such a mind, there was necessarily a conflict between faith and country, and one was only a running-dog if one insisted on following alien religion.

This was why, under the People's Republic, the Chinese Protestant Church had to adopt the policy of the Three-Selfs: to be self-governed, self-supporting, and self-propagating. It is a Chinese instinct to assimilate foreign ideas to familiar themes from the native tradition. The suspicion of foreign faiths, encapsulated in the slogan 'One Christian more, one Chinese less', is by no means entirely dissipated. But in the meantime, the churches are full all over China.

# Epilogue

I shall begin with a story.

It is the year 2000. The population of China has grown to 1·5 billion. Deng Xiaoping has been dead two years, and in the ensuing power struggle, many of his colleagues die mysteriously, some in car accidents, others in air crashes. The Central Committee's investigations conclude that Deng's surviving supporters are to blame, and show trials of these people are conducted. A purge mounted by the new rulers to 'liquidate the social foundation at the grassroots level of the counter-revolutionary con-spiratorial group' (that is, Deng and his supporters) is soon in full swing in Peking. Side by side with this go the resurrection of Mao Zedong's personality cult, the breaking of economic and cultural ties with the West, the reinforcement of police powers, the heightening of ideological vigilance, a wage freeze, and other typically 'leftist' policies. Along with the public condemnation of Deng's 'erroneous line' of the past twenty years, cer-emonies are held to rehabilitate those 'leftists' who died in disgrace during his period in power.

While this is happening a poster appears on Democracy Wall. It turns out to be a copy. The original was posted in 1978, the inaugural year of Deng Xiaoping's regime, and it warned its leaders that unless they created a democratic base for support, their reform measures would not survive them—at some point they would be up-ended. At the time Deng did not heed this advice, and now what was predicted has all come to pass.

Fatefully, the author of the poster himself is arrested and sentenced to life in a labour camp, where an arranged accident soon befalls him. His wife immolates herself before Democracy Wall shortly before it is bulldozed. Presently a garland appears at the site, placed there by a certain politburo member, who is glimpsed to drive up in his deluxe sedan. Around the Great Hall of the People in Peking, troops are suddenly seen to gather. A mysterious work conference begins. Another twist in the political line seems to be in the offing, a return perhaps to Deng-style policies. Thus the wheel of history turns full circle.

The message of this futuristic tale, written by an anonymous author and published in the samizdat *Peking Spring* in May, 1979, is quite clear: it is that in a situation where all authority is concentrated in the hands of a few people, power struggles at the top—and the shifts of fortune these imply for policies—are inevitable. All efforts to make the Chinese better off, the story suggests, will come to nothing if politically China goes on just the same.

This is one image of China's future. There is another, not entirely dissimilar. This takes the stance that Chinese society never changes and always follows the same pattern. In some observers' gloomy view, the Chinese will, as a matter of reflex, and out of immemorial habit, go on repeating the mistakes of the Self-Strengtheners and the Hundred Day reformers, and fail in this latest attempt at regaining their national self-esteem. To a far greater degree than most people, the Chinese look back to older forms, in the certainty that historical patterns repeat themselves. There is an extraordinary passage in the published diaries of the writer Liu Binyan which illustrates this Chinese sense of fatefulness. He is writing of a time in 1975, months before the Gang of Four are arrested. Deng Xiaoping has already taken charge of national affairs, and from the grapevine in Peking, Liu Binyan hears that the days of the Gang are numbered. This leads him to conjure up scenarios for China's political future. 'How will this chunk of history end?' he asks himself. 'In disorder? In yet another civil war?' He turns to history for his answer; and, 'like a lot of other comrades,' he tells us, 'I began to talk of the *General Mirror for the Aid of Government*.'

The title Liu mentions is a celebrated Chinese work, dating from the eleventh century, and vividly evoking the rise and fall of dynasties and the alternation of order and disorder as the established pattern of things. It covers 1300 years of Chinese history, and in its pages later historians are said to find all things of past and present. Is it surprising that many Chinese take the repetitiveness of history for granted, when even one of their best known writers foresees the future in this way, in terms of China's past and not via any Marxist analysis? Marxist as he is, Liu has the Chinese consciousness of history.

Those who hold that China never changes believe that modernisation will be slow in coming—modernisation is after all the struggle against the past. It certainly had bad beginnings in China, for to achieve it she had to defy her traditions, and this was inconceivable to the mass of the Chinese. Because no nation has had as long an uninterrupted history of success in meeting the challenges of survival, the Chinese are not easily persuaded to order their lives differently from the past. Unlike the Japanese, who are used to alien cultural transplants—they borrowed massively from China long before they ever absorbed modern European patterns—the Chinese have always westernised half-heartedly. Like the British perhaps, they are the victims of their past success, sticking to what they know to have worked yesterday.

One feels in China the old ideas and habits watching and waiting, to emerge the moment the ideological control relaxes. Mao recognised their power, and did his best to drive them out, but they outlived all his class struggles, his thought reform campaigns and rectification movements. At the end of the day, old peasant China proves irrepressible, and looking back on the thirty-eight years of the Chinese Communist Party's rule, one cannot help recalling Lenin's advice to Asian socialists to concern themselves with the practical realities of their countries, rather than applying Russian experience indiscriminately. 'You now face,' he had said, 'a task which has not confronted communists anywhere in the world until now: relying on general communist theory and practice, you must adapt yourselves to the specific conditions of a government not met with in European countries; you must learn to apply that theory and practice to a situation in which peasants form the bulk of the population, and in which the object is to struggle against medieval survivals, not capitalism.'

It is only now that the Chinese have been offered the kind of change in the circumstances of life which makes a change in outlook and mores possible. The change to a twentieth-century view can only take place as the peasant stops wearing the sandals depicted in twelfth-century paintings. Industrialisation, in both the economic and sociological sense, will do more to expunge the 'medieval survivals' Lenin mentioned than any amount of Red Guard assault upon the Four Olds. Whatever has kept China poor has also kept her medieval, and it is only when she sloughs off her poverty that she will begin to lose her anachronisms. If Deng Xiaoping's 'second revolution' does that, then it will perhaps be the most revolutionary of all the revolutionary changes that China has undergone this century.

Will she slough off her poverty? Like the author of the futuristic story I recounted, many people would say that that depends on her political structures, and that only decentralisation of power and popular participation will ensure stable economic policies. There is nothing wrong with the Chinese as a race, they say—look at the economic miracles they have wrought in Hong Kong, Singapore and Taiwan; it is only the political system in China that stifles them. Attachment to Confucian values, they maintain, is not detrimental to modernisation. Indeed the opposite is true— look how well it has served all the new nations of East Asia. It is not like Hinduism and the caste system, it is not Mohammedanism and purdah. Only let the diligent and canny Chinese remain themselves, these onlookers say, instead of forcing them into the straitjacket of Soviet-style planning, and they will thrive in no time, just as they have thrived throughout the world, from Melbourne to San Francisco. (My own view, for which I hope fellow-Chinese will forgive me, is that the millions of Chinese who have made it abroad have largely come from the small stretch of coast running from Shanghai to Canton, and that one must not suppose that all Chinese, northern and southern, littoral and inland, will succeed as well.)

People who condemn the effects of China's political system on her people generally consider economic growth under capitalist market conditions to be the most effective engine of development, so they will not see China achieving much prosperity without the magic of free enterprise and private ownership. All predictions of the future carry biases in favour of capitalist or socialist models of development. Nobody knows how it will go with the People's Republic. China's economic reforms are bound to increase the pressures for political pluralism, and since such pluralism will imply the loss of the Party's control over all spheres of life, whether economic, social or cultural, one may expect conservative resistance. Fears that economic decentralisation would bring demands for political liberalisation unarguably prompted the Soviet invasion of Czechoslovakia in 1968, which brought to an end what might have been a great reform experiment. Of course there is no likelihood at all of a similar threat being posed to China, and China has many well-wishers among the world's great nations; but still maintaining the momentum of change will be a tricky task for her leaders for many years to come. A nation whose citizens live by buying and selling will be materially more unequal than one where people are allocated the essentials of existence by the State. When such disparities increase, and with them social divisiveness and grievance, will the government have the political nerve to abstain from intervening?

This remains to be seen, but one thing Deng Xiaoping's government has demonstrated beyond a shadow of doubt is its nerve. The pulse of change and the degree of power risked have been staggering. When one thinks of the crises the government faced between 1984 and 1985—the runaway economy, the loss of control over credit and foreign exchange, the dip in grain yield and foreign currency reserves, the plethora of revelations of corruption and crime among cadres—one can only marvel at the way in which it stayed its course. Seldom was a government's will so severely tested. It made no odds with the opponents of its policies that the fault lay not in the open door or the reforms as such, but in the inexperience with which these innovations were administered; they were out for the reformers' blood. The government did draw back, it is true, and there did follow an andante to the allegro of the year before; but it has soldiered on none the less, and the next thing we have heard is that it has called for *political* reform. Regardless of whether it endures into the future or not, in that trial of strength, we may sense the momentousness of the Chinese experiment— its purpose, its risk, its possibility.

But the success of the experiment does not depend on China alone. Now that she has come round to believing in competitive exports as the surest way to becoming less poor, her future prospects will be affected by changes in the global economy. Look what happened to her plans to earn foreign exchange with oil exports to pay for her imports of technology: even as she was laying these plans, world oil prices collapsed. In the face of so much uncertainty, perhaps the only course for the forecaster to take is to make his prediction quickly, and then go into hiding—or alternatively to hedge his speculations about with many qualifications.

This is what the World Bank has done. A report it presented to the Chinese government concludes that China's goals of increasing per-capita income from $300 to $800 by the year 2000 and to quadruple her gross output value are, with reservations, attainable. But success is subject to her carrying out a number of changes: the reform of her system of economic management, a greater use of market mechanisms to foster efficiency, and alterations in her social institutions and policies to maintain the equitable distribution of development programmes. At the same time, the report suggests a step-up in the service sector and the promotion of efficiency in the use of resources. Being labour-intensive, services will make it easier for China to reduce the number of workers tied to agriculture, and to mop up the ten million extra people who will swell her labour force every year for the rest of the century.

If China does move in the direction of a bigger service sector, now accounting for only 18 per cent of her Gross Domestic Product, it will mean she has reconciled herself to middlemen and private business—and taken a further step along the materialist path. Suppose she were to plump for that path for good, or at least for the rest of the century, what kind of economy will hers be in 2000?

*The Economist* made some projections in December 1985 based on certain assumptions. If China's GDP growth averages 8 per cent a year from 1985 to 2000 (a pace the journal considers feasible), and if the largest economies of Western Europe were to grow at the same rate during that period as they did in 1970–82 (that is, West Germany at 2·2 per cent a year, France at 3·2, Britain at 1·6 and Italy at 2·6), then by 2000 China's GDP will have raced far ahead of Italy's and Britain's, and be only 30 per cent smaller than France's. By 2003, assuming that the same rates hold, China's will have become a bigger economy than West Germany's.

But one must hasten to add that big does not mean prosperous. Even if the population were to rise by only a little, it still will not be possible to be other than pessimistic about the standard of living in China over the next two decades. Most Chinese will remain very poor over the remaining years of this century, and even by 2000, when per-capita GDP is expected to rise to $875, the average Chinese's portion of the total economic pudding will only be one-fifth to one-fourteenth of the average Briton's.

Nor is population the only constraint on China's future prosperity. To industrialise quickly, she will need vast supplies of raw materials. Though well endowed with coal reserves, China's share of other natural resources, including agricultural land, is well below her share of world population. There has been much talk of late of China becoming another Japan, a nation whose population is one-tenth the size of China's. But Professor J P Cole of the University of Nottingham is quick to remind us, in a recent geographical study of China, that if present trends continue, there will be fewer and fewer regions in the world with primary products to spare. One cannot easily see China becoming another Japan, he argues, if only for the reason that there will not be enough primary products available to satisfy eight Japans, let alone ten. He forecasts that in order to consume energy per inhabitant at levels reached in the United States, whose per capita energy use was twenty times as high as China's in 1980, the People's Republic would need roughly the equivalent of all the official oil reserves of the Middle East in five years. Even if her energy use is to be less wasteful than it is at present, she will still need to increase her supplies phenomenally if she is to attain the levels of advanced industrial economies.

In all these projections one is working with arithmetical averages, dividing everything up among the billion-odd people and ending up with a tiny per capita share. But the picture could be different if one were to plan for greater productivity rather than equity. The pattern of industrial development in China has been influenced by the interaction of political ideologies and practical realities; for decades, we saw, government funds were channelled away from the coast to inland regions. China is not the first Third World country to be confronted with a choice between policies to promote economic growth and policies to promote greater economic equality. We know, from the slogan 'Let some people get rich first', that the Chinese policy-makers have reconciled themselves to the notion that the coexistence of wealth and poverty is a necessary stage in the process of development, the stage during which capital must be rapidly accumulated (the economic pie made bigger), in preparation for the economic 'take-off'. But how far will they translate this into spatial terms—that is, concentrate development resources where the returns will be greatest (in the eastern coastal regions), in the hope that the 'trickle-down' effect will spread to the rest of the country? The evidence of the Third World where this strategy has produced 'two nations' within a single country—the one relatively well-off and modern, the other miserably poor and stagnant—is not encouraging, but one of the reasons for the success of Japan's modernisation has been that almost all her industrial centres are located on or close to the coast. Were China also to locate her modern sector in or around her pre-revolution manufacturing centres along the seaboard, the region with the highest concentration of skilled labour, would she succeed better? Professor Cole, for one, thinks that the only way she could conceivably become another Japan is if she followed this course. He envisages the result of such a development strategy to be 'a zone of China like a watered-down version of Japan and an interior not greatly changed from the present state.' If, however, China's modernisation efforts were spread uniformly, then what he foresees is something 'between shared poverty and shared minimal affluence.'

Those who feel the greatest optimism about China's long-term prospects base themselves partly on general trends in the East Asian or Pacific Rim region, and partly on their perceptions of China's potential. One of the most interesting speculations I have come across is that of Michael Ratcliffe, an economist with the Lloyds of London Press. To set China's prospects in the context of world trade, he invokes a theory expounded by the Russian economist Kondratieff. Looking back to the eighteenth century, Kondratieff detected long-term fifty- to sixty-year business cycles in British, French and American statistics. He noticed peaks in these cycles around 1800, 1860 and 1920, and predicted that the next climax would occur some time in the 1970s. A number of economists took the post-second-world-war boom, culminating in the oil crisis of 1973, to be the peak Kondratieff had predicted, and on that basis foresaw a global economic decline until the mid-1990s.

Elaborating on Kondratieff's theory, Michael Ratcliffe invokes that other theorist of business cycles, Joseph Schumpeter, who saw these super-booms to be driven by the introduction of revolutionary new technology—steam power in the first cycle, the railway in the next, the internal combustion engine and electricity in the third, and cheap oil in the last. It is reasonable to suppose that some economies will be in a better position to take advantage of the new technology than others, and that the nation which makes the most of it will have the industrial lead. Britain had her day in the nineteenth century, America has nearly had hers in the twentieth. Looking at the leap in China's cargo sailings since 1976, Michael Ratcliffe envisages the Pacific Basin trades in the 1990s to be dominated by three, not two economies—the United States, Japan, and China. If Japan is today's rising star, he is led to ask, is China tomorrow's?

I found few takers for this view of China as the world's next colossus, when I canvassed opinions in Hong Kong's business community in early 1986. But the scenario was by no means rejected by all. Those who envisage it as a distinct possibility do not see it happening this century; but give her another fifty or sixty years, they say, and China will have overtaken Japan. That is about the time that the Chinese Communist Party completes its current cycle of Cathay and embarks upon the next. It is very unlikely that many of us will live to see it. But sixty years is but a flash in the Chinese centuries.

for one, thinks that the only way she could conceivably become another Japan is if she followed this course. He envisages the result of such a development strategy to be 'a zone of China like a watered-down version of Japan and an interior not greatly changed from the present state.' If, however, China's modernisation efforts were spread uniformly, then what he foresees is something 'between shared poverty and shared minimal affluence.'

Astonishingly, it is among foreign trade and business circles that I found the greatest optimism about China's long-term prospects. These base themselves partly on general trends in the East Asian or Pacific Rim region, and partly on their perceptions of China's potential. One of the most interesting speculations I have come across is that of Michael Ratcliffe, an economist with the Lloyds of London Press. To set China's prospects in the context of world trade, he invokes a theory expounded by the Russian economist Kondratieff. Looking back to the eighteenth century, Kondratieff detected long-term fifty- to sixty-year business cycles in British, French and American statistics. He noticed peaks in these cycles around 1800, 1860 and 1920, and predicted that the next climax would occur some time in the 1970s. A number of economists took the post-second-world-war boom, culminating in the oil crisis of 1973, to be the peak Kondratieff had predicted, and on that basis foresaw a global economic decline until the mid-1990s.

Elaborating on Kondratieff's theory, Michael Ratcliffe invokes that other theorist of business cycles, Joseph Schumpeter, who saw these super-booms to be driven by the introduction of revolutionary new technology—steam power in the first cycle, the railway in the next, the internal combustion engine and electricity in the third, and cheap oil in the last. It is reasonable to suppose that some economies will be in a better position to take advantage of the new technology than others, and that the nation which makes the most of it will have the industrial lead. Britain had her day in the nineteenth century, America has nearly had hers in the twentieth. Looking at the leap in China's cargo sailings since 1976, Michael Ratcliffe envisages the Pacific Basin trades in the 1990s to be dominated by three, not two economies—the United States, Japan, and China. If Japan is today's rising star, he is led to ask, is China tomorrow's?

I found few takers for this view of China as the world's next colossus, when I canvassed opinions in Hong Kong's business community in early 1986. But the scenario was by no means rejected by all. Those who envisage it as a distinct possibility do not see it happening this century; but give her another fifty or sixty years, they say, and China will have overtaken Japan. That is about the time that the Chinese Communist Party completes its current cycle of Cathay and embarks upon the next. It is very unlikely that many of us will live to see it. But sixty years is but a flash in the Chinese centuries.

# The Politburo, November 1987

*Standing Committee
Members*

Zhao Ziyang
Li Peng
Qiao Shi
Hu Qili
Yao Yilin

*Re-elected Members*

Hu Yaobang
Tian Jiyun
Wan Li
Wu Xueqian
Yang Shangkun

*New Members*

Jiang Zemin
Li Ruihuan
Li Tieying
Li Ximing
Qin Jiwei
Song Ping
Yang Rudai

*Alternate*

Deng Guanger

# A Note on Sources

Footnotes and references would not be appropriate in a book of this kind, especially as some of my sources were not directly related to my subject, and I have used materials as diverse as local Chinese tabloids and learned American treatises. Much of my information has come from my travels about China, but still I must acknowledge my debt to a number of works which have given me particular insights, or which I have directly quoted in my text.

My first chapter quotes from Steven N. S. Cheung's Hobart essay 'Will China Go Capitalist?' (London: The Institute of Economic Affairs, 1982), and Leslie's Sklair's paper 'Shenzhen: A Chinese "Development Zone" in Global Perspective' (London, Beverly Hills and New Delhi: *Development and Change*, vol. 16, 1985, 571–602). Among historical works I have found Jerome B. Grieder's *Intellectuals and the State in Modern China* (New York: The Free Press, 1981) and Immanuel C. Y. Hsu's *The Rise of Modern China* (Hong Kong: Oxford University Press, 1970) to be the most useful.

The views expressed by Steven N. S. Cheung in Chapter Two have since been published in a paper entitled *China in Transition* by the Institute of Economic Affairs (1986). In this chapter, as in others, I have taken some characters from Zhang Xinxin's *Beijing Ren* ('Peking Man', published in various Chinese literary magazines, 1984–85, and to be published in English as *Chinese Lives*). Reading Richard Kirkby's *Urbanisation in China: Town and Country in a Developing Economy, 1949–2000 A.D.* (Beckenham: Croom Helm, 1985) has helped to clarify my views on the subject-matter of this chapter and the next. I have also been helped by Fei Xiaotong's *Xiao chengzhen, da wenti* ('Small Town, Big Issue', Jiangsu People's Publishing, 1984), and Jean C. Oi's essay 'Peasant Grain Marketing and State Procurement: China's Grain Contracting' (London: *China Quarterly*, 106, June 1986).

The World Bank study mentioned in Chapter Three is *Recent Chinese Economic Reforms: Studies of Two Industrial Enterprises* (Washington: The World Bank Staff Working Paper no. 652, 1984). This chapter has also benefited from Bruce Reynold's essay 'China in the International Economy' in *China's Foreign Relations in the 1980s*, edited by Harry Harding (New Haven: Yale, 1984), and from Wen Yuankai's *Zhongguo de da qushi* ('China's Megatrends', Shanghai People's Publishing, 1984).

Chapter Four contains information from David Goodman's essay 'The National CCP Conference of September 1985 and China's Leadership Changes' (London: *China Quarterly*, 105, March 1986), Hong Yung Lee's paper 'Political Implications of the Reforms in China' (New York: *Journal of International Affairs*, vol. 39/2, Winter 1986), and Richard Baum's paper 'China in 1985: The Greening of the Revolution' (Berkeley: *Asian Survey*, vol. 26, no. 1, January 1986).

Harry Harding's remarks in Chapter Five are taken from his contribution 'China's Changing Roles in the Contemporary World' to his own book, mentioned above.

The description of Hainan in Chapter Six comes from the Nagel Encyclopaedia Guide to China (Geneva: Nagel, 1973). The American missionary mentioned was the Rev. Philip Wilson Pitcher, to whose book, *In and about Amoy* (Shanghai and Foochow: The Methodist Publishing House, 1912), I am greatly indebted.

Chapter Seven owes something to Orville Schell's *To Get Rich is Glorious* (New York: Pantheon, 1984), and to *Young Children in China*, by Rita Liljestrom et al. (Clevedon: Multilingual Matters, 1982).

Sun Longji's book, referred to in Chapter Eight, is *Zhongguo wenhua de shenceng jiegou* ('The Deep Structure of Chinese Culture', Hong Kong: Yishan, 1983). Gertrud Schyl-Bjurman's account may be found in *Young Children in China*, which I have already mentioned.

In Chapter Nine, I have made some use of David R. Arkush's *Fei Xiaotong and Sociology in Revolutionary China* (Cambridge, Mass: Harvard, 1981).

Chapter Ten owes a debt to Andrew J. Nathan's *Chinese Democracy: The Individual and the State in Twentieth-Century China* (London: I. B. Tauris).

Chapter Eleven has drawn gratefully from *Trees on the Mountain*, edited by Stephen C. Soong and John Minford (Hong Kong: The Chinese University Press, 1984), and from *Essays on Modern Chinese Literature and Literary Criticism*, edited by Wolfgang Kubin and Rudolf G. Wagner (Bochum: Papers of the Berlin Conference, 1982).

For Chapter Twelve, I have consulted A. J. Broomhall's *Strong Tower* (London: China Inland Mission, 1947), and Colin Mackerras' essay 'The Minority Nationalities: Modernisation and Integration' in *China: Dilemmas of Modernisation* edited by Graham Young (Beckenham: Croom Helm, 1985).

Finally, for the epilogue, I have made much use of J. P. Cole's *China 1950–2000: Performance and Prospects* (Nottingham: The University, 1985), and K. Michael Ratcliffe's paper 'Perspective of Pacific Basin Trade in the 1990s', given at the Marintec China '85 Conference in Shanghai (December, 1985).

Among newspapers and periodicals I have learnt much from are *The Economist* (London), the *China Daily* (Peking), the *Shijie jingji daobao* (Shanghai), the *Dagong bao* and *Jiushi niandai* (both of Hong Kong). The Hong

Kong monthly magazine *Zhengming*, with its revelations of the latest scandals in the Chinese Communist Party, has been compulsive reading, as well as an up-to-date barometer of the political climate in Peking.

# Index

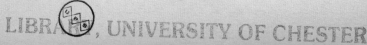